Information for the reader

This edition of European Community environment legislation was compiled on the basis of the official texts in force most of which were published in the Official Journal of the European Communities between 1 October 1991 and 30 June 1994. A number of previous texts, omitted in the preceding edition, have been included in the present edition and are published in German, English, Danish, Spanish, French, Greek, Italian, Dutch and Portuguese.

The laws are presented in chronological order of adoption. If applicable, the principal legislation is directly followed by the amending legislation. Occasionally, technical Annexes have been deleted for reasons of their length and the highly technical information provided for specialists who have access to these texts in other publications. These deletions are indicated at the end of each act concerned.

The EEC Treaty establishes different requirements for each type of Community legislation to become effective:

- Regulations take effect on the date specified in them or, failing this, on the twentieth day following their publication in the Official Journal of the European Communities;

- Directives and decisions must be notified to those they are addressed to and take effect upon their notification. Directives often give a deadline by which the Member State must have implemented them;

- International treaties take effect when they have been ratified by a certain number of States.

Every effort has been taken to assure the completeness and accuracy of the legislation presented herein. Neither the editor nor the institutions of the EC will assume any liability for its usage.

European Community environment legislation

Volume 6 — Waste

European Commission
Directorate-General XI
Environment, Nuclear Safety and Civil Protection

Cataloguing data can be found at the end of this publication

Luxembourg: Office for Official Publications of the European Communities, 1996

ISBN 92-827-6882-1 (Volume 6)
ISBN 92-827-6828-7 (Volumes 1-7)

Printed in Belgium

Table of contents

Preface

Legislation has long been the main pillar of the European Union's environment policy. As long ago as 1973, when environmental action first got under way, the Commission adopted a large number of measures aimed at protecting the environment and combating pollution. More often than not these were directives setting limits for emissions and standards for environmental quality, and requiring governments to help implement plans, projects and programmes for safeguarding the environment and for regulating industrial activities and products.

Environmental legislation gathered pace during the1980s: the completion of the Single Market meant that environmental rules and standards had to be harmonised to allow goods and services to move freely between the Member States.

At the same time, the general approach to environmental problems was changing and the Community introduced new instruments to modernise its action. The Treaty as amended in 1987, and the 1992 Maastricht Treaty, proclaimed the integration of environmental protection into the Community's other policies. Also in 1992, the 5th Action Programme entitled 'Towards Sustainability' was adopted. It provides for the implementation of fiscal, economic and financial instruments and opens up channels of information, communication, education and consultation. Today, more than ever, the Community needs dialogue, cooperation and partnership with national, regional and local authorities, with social and economic agents, associations and citizens, so that everyone can be involved in safeguarding our environment and natural resources.

Nevertheless, legislation remains an important instrument. In several of the spheres in which the European Union is competent, by virtue of the principle of subsidiarity, environmental assessment leads to the introduction of new legislation — as does the carrying out of international obligations.

So it is still very useful to publish these volumes of *Community legislation on the environment*. The first edition was in 1993, and this second edition is the first update. As before, it is being published in all the official languages of the European Union, for use by the growing number of individuals responsible for environmental issues within governments, industry, educational establishments and private organisations. It is hoped that these volumes will provide a useful tool for all those wishing to be involved in the vital task of protecting the environment, safeguarding natural resources and promoting sustainable development.

Ritt Bjerregaard,
Member of the Commission

General introduction

Environment protection in the framework of the Community law

In accordance with the original intentions of the founders, the European Community has developed into a supranational government which — as it approaches its 40th year — is in the process of increasing its membership, thus deepening its democratic structure and strengthening its powers.

Six European states (Belgium, France, Italy, Luxembourg, the Netherlands and the Federal Republic of Germany) — determined to lay the foundations of an ever closer union among the peoples[1] of Europe — joined together on 1 January 1958 to create the European Economic Community[2]. Denmark, the United Kingdom and Ireland joined in 1973, Greece in 1981, and Spain and Portugal in 1985. Finally, in 1995, Austria, Finland and Sweden brought EC Membership to fifteen countries. Today, the list of countries which have declared their intention to seek membership in the European Community would include most of Europe, especially the Central European States which see close ties to the community as a crucial source of economic growth and democratic stability.

Where early post-war proposals for European union failed, Jean Monnet and French Foreign Minister Robert Schuman's pragmatic approach succeeded. 'A united Europe will not emerge overnight or in one grand design. It will be built on practical achievements, creating first a *de facto* interdependence.' Schuman declared.

---

[1]   Preamble to the Treaty establishing the European Economic Community, Treaties establishing the European Communities, Office for Official Publications of the European Communities (Luxembourg : 1987), p 217. References in the text to the Treaty mean the EEC Treaty. The EEC Treaty together with the 1951 Treaty establishing the European Coal and Steel Community and the 1957 Treaty establishing the European Atomic Energy Community make up the Constitution of the European Community.

[2]   The European Parliament resolved to use the term 'European Community' in 1975 to refer to the supranational political entity created by the founding Treaties. This term is increasingly used in Community documents, e.g. in Article 130r which refers to 'action by the Community relating to the environment'. However, while it is an appropriate designation for the political entity, it occasionally comes into conflict with legal texts under the Treaties, each of which established a separate 'Community', and in formal references to the Community institutions. For example, the formal title of the Commission is : 'Commission of the European Communities', meaning that it is the sole executive authority for the three founding Treaties.

From the outset, the Member States delegated powers to the Community to legislate, implement and enforce the Community's legislation that went beyond the powers of any other international organisation.

The EC is characterised by a number of features which make it unique:

1) legislative, executive and judicial organs of government;
2) a transfer of powers from the Member States to the Community by virtue of treaties;
3) supremacy of Community law over national law, which is subject to exclusive review by the Community's Court of Justice.

Two milestones on the road to a united Europe were the agreement in 1967 to merge the separate organs of government of the three founding treaties which together provide the Community's constitutional framework, and the 1976 Act introducing the direct election of the members of the European Parliament[1].

Another major step forward came on 1 July 1987 when the Single European Act amending the Treaties came into effect[2]. The Single European Act reiterates the objective of economic and monetary union formally declared by the Heads of State at the 1972 Paris Summit, amends and completes the Founding Treaties and contains provisions which codify principles of political cooperation, in particular the endeavour 'to jointly formulate and implement a European foreign policy'[3].

These amendments introduced the aim of achieving an internal market without national frontiers before 31 December 1992. They also introduced for the first time two explicit references to the Community's powers concerning environmental protection: Article 100a stipulates the criteria for environmental protection legislation affecting the internal market and allows legislation to be adopted by qualified majority in the Council. Articles 130r, 130s and 130t lay down the objectives, means and procedures for the adoption of legislation regarding the environment, specifying, however, that these decisions must be taken unanimously.

The Treaty of the European Union, which was signed by the Heads of State and Government of the European Community Member States in Maastricht on 7 February 1992 and which must be ratified by the Member States in 1992, extended the application of the cooperation procedure to environmental legislation generally under Articles 130s. Unanimity is still required in three areas:

---

[1] Act concerning the election of the representatives of the European Parliament by direct universal suffrage, annexed to Council Decision 76/787/ECSC, EEC, EURATOM (OJ L 278, 8.10.1976).
[2] Single European Act (OJ L 169, 29.6.1987, p. 1).
[3] Article 30 (1).

- provisions primarily of a fiscal nature;

- measures concerning town and country planning, land use with the exception of waste management, measures of a general nature and the management of water resources; and

- measures significantly affecting a Member State's choice between different energy sources and the general structure of its energy supply.

The EC's powers regarding the environment

The European Community is an institution with limited powers delegated to it through the Treaties defining both the areas of the Community's exclusive power and the areas where the Community and the Member States jointly decide. Other areas are by definition the competence of the Member States. The environment is one of the areas in which competence is shared and the area of external relations is another. Member States are thus free to adopt legislation in the absence of Community legislation, but where the Community has acted, Community legislation is supreme and binding on both past and future Member State actions.

The European Community can and does actively participate in the preparation of international conventions on the environment and in their implementation. In addition, the Court of Justice has upheld the direct effect of international agreements to which the Community is a part[1]. Community regulations, decisions and directives must be enforced in national courts if the obligation at issue is expressed in a sufficiently precise and unconditional manner.

Types of Community legislation

The European Community can adopt:

- Non-binding **recommendations** and **resolutions**;

- **Regulations** that are binding and directly applicable in all Member States;

- **Decisions** that are directly binding on the persons to whom they are addressed, including Member States, individuals and legal persons.

- **Directives** which must be implemented by the national laws or regulations of the Member States within a designated time limit (normally 18 months to two years).

---

[1] Case 87/75 Bresciani, [1976] ECR 129.

For more than 20 years, the Directive was the main tool of the Community's environmental policy. The Community defines objectives, standards and procedures allowing the Member States some flexibility in integrating them into their national systems of administration and law. Thus, where one Member State may choose to enact a new law virtually reproducing the text of the Directive, another Member State which already has legislation in the sector covered by the Directive may choose to implement it by amending the previous law or by means of administrative regulations.

Because it sometimes takes years to fully implement directives and Member States may differ concerning the transformation of the directives into national law, the Community has recently turned to the adoption of regulations because of their taking effect more rapidly and applying directly throughout the Community.

The EEC Treaty establishes different requirements for the entry into force of each type of Community legislation:

- Regulations must take effect on the date specified in them or, failing that, on the twentieth day following their publication in the Official Journal of the European Communities.

- Directives and decisions must be notified to those they are addressed to and take effect upon their notification. The notification dates are indicated in the footnotes. Directives often give a deadline by which the Member State must have implemented them.

- International treaties take effect when they have been ratified by a certain number of countries. The dates on which these treaties took effect in the Community are indicated in the footnotes.

The institutions of the European Community

The main institutions of the EC include:

- the directly elected **European Parliament**;

- the **Council of Ministers** which has the fundamental power to adopt legislation;

- the **Commission of the European Communities** which has the sole power to propose legislation and which also implements and enforces it; and

- the **Court of Justice** which assures that Community law and the treaties are respected.

⚄ The Commission

The European Commission is the executive organ of the European Community. It consists of 20 Commissioners proposed by the Member States and serving a collective 5-year term of office. It employs about 15,000 civil servants. All must swear allegiance to the European Community and declare that they are free from influence by their national governments. Only the Commission has the power to propose legislation. Before doing so, it generally consults with experts from the Member States, from industry and from the groups concerned. Its proposals are published in the *Official Journal of the European Communities*.

Moreover, the Commission is also responsible for implementing, monitoring and controlling the enforcement of Community law and policy. In this respect, it may well bring a Member State before the Court of Justice for not complying with Community law. Finally, it administers the Community budget.

In certain specific cases, the Council can in addition authorise the Commission to adopt complementary legal texts to assure the Community legislation's implementation. This power is generally used to amend the technical Annexes to the original legislation. The Member States participate in the process through one of a series of procedures laid down in Council Decision 87/373/EEC[1].

The Commission consists of 23 Directorates-general, a legal service and a general secretariat. Directorate-General XI (DG-XI) is responsible for environment, nuclear safety and civil protection. Worker protection, industrial technical regulation, regional development and aid to third countries are the responsibility of other DGs. Support for the DGs is provided by a number of other specialised services of the Commission.

The role of the Commission in the law-making process regarding the environment has become increasingly important over the years. Member States must notify the Commission before adopting any legislation that could possibly affect the common market, including most of the environmental legislation aimed at industry and which gives the Community the possibility to adopt Community-wide measures[2]. When the environment is concerned, it is increasingly common for a Member State to take the lead and for other Member States to turn to the Commission to work out a proposal to harmonise the environmental standards within this sector in all Member States rather than adopting their own national policy.

---

1   Council Decision 87/373/EEC of 13 July 1987 laying down the procedures for the exercise of implementing powers conferred on the Commission (OJ L 197, 18.7.1987, p. 33).

The Commission also plays an increasing important role in international environmental policy-making. For example, it participates in the work of the Organisation for Economic Cooperation and Development (OECD) and regularly receives mandates from the Council for the negotiation of international treaties on the environment. The European Environmental Agency and its environmental information and observation network were established by the Council to provide the Community, the Member States and other European countries with reliable and comparable information to enable them to take the necessary measures to protect the quality of the environment. The Commission also manages the budget allocated by the Community for aid to Central and Eastern Europe (PHARE) and has been given the task of coordinating all of the aid programmes of the G-24 (OECD) countries.

Once legislation has been adopted, the Commission's fundamental task is to ensure that it is correctly applied by the Member States, formally as well as in practice.

Environmental legislation often provides the Commission with responsibilities that go beyond its duty to monitor and control, for example the development and management of an information system, the defining of guidelines, the organization of technical training, etc. The Commission also convenes regular meetings in Brussels of the national authorities responsible for the implementation of environmental legislation in order to discuss practical problems arising during the implementation of the legislation, needs of information and education or the amendment or adaptation of the legislation to scientific and technical developments.

---

[2] Council Directive 83/189/EEC of 28 March 1983, laying down a procedure for the provision of information in the field of technical standards and regulations (standstill) (OJ L 109,26.4.1983, p. 8). This Directive stipulates that Member States should notify the Commission well in advance about the adoption of measures liable to affect the Community's or the Member States' policy or the workings of the internal market so as to enable the Commission to propose a harmonised legislation dealing with the subject in question. The Directive 83/189/EEC includes a procedure for Member states to follow in case of creating national standards or technical regulations liable to affect the Common Market by creating non-tariff trade barriers. A large number of national environmental measures is included in this Directive for they impose regulations or define standards applicable to either the process of industrial production or the products, implying a direct or indirect impact on industry and trade.

The Council

The Council is the main legislative organ of the Community and represents the interests of the Member States. It is composed of one representative from each of the governments of the Member States, generally at ministerial level. The foreign affairs minister usually represents the Member State on general matters. The 'Environmental Council' is composed of the ministers responsible for the environment. The presidency of the Council passes from one Member State to another every six months according to an order defined unanimously by the Council. The Member States maintain a permanent representation in Brussels.

The Council is assisted by a standing Committee of Permanent Representations (COREPER) who carry out the day-to-day political work preceding agreements and a Committee of the Regions for consultation.

The European Parliament

The European Parliament represents the interests of the citizens of the European Community but has neither the power to propose legislation nor to adopt it. It does, however, have the power to approve the budget and to dismiss the Commission. Nevertheless, its role has steadily gained importance over the years. The Treaty of the European Union has significantly increased, its powers no longer being merely consultative and controlling. From now on it will exercise " the powers attributed by the present Treaty"[1].

The European Parliament participates in the process of adopting Community Acts both by exercising its powers within the framework of the procedures defined in Articles 189 B and 189 C and by giving either confirming or consultative opinions.

Moreover, it has acquired an official role in the adopted legislation by virtue of the procedures of cooperation and co-decision introduced by the Single European Act and by the Treaty of the European Union respectively. This procedure of cooperation applies, by virtue of Article 130 S (1) of the Treaty, to the actions undertaken by the Community in order to bring about the objectives put forward by the Community's environmental policy.

Members of the European Parliament are elected every five years and are divided into political groups organized at community level.

The Parliament meets for one week a month, usually in Strasbourg (France). Its sessions are open to the public. The commissions usually meet in the pre-

---

[1]   Article 137.

ceding week in Brussels. Many commission meetings are open to the public, including those of the Environment, Public Health and Consumer Affairs Commissions.

The legislative procedures

Under the **consultation procedure**, the Commission must send its proposals to the Council, which is usually required to request the opinions of the European Parliament and the Economic and Social Committee. After counselling the European Parliament and the Economic and Social Committee, the proposal is returned to the Council where it will be examined by the COREPER working group concerned. Once the report of this working group has been drawn up, the proposal is studied by COREPER and is then returned to the Council. When COREPER reaches an agreement concerning the Commission's proposal, it is entered into the Council's agenda as item A. Item As are generally adopted by the Council without preliminary discussion. When, on the other hand, no consensus can be reached, the proposal is entered in the Council's agenda as item B implying that the proposal needs to be discussed and negotiated before it is voted or amended by the Council. Whether a simple majority, qualified majority or unanimity is needed depends on the authorizing provision on which the proposal is based.

If the Council is unable to adopt the proposal in accordance with the voting system mentioned in the provision concerned, the proposal is not completely overruled but is merely suspended or, as is increasingly the case, amended or withdrawn by the Commission. Occasionally, an appeal is made to the Council to resolve the deadlock.

This type of consultation applies to the environmental legislation for:

- Provisions primarily of a fiscal nature;

- measures concerning town and country planning, land use with the exception of waste management, measures of a general nature and the management of water resources;

- measures significantly affecting a Member State's choice between different energy sources and the general structure of its energy supply.

The **cooperation procedure** *(figure 1)* was introduced through the Single European Act in order to accomplish two objectives: on the one hand, it was meant to strengthen the role of the Parliament in the law-making process and, on the other hand, to accelerate the legislative process, requiring the Council to adopt a large number of acts by qualified majority and imposing deadlines on the present phase of the procedure's cooperation.

The cooperation procedure also stipulates that the Commission must send its proposals to the Council, which again is obliged to counsel the European Parliament and the Economic and Social Committee. Upon receiving the Parliament's opinion, the Council agrees a common position which is sent back to the Parliament for a second reading. Within three months following this transmission, the European Parliament may approve the common position, not pronounce its opinion, reject it by absolute majority of the constituent members or propose amendments to the Council's common position by the same majority.

If one of the two first-mentioned alternatives is chosen by the Parliament, the Council decides upon the act in accordance with its common position. If the act is rejected, however, the Council can only decide by unanimity. Finally, when the European Parliament opts for to amend the text of the common position, the Commission has three months to re-examine the proposal it based its common position on, starting from the amendments proposed by the European Parliament. Afterwards, the Commission sends not only its re-examined proposal to the Council but also the amendments that have not been accepted, together with the Commission's opinion on them. The Council can adopt these amendments by unanimity and enact the Commission's re-examined proposal by qualified majority of its members. It can also modify the Commission's re-examined proposal by unanimity. The Council is required to decide within three months. If no decision has come through by that time, the proposal is considered not-adopted.

The Treaty of the European Union has significantly enlarged the application of this legislative procedure. Within the framework of the environmental policy, actions to be undertaken by the Community to bring about the objectives mentioned in Article 130R will be decided upon according to the cooperation procedure defined in Article 189c of the Treaty.

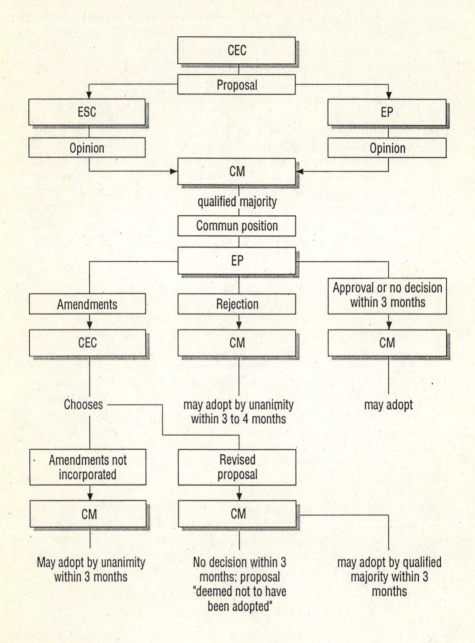

The **co-decision procedure** *(figure 2)* was first introduced by the Treaty of the European Union. This procedure allows the European Parliament to amend or to use its veto regarding certain acts of the Council. Thus, the Parliament is certain to play a more active role in the adoption of Community Legislation. Article 189 B of the Treaty describes the way in which the Parliament exercises its power of co-decision.

Upon submission of a Commission's proposal to the Council and the Parliament, the Council adopts a common position by qualified majority after counselling the Parliament. This common position is subsequently transmitted to the European Parliament. Within a period of three months after this transmission, the European Parliament may approve the common position, not pronounce its opinion, reject it by absolute majority of its constituent members or propose amendments to the common position by the same majority.

If one of the two first-mentioned alternatives is chosen by the Parliament, the Council decides upon the act in accordance with its common position. If the Parliament intends to reject the common position, it is required to inform the Council immediately. The Council can subsequently make an appeal to the Conciliation Committee[1] to fine-tune its position. Subsequently, the European Parliament either confirms the rejection of the common position by absolute majority of its constituent members implying that the act will not be adopted, or proposes amendments. Amendments to the common position need the Parliament's absolute majority of its members after which the amended text is transmitted to the Council and the Commission which have to reach an opinion on it.

If the Council approves the Parliament's amendments by qualified majority within three months, it consequently modifies its position and decrees the act concerned.

If the Council does not decree the act concerned, a meeting of the Conciliation Committee is convened. The Conciliation Committee must reach an agreement on a common project by qualified majority of its members. The Conciliation Committee must approve a common project within six weeks following its convocation. In this case, the Parliament, having decided by absolute majority and the Council, having decided by qualified majority, have another six weeks upon this approval to decree the act concerned in accordance with the common project. If one of the two institutions fails to approve the common project, the act is considered not-adopted which is also the result if the Conciliation Committee has not been able to agree on a common project. However, during the second six-week period starting immediately after the expiry of the six weeks

---

[1]   The Committee of Reconciliation consists of the members of the Council or their representatives and an equal number of representatives of the European Parliament.

granted to the Conciliation Committee, the Council may confirm, by qualified majority, the common position it had agreed upon before the procedure of reconciliation was initiated. This confirmation may possibly include the amendments put forward by the European Parliament. In this case, the act concerned is finally decreed but the European Parliament always has the final word enabling it to reject the text by absolute majority of its members within six weeks following the Council's confirmation, thus causing the act to be considered not-adopted.

Article 130S (3) of the Treaty enables the co-decision procedure to be applicable to the Council's decisions concerning decreeing general action programmes concentrating on environmental priority objectives. The measures needed to implement these programmes are agreed upon according to the procedure of consultation or cooperation, depending on the case.

The legislative procedure also implies numerous direct consultations with the national governments through COREPER and private organisations, both at national and community level. Before expressing their stances regarding proposals for Community legislation, Member States often officially consult their national parliaments and proceed with informally consulting national interest groups.

This complicated consultation process is absolutely necessary to draw up a legislation to:

- assure a 'high level of protection' of public health and the environment;
- harmonise industrial standards and procedures Community-wide;
- be integrated in the various legal systems of the Member States; and
- be implemented by the various administrations and by the various levels of government.

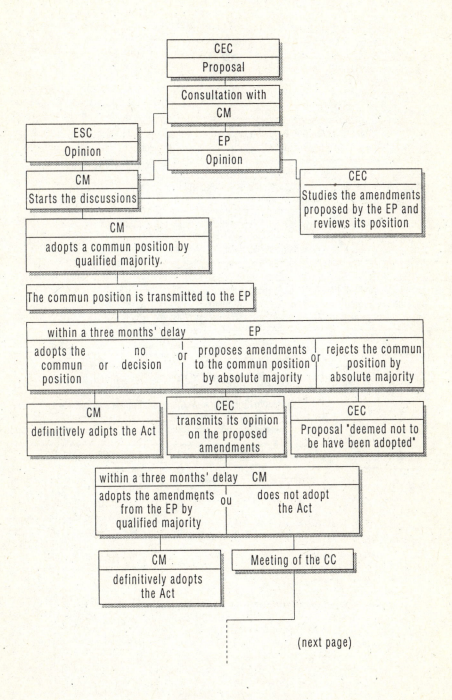

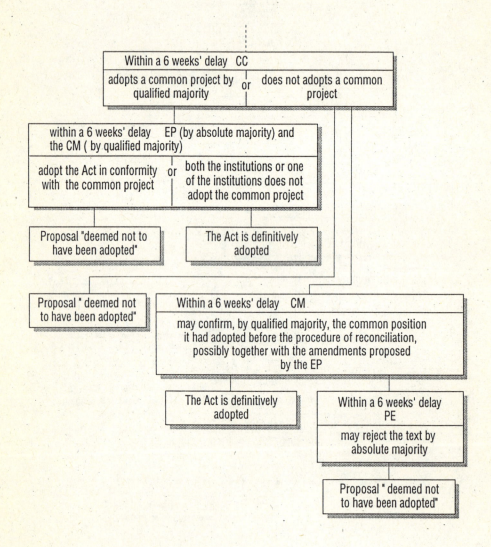

The Court of justice

The Court of Justice is the guardian of the Treaties of Community law. It is composed of judges appointed by agreement with the Member States. The judges are assisted by advocates general, who analyse and propose decisions on the cases before it.

Cases may be brought by the Community institutions against each other, by the Commission against a Member State or vice versa. Cases may also be brought by natural or legal persons against Member States or the Commission under Community law.

Regarding the Court of Justice, the major change introduced by the Treaty of the European Union, is the power granted to the Court to impose fines on Member States[1]. When a Member State fails to take the measures included in the execution of a decree established by the Court of Justice, the Commission may go to Court. The Commission determines the amount of the fine or the penalty to be paid by the Member State, taking into consideration the circumstances. If the Court of Justice finds that a Member State is not complying with its decree, it may impose the payment of the fine or the penalty.

The national courts have the power to review actions taken by their governments for the implementation and enforcement of Community legislation. They may apply to the Court of Justice for a preliminary ruling on an issue of EC law before taking a decision. Moreover, national courts have the power to enforce the decisions of the Court of Justice.

The Court of Justice has rarely ruled on the substance of Community environmental law but several decisions are of fundamental importance in defining the power of the Community to limit the lawmaking authority of the Member States.

The principle of the direct applicability of Community law to individuals was first enunciated in 1963, when the Court stated: 'The Community constitutes a new legal order of international law for the benefit of which the States have limited their sovereign rights, albeit within limited fields", and 'independently of the legislation of Member States, Community law not only imposes obligations on individuals but is intended to confer upon them rights which become part of their legal heritage. These rights arise not only where they are expressly granted by the Treaty but also by reason of obligations which the Treaty imposes in a clearly defined way upon individuals as well as upon the Member States and upon the institutions of the Community"[2].

---

[1] Article 171 (2).
[2] Case 26/62 Van Gend & Loos [1963] ECR 10 ; Case 8/81 Becker vs Finanzamt Münster [1982] ECR 50 ; see also Jean-Victor Luis, The Community Legal Order, 2nd ed., Office for Official Publications of the European Community (Luxembourg : 1990).

Hence, in spite of the fact that a Member State has not implemented (or not properly implemented) a Community environmental directive in violation of Article 189 (13) of the Treaty, the Directive may take direct effect. However, the provisions of the Directive regarding the obligations of the Member State must be sufficiently precise and unconditional in order to have the direct effect of national law vis-à-vis the citizen[1]. They must also be capable of being enforced as law by the national courts.

A landmark environmental ruling came in September 1988 when the Court upheld a Danish law requiring all beer and soft drinks to be sold in reusable containers with a deposit. The ensuing trade barrier to non-resident producers (which for reasons of weight and cost prefer to use throw-away containers) was justified because of the 'imperative requirement' to protect the environment in the absence of a Community law covering this issue. The Court nevertheless struck down a clause of the Danish law which limits the quantity of beverages that non-resident manufacturers may import in bottles that do not conform to Danish standards taking the view that this was a significant trade barrier insofar as Danish exporters faced no similar restrictions in other Member States[2].

Evolution of EC Environmental protection policies

In the 1950s, European politicians sought to rebuild European prosperity and secure peace in the future by creating a common trading area. The core objective of the 1957 Treaty of Rome, establishing the European Economic Community, was 'the constant improvement in the living and working conditions' of the European peoples.

Protection of the environment as such did not appear in the EEC Treaty. However, not so many years later, Community lawmakers recognised the need to create common standards to protect consumers in order to assure the free circulation of goods among the Member States. Thus, the first Community environmental legislation dealt with products (dangerous chemicals, motor vehicles and detergents). Product and later industry-related environmental legislation was based on Article 100 of the Treaty, which covered the harmonisation of laws 'in Member States as having a direct impact on the establishment or functioning of the common market.' In addition, environmental legislation was based on Article 235, covering measures which 'prove necessary to attain... one of the objectives of the Community' in the absence of a specific

---

[1]   Ludwig Krämer, 'Effet national des directives communautaires en matière d'environnement', 1990 RJE 3, pp. 325 — 349.

[2]   Case 302/86 Commission vs Denmark [1988] ECR 4607.

delegation of power by the Treaty. Until 1987, all Community environmental legislation was based upon one or the other or both of these Articles.

In the late 1960s, it became obvious that drastic and comprehensive measures would be needed to protect the Community's environment from the demands imposed on it by economic growth. By the end of the 1970s, the global dimensions of environmental pollution were becoming apparent. In 1972 (the year of the first United Nations conference on the environment), the European Community adopted its first five-year environmental action programme (1973 — 1977) setting out the principles and priorities that would guide its policies in the future.

The first and second environmental action programmes[1] set out detailed lists of actions to be taken to control a broad range of pollution problems. Eleven principles were listed, which have remained valid in subsequent action programmes[2]:

1) Prevention is better than cure. This principle has become paramount under the fourth environmental action programme.

2) Environmental impacts should be taken into account at the earliest possible stage in decision-making.

3) Any form of exploitation of resources and of the natural environment which causes significant damage to the ecological balance must be avoided.

4) Scientific knowledge must be improved to enable efficient action to be taken in this field.

5) The 'Polluter pays' principle: that is, the cost of preventing and repairing environmental damage should be borne by the polluter.

6) Activities in one Member State should not cause deterioration of the environment in another.

7) Environmental policy in the Member States must take into account the interests of the developing countries.

8) The EC and its Member States should promote international and world-wide environmental protection through international organisations.

9) Environmental protection is everyone's responsibility, therefore education is necessary.

---

[1] OJ C 112, 20.12.1973, p. 1 ; OJ C 139, 13.6.1977, p. 1.

[2] A number of these principles have been reiterated in Articles 100a and 130r, 130s and 130t of the Treaty.

10) Environmental protection measures should be taken at the most 'appropriate level', taking into account the type of pollution, the action needed and the geographical zone to be protected. This is known as the "subsidiary principle".

11) National environmental programmes should be coordinated on the basis of a common long-term concept and national policies should be harmonised within the Community, not in isolation.

The third environmental action programme, adopted in 1983[1], tried to provide an overall strategy for the protection of the environment and natural resources in the European Community. It shifted the emphasis from pollution control to pollution prevention, and broadened the concept of environmental protection to include land use planning and the integration of environmental concerns into the other EC policies. The areas affected include the funds for agricultural activities, regional economic development, and aid to African, Caribbean and Pacific countries within the framework of the Lomé Convention.

The fourth environmental action programme[2] (1987 — 1992) sought in part to give substance to the new obligations for integration of the environmental dimension into other Community policies by emphasising four areas of activity:

1) Effective and complete implementation of existing Community Legislation;

2) Regulation of all environmental impacts of 'substances' and 'sources' of pollution;

3) Increased public access to and dissemination of information;

4) Job creation.

The fifth environmental action programme[3] (1993 — 2000) signifies a watershed for the Community. As in the 1980s the major challenge consisted in bringing about the internal market, in the present decade it consists of the reconciliation between environment and development.

In order to achieve tangible results in this respect within the time limit of the fifth programme, the following fields of action have priority:

---

[1] OJ C 46, 17.2.1983, p. 1.
[2] OJ C 328, 1987, p.1.
[3] OJ C 138, 17.5.1993, p .1.

1) Long-term management of natural resources: soil, water, nature reserves and coastal areas.

2) The overall fight against pollution and preventive action concerning waste.

3) Reducing the consumption of non-renewable energy sources.

4) Improving mobility management, notably by opting for more efficient and environmental-friendly locations and means of transport.

5) Health and security improvements, particularly regarding the assessment and management of industrial hazards, nuclear safety and protection against radiation.

Tackling these challenges implies adopting new strategies which aim at breaking the tendencies set out by preceding action programmes and turning towards long-term development.

These strategies imply an active commitment of all the major participants and provide access to a wider range of resources including, notably, economic instruments and the improvement of information aimed at contributing to the identifiable and measurable environmental improvements or aim at changing consumer habits which is the principal source of our planet's deterioration.

The Single European Act

The amendments to the Treaty of Rome, which took effect on 1 July 1987, introduced a series of new articles on the environment in the third part of the Treaty which covers the 'foundation and policy of the Community'. Three articles (130r, 130s and 130t) set out the objectives and elements of environmental protection actions by the Community. The objectives of this action are defined as follows:

• to preserve, protect and improve the quality of the environment;

• to contribute towards protecting human health,

• to assure a prudent and rational utilisation of natural resources.

EC environmental protection actions must become integrated into other EC policies, the most important of which are agriculture, regional development and energy and must be based on three principles:

• preventive action;

• environmental damage must be rectified at source;

• the polluter pays.

The integration principle is by far the most significant provision in the new article. Environmental protection is the only area of EC policy that imposes such a sweeping requirement; and the Community must adopt procedures to implement and enforce it[1].

Article 130s stipulates the requirement of unanimity on the Council[2]. However, the Commission and the Court of Justice have made it clear that Community environmental legislation sets minimum standards, but may not be used to prevent the Member States from going further: 'The protective measures adopted in common pursuant to Article 130s shall not prevent any Member State from introducing more stringent protective measures compatible with this Treaty[3].'

The Single European Act recognised the complicated relationship between the environment and trade in a new Article 100a which states that when the Commission proposes a law concerning health, safety, environmental protection and consumer protection affecting the common market, that proposal must 'take as a base a high level of protection'. Again, Member States are given the opportunity to adopt more stringent standards if they deem it necessary.

The cooperation procedure under Article 100a was first used to break the deadlock on emission limits for medium and large-engine motor vehicles. In April 1987, the Parliament amended the Council text to impose stricter controls on emissions from small-engine cars and managed to convince the Commission to introduce the same standards instead. The Council was forced to agree.

In June 1991, the Court of Justice issued a judgement[4] regarding the legal basis of Directive 89/428/EEC on a progressive phase-out programme for the disposal of titanium dioxide wastes. Through this judgement, the Court cleared the way for the Community to adopt environmental legislation affecting industry by qualified majority instead of unanimity.

The Commission based its proposed Directive on Article 100a of the Treaty (measures furthering the single market) but the Council disagreed and opted for Article 130s on the environment.

---

[1] Pascale Kromarek, 'The Single European Act and the Environment', in European Environment Review 1, 1986, pp. 10 — 12.
[2] It also allows the Council to define matters on which decisions will be taken by majority opinion.
[3] Article 130t.
[4] Case 300/89 Commission vs Council [1991].

Under Article 100a, the European Parliament would have two readings of a proposal which could be adopted by qualified majority. In practice, basing legislation on Article 100a gives the more environmentally progressive forces in Parliament and the Council greater influence over the final text, but this practice has been strongly fought against by some Member States which are concerned about the Parliament's increased power and the loss of national legislative authority to the Community.

Under the terms of Article 130s, the Parliament has only one "consultative" reading and the Council must decide by unanimity (which is sometimes difficult to achieve).

The Court struck down the Directive, accepting the Commission's argument that since national environmental laws regulating this industry could lead to distortions in competition, Article 100a was the correct legal basis for creating a harmonised Community system. Since Article 100a (3) states that such laws affecting the environment must achieve 'a high level of protection', it is clear that, according to the Court, 'the objectives of environmental protection cited in Article 130r can be efficiently pursued through harmonisation measures based on Article 100a'.

This decision cleared up a knotty problem that had been pending since July 1987 when the amendments to the Treaty took effect. It means that the Commission is free to base other environmental proposals on Article 100a without fear of upset in the Council.

The Treaty of the European Union

The Treaty of the European Union significantly modifies the 'environment' sector of the EEC Treaty adding a fourth objective of the environmental policy to Article 130r. Community policy should 'contribute to promoting on an international scale measures taken to deal with regional or global environmental problems.'

Concerning the environment, the Treaty also implies a policy of high-level protection, taking into account the diversity of the Community's regions.

The new Article 130r (2) strengthens the existing provision that environmental needs must be integrated in the definition and implementation of all other Community policies. Measures of harmonisation dealing with these needs may include a safeguard clause, authorising Member States to take temporary measures based on non-economic environmental reasons, under a Community procedure of supervision.

The Treaty deletes the fourth paragraph of Article 130r which stipulates that "the Community acts in environmental matters whose objectives can easier be achieved at Community level than at national level". Nevertheless, the environmental policy generally remains submitted to the subsidiary principle in Article 3 B of the Treaty. It also stipulates that Decisions are to be made as close to citizen-level as possible[1].

Article 130s stipulates that concerning its contents, the Council must decide by qualified majority[2] in accordance with the procedure of cooperation determined in Article 189c in order to attain the objectives stipulated in Article 130r. Unanimity, however, is required for:

- provisions primarily of a fiscal nature;

- measures concerning town and country planning, land use with the exception of waste management, measures of a general nature and the management of water resources;

- measures significantly affecting the choice of a Member State between different energy sources and the general structure of its energy supply.

Action programmes of a general nature regarding priority objectives are adopted by the Council in accordance with the cooperation procedure established in Article 189 B of the Treaty.

The Member States have to assure the funding and execution of the Community's environmental policy. If the policy's implementation implies funds going beyond the Member State's means, the Council includes in the act containing the measure taken in order to achieve the objectives set out in Article 130r (1) the appropriate provisions by means of a temporary derogation and/or financial support from the Cohesion Fund.

Financial instruments for the environment

On 26 May 1994, the Cohesion fund[3] replaced the financial instrument of cohesion[4], introducing a financial backing to both environmental projects and transeuropean networks of transport in the Member States whose Gross

---

[1] Article A.
[2] The Council is authorised by Article 130s to determine the matters to be voted by qualified majority.
[3] The Council's Regulation (EEC) 1164/94 from 16 May 1994 establishing the Cohesion Fund (OJ L 130,25.05.1994, p.1).
[4] The Council's Regulation (EEC) 792/93 from 30 March 1993 establishing a funding instrument of cohesion (OJ L 97, 01.04.1993, p. 74).

National Product per capita is less than 90% of the Community's average: i.e. Greece, Spain, Portugal and Ireland.

In order to be eligible, environmental projects must contribute to the completion of the objectives mentioned in Article 130r of the Treaty, including the measures taken in conformity with Article 130s and the objectives which have priority within the Community's environmental policy. A project's funding by the Cohesion Fund is agreed upon by the Commission consonant with the Member State in question. The funding rate is between 80 and 85% of public spending and is in line with the interventions to be made. In order to make sure that the projects financed by the Cohesion Fund are correctly carried out and in order to avoid any irregularity whatsoever, a control system was introduced by the Member States.

The financial instrument for the environment (Life) introduces a financial backing to actions contributing to the implementation of the Community's environmental policy based on the principle of "the polluter pays". Also eligible are projects of technical support to third countries around the Mediterranean and the Baltic sea and, more exceptionally, to regional and global actions regarding environmental problems as established international agreements.

Financial backing is either agreed upon as co-financing, the level of which varies between 30 and 100% according to the kind of action or as an interest reduction.

Proposals of actions to be financed must be submitted to the Commission by the Member State concerned. These proposals are then studied by a committee made up of representatives from the Member States and the Commission and are adopted, in most cases, by the Commission.

The Commission is also responsible for the success of the projects financially supported by the Community. If any irregularities are found, it has the right to decrease, suspend or reclaim the funds awarded.

Communication 94/C 139/03[1] defines the priority actions to be implemented in 1995 within the framework of LIFE.

Finally, the new provisions included in the modified regulations concerning the Structural Funds, adopted in July 1993[2], increased the attention given to

---

[1] The Commission's communication 94/C 139/03 in conformity with the Council's regulation (EEC) 1973/92 containing the creation of a funding instrument for the environment (Life) regarding the priority actions to be carried out in 1995 (OJ C 139, 21.05.1994, p. 3).

[2] OJ L 215, 30.07.1992, p. 85.

environmental problems. These provisions want these national and regional funding programmes to bring about a revaluation of the national and regional environmental situation as well as the results of the actions aimed at. It also specifies that these programmes must specify the provisions agreed upon with the authorities concerned.

Citizen rights under Community Law

The Treaty of the European Union introduces a European citizenship. "Every person with the nationality of a Member State is a citizen of the Union'.

Citizens of the Union have five general rights:

1) The right to travel and reside unconditionally on the territory of a Member State;

2) The right to vote as well as the eligibility in both municipal elections and elections for the European Parliament in the Member State in which they reside under the same conditions as the nationals;

3) The right to protection from the diplomatic and consular authorities of every Member State on the territory of a third country where his country is not represented;

4) The right to petition the European Parliament about a matter within the Community's competence which directly concerns him; and

5) The right to complain to the ombudsman, appointed by the European Parliament, regarding wrong administration of the Community's institutions or organs except for the Court of Justice and the Court of First Instance concerning the exercise of their judicial powers.

In addition to these rights directly related to Union citizenship, citizens also have the right to formally complain to the Commission about a violation of Community law; this may form the basis of an infringement proceeding by the Commission against the Member State concerned.

European citizens only have the right to bring a complaint directly before the Court of Justice under decisions or regulations addressed directly and individually to them. Since directives are addressed to the Member States, no standing arises for citizens or citizen groups. However, citizen groups have the right to appear before the Court of Justice in support of a case already before the Court, if the Court agrees that the group has a legal interest in supporting the case (e.g. a consumer organisation in a consumer protection case).

Introduction

Framework Directive concerning waste

Directive 75/442/EEC[1] defines waste as any substance or any object which the owner disposes of or intends to dispose of. This definition implies that the Directive does not apply to waste gas emitted into the atmosphere. Neither does the Directive apply to radioactive waste, waste from mines and quarries, animal cadavers, agricultural waste, waste water and downgraded explosives as they are already being covered by other legislation. The Member States adopt the necessary measures to promote the prevention and the reduction of waste production and to promote the reclamation or elimination of the waste produced. They also ensure that waste is being reclaimed or eliminated without endangering public health and without creating any risks for water, soil and air or for plant and animal life. In addition, they must prevent noise pollution, diffusion of foul odours and damage to the landscape and sites of a particular interest.

On 23 February 1994[2] it was judged that, concerning private individuals, the aforementioned provisions do not imply rights which must be safeguarded by the national jurisdictions. According to a constant jurisprudence, the provisions of a Directive are directly enforceable insofar as they are, with respect to their contents, unconditional and sufficiently precise. However, the provisions concerned do not appear to meet these requirements. They must be considered as a framework within which the Member States are expected to deal with waste treatment and do not impose the adoption of specific measures or methods of waste elimination.

The Member States appoint the competent authorities entrusted with the task of drawing up waste management plans. These plans concern the types of waste to be disposed of or reclaimed, the appropriate locations and installations for waste elimination, the persons authorised to carry out waste management and the estimated operation costs. The companies entrusted with waste reclamation and elimination need a special licence. The companies responsible for the collection and transport of waste or responsible for monitoring its reclamation or elimination on behalf of a third party are required to register with the competent authorities. These companies are also subject to regular inspec-

---

[1] Council Directive 75/442/EEC, of 15 July 1975, on waste (OJ L 194, 25.07.1975, p. 39). See also Community Legislation concerning the environment, Volume 6, Waste, first edition, p. 14 and xxvi.

[2] Case C 236/92, Comitato di Difensa vs. Lombardia, 23.02.1994, Rec. 1994, I-483.

tions. In conformity with the "polluter pays" principle, it is the owner of the waste who is required to finance the waste disposal when it is brought to a collector. However, it may also be the previous owners or the manufacturer of the waste-generating product who must foot the bill.

Directive 91/156/EEC[1] concerns a number of significant modifications to Directive 75/442/EEC which are based upon the experience acquired from its implementation. These changes are intended to maintain a high level of environmental protection. The adoption of this Directive was based upon Article 130 S of the treaty of which the rescission was requested by the Commission in view of Article 173, first paragraph of the Treaty. The Commission stated that the Directive's sufficient legal ground was Article 100 A. In the case of the Commission versus the Council[2], it was judged by the Court of Justice that the ground for claiming the wrong choice of legal basis could be overruled as the fact alone that the Directive only incidentally contributes to the harmonisation of market conditions in the Community is not sufficient for Article 100 A of the Treaty to be enforceable.

Decision 94/3/EEC[3] establishes a List of waste which belongs to the categories mentioned in Annexe I to Directive 75/442/EEC.

Toxic and dangerous waste

Toxic and dangerous waste

Directive 78/319/EEC[4] concerns toxic and dangerous waste containing or contaminated by substances or products mentioned in the Annexe to the present Directive in quantities or amounts that involve a risk to public health and to the environment. Similar obligations to those mentioned in framework Directive 75/442/EEC on waste are imposed: the authorisation for companies entrusted with the storage, treatment and deposit of toxic and dangerous waste; regular inspection of the companies transporting such waste; elimination programmes

---

[1]   Council Directive 91/156/EEC, of 18 March 1991, amending Directive 75/442/EEC (OJ L 78, 26.03.1991, p. 32). See also Community Legislation concerning the environment, Volume 6, Waste, first edition, p . 217.

[2]   Case C 155/91, Commission vs. Council, 17.03.1993, Rec. 1993, I-939.

[3]   Commission Decision 94/3/EC, of 20 December 1993, establishing a list of wastes pursuant to Article 1 (a) of Council Directive 75/442/EEC on waste OJ L 5, 07.01.1994, p. 15).

[4]   Council Directive 78/319/EEC, of 20 March 1978, on toxic and dangerous waste (OJ L 84, 31.03.1978, p. 43). See also Community Legislation concerning the environment, Volume 6, Waste, first edition, p. 44 and xxviii.

for toxic and dangerous waste,... Directive 78/319/EEC was replaced by Directive 91/689/EEC[1] on dangerous waste on 27 June 1994[2].

The obligations included in Directives 75/442/EEC and 78/319/EEC are mandatory. In two recent cases[3], it was found by the Court of Justice that Italy and Greece failed to comply with the aforementioned obligations. Italy and Greece did not adopt measures to ensure that the disposal of waste and toxic and dangerous waste would not affect human health and the environment in the regions of Campania and Chania respectively. These regions also lacked elimination plans or programmes for this waste.

Dangerous waste

Directive 91/689/EEC[4] on dangerous waste, concerns the approximation of the legislations of the Member States on the controlled management of this waste.

Waste is registered and identified in every location of waste deposit. Mixing dangerous waste and other waste is only allowed when it is required for the prevention, recycling and transformation of dangerous waste.

Any person assuring the disposal of dangerous waste is from now on subject to the authorisations defined in Directive 75/442/EEC. Only companies assuring the reclamation of dangerous waste do not need an specific licence, provided that they have been registered with the national authorities.

The monitoring measures in Directive 75/442/EEC also apply to the producers and transporters of dangerous waste.

The national authorities must define management plans for dangerous waste. However, emergencies allow them to deviate from the provisions of the present Directive in order to prevent dangerous waste from affecting public health and the environment.

---

[1]   Council Directive 91/689/EEC, of 12 December 1991, on hazardous waste (OJ L 377, 31.12.1991, p. 20).

[2]   As it has not been possible to implement Directive 91/689/EEC within the established limits, Directive 94/3.   ˜ (OJ L 168, 02.1994, p. 28) withdraws Directive 78/319/EEC on 27 June 1995.

[3]   Case C 45/91, Commission vs. Republic of Greece, 07.04.1992, Rec. 1992, I-2509.

[4]   Council Directive 91/689/EEC, of 12 December 1991, on hazardous waste (OJ L 377, 31.12.1991, p. 20).

Waste transfers

Cross-border transfers of dangerous waste

Directive 84/631/EEC[1] concerning the supervision and control in the Community of cross-border transfers of dangerous waste was adopted after it was found that the control of waste transfers ended at the borders of the Member States. In 1986, Directive 94/631/EEC was significantly changed[2] in order to take into consideration pollution risks beyond the Community's borders when waste shipments are intended for a third state. The changes emphasise the measures for the prevention of illegal transfers of dangerous waste from industrialised countries to developing countries for the latter do not have the technical capacities to dispose of this waste.

Directive 84/631/EEC, as amended by Directive 86/279/EEC, applies to cross-border transfers of dangerous waste within as well as from or to the Community. The dangerous waste concerned in the present Directive is the dangerous and toxic waste from Directive 78/319/EEC, except for chlorinated and organic solvents and the PCBs which are defined in Directive 76/403/EEC. A notification to all the competent authorities of the Countries concerned is required by means of a transfer note in the following cases: the owner of waste intends to transfer waste from one Member State to another; he intends to transit waste through one or several Member States; he wants to import waste from a third country into a Member State or export it from a Member State to a third country. Transferring waste from a Member State into a third country requires the owner of the waste to obtain the authorisation of the third country before initiating the notification procedure. Cross-border transfers may only be started when the country of destination acknowledges receipt of the notification. The competent authorities of the country of destination are allowed to object to the shipments of waste. However, objections must be based upon legislative and regulatory provisions regarding environmental protection, public order, public safety or the protection of public health.

The waste thus shipped is subject to strict regulations: the waste must be appropriately packed and labelled. The labels must indicate the nature, the composition and the quantity of the waste as well as the names and telephone numbers

---

[1]   Council Directive 84/631/EEC, of 6 December 1984, on the supervision and control within the European Community of the transfrontier shipment of hazardous waste (OJ L 326, 13.12.1984, p. 31). See also Community Legislation concerning the Environment, Volume 6, Waste, first edition, p. 76 and xxxi.

[2]   Council Directive 86/279/EEC, of 12 June 1986, amending Directive 84/631/EEC on the supervision and control within the European Community of transfrontier shipment of hazardous waste (OJ L 181, 04.07.1986, p. 13). See also Community Legislation concerning the Environment, Volume 6, Waste, first edition, p. 224.

of the people from who instructions can be obtained during the transfer or in case of an accident. The implementation of the procedure of notification must be funded by the owner and/or producer of the waste, in accordance with the "polluter pays" principle. However, the owner or the producer of the waste can only be required to foot the bill when the costs are comparable with those of similar operations for the same kind of waste which is entirely transferred within his own Member State.

Directive 84/631/EEC has established a complete system for cross-border shipments of waste which are based on the obligation of the owner of the waste to give prior notification. The national authorities concerned have the possibility to object to, and consequently ban, a specific transfer of dangerous waste (contrary to dangerous waste transfers of a general nature). The system thus prevents the Member States from issuing a blanket ban on such shipments. This was also the reason why the Court of Justice found that the Belgian prohibition to store, deposit or dump dangerous waste from other Member States on the Walloon provinces of Belgium did not fulfil the conditions for the implementation of the procedure established by Directive 84/631/EEC. Belgium thus failed to abide by the obligations imposed by virtue of this Directive[1].

Supervision of waste transfers to and from the Community

Decision 93/98/EEC[2] approves, on behalf of the Community, the Convention on cross-border shipments of dangerous waste and its elimination (Basel Convention). This Convention intends to contribute to the protection of the environment by imposing more strict controls on cross-border shipments of dangerous and other waste and by environmentally-responsible management of this waste.

Turning this international agreement into Community Law required the adoption of amendments to the existing system of supervision and control of shipments of waste. Regulation (EEC) n° 259/93[3] stipulates new monitoring procedures for the importation, exportation and transit of waste. This Regulation replaces Directive 84/631/EEC on the supervision and control of cross-border shipments of dangerous waste in the Community.

---

1   Case C 2/90, Commission vs. Belgium, 09.07.1992, Rec. 1992, I-4431.

2   Council Decision 93/98/EEC, of 1 February 1993, on the conclusion, on behalf of the Community, of the Convention on the control of transboundary movements of hazardous wastes and their disposal (Basel Convention) (OJ L 39, 16.02.1993, p. 1).

3   Council Regulation (EEC) N° 259/93, of 1 February 1993, on the supervision and control of shipments of waste within, into and out of the European Community (OJ L 30, 06.02.1993, p. 1).

The exporting country informs the importing country and the transit countries about waste shipments within, to and from the Community. The importing and transit countries acknowledge receipt of the notification and authorise the transfer, under certain conditions or otherwise, or reject it. The shipment is not authorised unless the forwarder has the written authorisation of the importing and transit countries as well as the confirmation of the existence of a contract between the exporter and the consignee of the waste. This contract must specify an ecologically acceptable means of managing the waste concerned. The consignee must notify the exporter and the competent authorities of the receipt of the waste and its disposal in conformity with the stipulations agreed upon in the notification. If the waste cannot be shipped to its destination, the competent authorities ensure that the waste is disposed of or reclaimed by environment-friendly methods.

Transfers of waste which do not meet the stipulations of this Regulation are considered illegal and are subject to sanctions.

A financial guarantee to cover transport and elimination or reclamation costs is instituted and will be refunded once the arrival of the waste at its destination has been proved.

The adoption of Regulation (EEC) n° 259/93 on the basis of Article 130 S of the Treaty urged the European Parliament to request the rescission of Article 130 S, in view of Article 173, first paragraph of the Treaty. The Parliament stated that the appropriate legal basis of the Regulation was Article 100 A. In the case of the European Parliament versus the Council[1], it was judged by the Court of Justice that the ground for claiming the wrong choice of legal basis could be overruled as, taking into consideration its constant jurisprudence[2], the fact alone that the Directive only incidentally contributes to the harmonisation of market conditions in the Community is not sufficient for Article 100 A of the Treaty to be enforceable.

Specific substances

Polychlorinated biphenyls (PCBs) and polychlorinated terphenyls (PCTs)

Directive 76/403/EEC[3] requires the Member States to adopt the necessary measures to prohibit the uncontrolled discharge, dumping and storage of PCBs and of objects and equipment containing such substance, and to make compul-

---

[1] Case C 187/93, European Parliament vs. Council, 28.06.1994, Rec. 1994, I-4109.

[2] See case C 155/91, Commission versus Council above.

[3] Council Directive 76/403/EEC, of 6 April 1976, on the disposal of polychlorinated biphenyls and polychlorinated terphenyls (OJ L 108, 26.04.1976, p. 41). See also Community Legislation concerning the Environment, Volume 6, Waste, first edition, p. 27 and xxvii.

sory the disposal of waste PCBs. This disposal must be carried out without endangering human health and without harming the environment. The establishments responsible for the elimination of PCBs on their own account or on behalf of third parties, must be designated by the competent national authorities. In accordance with the "polluter pays" principle, the cost of disposing PCBs must be borne by the holder who has the PCBs disposed of by an agency responsible for its disposal, by the previous holder or the producer of PCBs or of equipment containing PCBS.

Waste oils

Directive 75/439/EEC[1], as amended by Directive 87/101/EEC[2], prohibits any discharge of waste oil and waste oil treatment which results in environmental pollution. When these discharges and treatments cannot be avoided, it is required for the Member States to adopt the necessary measures to ensure that waste oils are collected and disposed of without endangering human health and the environment. The companies responsible for collecting waste oils are required to register with the national authorities which are responsible for an appropriate control on these companies. The companies responsible for the disposal of waste oils need a specific licence for this purpose.

The present Directive runs counter to a national regulation instituting a system for the collection and disposal of waste oils in favour of the companies having a licence issued by the authorities for a specific area as the aforementioned licence may only be awarded to national companies. This issue is concerned in a ruling[3] issued by the Court of Justice about a prejudicial question regarding a penal procedure against two Belgian citizens sued for collecting and transporting waste oils into France without the licence required by the applicable regulations. These deeds were dealt with under the regulation and consequently punished.

---

[1]   Council Directive 75/439/EEC, of 16 June 1975, on the disposal of waste oils (OJ L 194, 25.07.1975, p. 23). See also Community Legislation concerning the Environment, Volume 6, Waste, first edition, p. 2 and xxvi.

[2]   Council Directive 87/101/EEC, of 22 November 1986, amending Directive 75/439/EEC, on the disposal of waste oils (OJ L 42, 12.02.1987, p. 43). See also Community Legislation concerning the Environment, Volume 6, Waste, first edition, p. 214.

[3]   Case C 37/92, Vanacker and Lesage vs. Baudoux combustibles S.A., 12.10.1993, Rec. 1993, I-4947.

Titanium dioxide

Directive 78/176/EEC[1] concerns the prevention and progressive suppression of pollution caused by waste from the titanium dioxide industry. This Directive bans the discharge, dumping, storage, tipping and injection of waste unless prior authorisation is issued. In addition, these operations are accompanied by regular inspections of the waste and of the environment concerned with regard to its physical, chemical, biological and ecological aspects. Concerning former industrial establishments, the Member States stipulate programmes for a progressive reduction, with a view to the elimination, of the pollution caused by liquid, solid or gaseous waste from such establishments. New industrial establishments require a licence which will only be issued if the company undertakes to use only materials, processes and technologies which cause the least possible harm to the environment.

Directive 82/883/EEC[2] stipulates the obligations imposed on the Member States regarding the supervision and control of the areas likely to be polluted by discharges from the titanium dioxide industry.

Within the framework of Directive 78/176/EEC, the programmes adopted to progressively reduce pollution caused by the titanium dioxide industry differ considerably between the Member States, particularly concerning waste reduction methods and anti-pollution investments. That is why Directive 92/112/EEC[3] on the harmonisation of the aforementioned programmes was adopted. From 15 June 1993 onwards, it is forbidden to discharge certain kinds of waste into the sea and into inland surface waters and to emit certain forms of waste into the air. Technical and economic difficulties may allow this date to be postponed until 31 December 1994 provided that a programme of waste reduction is established.

---

[1] Council Directive 78/176/EEC, of 20 February 1978, on waste from the titanium dioxide industry (OJ L 54, 25.02.1978, p. 19). See also Community Legislation concerning the Environment, Volume 6, Waste, first edition, p. 31 and xxviii.

[2] Council Directive 82/883/EEC, of 3 December 1982, on procedures for the surveillance and monitoring of environments concerned by waste from the titanium dioxide industry (OJ L 378, 31.12.1982, p. 1). See also Community Legislation concerning the Environment, Volume 6, Waste, first edition, p. 55 and xxx.

[3] Council Directive 92/112/EEC, of 15 December 1992, on procedures for harmonising the programmes for the reduction and eventual elimination of pollution caused by waste from the titanium dioxide industry (OJ L 409, 31.12.1992, p. 11).

Sewage sludge

Directive 86/278/EEC[1] concerns the regulation of the use of sewage sludge in agriculture in order to prevent harmful effects on soil, vegetation, animals and man, thereby encouraging the correct use of such sewage sludge.

Beverage containers

The purpose of Directive 85/339/EEC[2] is to provide for a series of measures relating to the production, marketing, use, recycling and refilling of containers of liquids for human consumption and to the disposal of used containers in order to reduce the impact of the latter on the environment and to encourage a reduction in the consumption of energy and raw materials in this field. In pursuance of these objectives, Member States are required to draw up programmes geared towards reducing the tonnage and/or volume of containers of liquids for human consumption in household waste to be finally disposed of. This implies adopting measures so as to make consumers more aware of the use of refillable containers, the recycling of these containers and the disposal of waste containers in household waste. These measures are designed to facilitate the refilling and recycling of beverage containers and, should this prove to be impossible, to promote both the selective collection of containers and to market new types of containers.

---

[1] Council Directive 86/278/EEC, of 12 June 1986, on the protection of the environment, and in particular of the soil, when sewage sludge is used in agriculture (OJ L 181, 04.07.1985, p. 6). See also Community Legislation concerning the Environment, Volume 6, Waste, first edition, p. 126 and xxxiii.

[2] Council Directive 85/339/EEC, of 27 June 1985, on containers of liquids for human consumption (OJ L 176, 06.07.1985, p. 18). See also Community Legislation concerning the Environment, Volume 6, Waste, first edition, p. 108 and xxxiii.

Municipal waste incineration plants

In 1989, the Council adopted two Directives[1] within the framework of Directive 84/360/EEC[2] which concerns the fight against air pollution by industrial plants. Directives 89/369/EEC and 89/429/EEC concern air pollution from existing and new municipal waste incineration plants. The distinction between the two depends on the date on which the operation authorisation was issued. If the authorisation was issued after 1 December 1990, the municipal waste incineration plant is considered a new unit.

The emission limit values of hydrochloric acid dust and hydrofluoric acid dust for new units are stipulated in accordance with the size of the unit. The emission limit values for cadmium, mercury and other heavy metals as well as sulphur dioxide are established in conformity with the general minimum standards. the awarding of an operating licence for a new municipal waste incineration plant depends on the unit meeting these limit values and the stipulations mentioned in Directive 89/369/EEC.

Existing units with a capacity greater than or equal to six tonnes of waste per hour will be subject to the same conditions as those for new municipal waste incineration plants on 1 January 1996 at the latest. The emission limit values for other existing units will be progressively reduced from 1 December 1995 onwards to make these units subject to the same conditions as those applicable to new municipal waste incineration plants with the same capacity.

Urban waste water

Directive 91/271/EEC[3] concerns the protection of the environment against pollution by discharges of urban waste water and waste water from certain industrial sectors. Built-up areas must therefore be equipped with collecting systems for urban waste water at the latest by 31 December 2000 or 31 December 2005

---

[1] Council Directive 89/369/EEC, of 8 June 1989, on the prevention of air pollution from new municipal waste incineration plants (OJ L 163, 14.06.1989, p. 32). See also Community Legislation concerning the Environment, Volume 6, Waste, first edition, p. 140 and xxxiv. Council Directive 89/429/EEC, of 21 June 1989, on the reduction of air pollution from existing municipal waste-incineration plants (OJ L 203, 15.07.1989, p. 50). See also Community Legislation concerning the Environment, Volume 6, Waste, first edition, p. 151 and xxxv.

[2] Council Directive 84/360/EEC, of 28 June 1984, on the combating of air pollution from industrial plants. See also Community Legislation concerning the Environment, Volume 2, Air, first edition, p. 109 and xxvii.

[3] Council Directive 91/271/EEC, of 21 May 1991, concerning urban waste water treatment (OJ L 135, 30.05.1991, p. 40). See also Community Legislation concerning the Environment, Volume 6, Waste, first edition, p. 192 and xxxviii.

depending on the size of the built-up area. The water entering the system must undergo a secondary treatment. This process generally involves a biological treatment with secondary settlement or another process in which the requirements established in table 1 of Annexe 1 are respected.

Certain circumstances allow water discharges to undergo a less stringent treatment provided that detailed studies ascertain that these discharges will not alter the environment. This is the case for waste water emitted in high-altitude areas where an efficient biological treatment is seriously impaired due to low temperatures. A similar case is the waste water emission from small built-up areas in regions where the environment is less prone to stress provided, however, that the waste water has at least undergone a primary treatment.

However, a more stringent treatment than the secondary treatment is imposed on waste water discharges from larger built-up areas in areas with a higher susceptibility.

Waste management strategy

In 1989, the Commission adopted a Communication[1] relating to a Community strategy for waste management. This document discusses , on the one hand, the customary proceedings for waste disposal and, on the other hand, the rules governing waste transfers within the framework of the internal market.

Within the framework of waste disposal, the Communication emphasises five main issues:

- the prevention of pollution by implementing clean technologies and manufacturing products which generate less waste;

- the reclamation of waste by implementing different methods such as reutilisation, recycling, regeneration, recovery of raw materials or generation of energy;

- optimisation of final disposal: dumping and incineration of waste is subject to strict standards;

- regulation of transport;

- remedial action, particularly regarding R&D on techniques for site-mapping and clean-up as well as on decontamination and rehabilitation.

---

[1] Commission Communication to the Council and to the Parliament, Community strategy for waste management (1989). The Council passed this Communication in its Resolution of 7 May 1990, on waste policy (OJ C 122, 18.05.1990, p. 2). See also Community Legislation concerning the Environment, Volume 6, Waste, first edition, p. 161 and xxxv.

With a view to the creation of an area without frontiers, the Commission stresses the principles which must regulate the transport and disposal of waste so as to discourage waste transfers to units operating at lower costs and located in regions where less stringent regulations are being implemented. For this reason, the Commission states that waste must be disposed of in the nearest suitable establishments using the most adequate technologies so as to guarantee high-level protection of the environment and public health. An exception for recyclable waste may be made regarding the principle of waste treatment in the nearest suitable establishment. The waste to be recycled will enter an economic circuit and the principles of free competition will then come into play provided that waste transfers are monitored and set out in a recycling contract between the holder of the waste and the recycler. In addition, both parties must be recognised and must have an operating licence.

Summary of the Legislation

Council Directive 91/689/EEC[1] — dangerous waste

This Directive modifies the Community Regulation on the elimination of dangerous waste and replaces Directive 78/319/EEC[2] from 27 June 1994 onwards.

Directive 91/689/EEC aims at bringing in line the Legislation of the Member States concerning the supervised management of dangerous waste. The Directive applies the concept of "dangerous waste" to the waste appearing in a List which must be drawn up in accordance with Article 18 of Directive 75/442/EEC[3] and based on Annexes I and II to this Directive. The aforementioned List must be available within a maximum delay of six months upon the implementation of the present Directive. Waste must meet one or several characteristics mentioned in Annexe III in order to be considered dangerous.

The Member States must make sure that on every dumping location, waste is both registered and identified. Blending dangerous waste and other waste is prohibited except when it is necessary for the prevention, recycling and transformation of dangerous waste. Such operations require an authorisation.

The entities responsible for the elimination of dangerous waste are subject to the authorisations concerned in Directive 75/442/EEC. The derogation granted to companies, ensuring the elimination of their own waste in the company proper, no longer applies to the waste concerned in Directive 91/689/EEC. Nevertheless, the Member States are still allowed to issue a derogation to the required authorisation for companies ensuring the reclamation of dangerous waste. This derogation implies a number of conditions, one of which is the company's registration at the national authorities.

The measures relating to monitoring, included in Directive 75/442/EEC also apply to the producers of dangerous waste. Not only the producer is required to draw up a register mentioning, among other things, quantity, nature, origin, and destination of dangerous waste, but so is the company transporting the waste.

---

[1] Council Directive 91/689/EEC, of 12 December 1991, on hazardous waste
[2] Council Directive 78/319/EEC, of 20 March 1978, on toxic and dangerous waste (OJ L 84, 31.03.1978, p. 43). See also Community Legislation concerning the environment, Volume 6, Waste, first edition, p. 44 and xxviii.
[3] Council Directive 75/442/EEC, of 15 July 1975, on waste (OJ L 194, 25.07.1975, p. 39). See also Community Legislation concerning the environment, Volume 6, Waste, first edition, p. 14 and xxvi.

The Member States also make sure that during the collection, transport or temporal storage of waste, the appropriate packaging and labelling is applied in accordance with the current international and Community standards.

The national authorities must design management programmes for dangerous waste. In urgent matters they are authorised to issue a temporal derogation to the provisions of the Directive with a view to preventing dangerous waste to become a threat to the population and the environment.

The Member States must submit a report on the implementation of the Directive to the Commission, which in its turn will report to both the European Parliament and the Council about the implementation of the Directive.

Council Directive 94/31/EEC[1] — Hazardous waste

It has been impossible to elaborate a binding List of hazardous waste within the limits mentioned in Directive 91/689/EEC. As this Directive's implementation depends on the establishment of such a List by the Commission, Directive 94/31/EEC includes the withdrawal of Directive 78/319/EEC on 27 June 1995.

Council Directive 92/112/EEC[2] — Titanium Dioxide

This Directive lays down the procedures for harmonising the programmes for the reduction and eventual elimination of pollution caused by waste from old industrial plants and intends to improve the competitive conditions of the titanium dioxide industry.

In order to protect the marine environment, it is prohibited, from 15 June 1993 onwards, by virtue of this Directive, to carry out any discharge of high-acidiferous, low-acidiferous or neutralised solid waste.

From 15 June onwards, it is prohibited to discharge solid, high-acidiferous waste from old industrial plants, which is treated by sulphate, in inland waters as well as in coastal waters, territorial waters and deep sea waters. A similar prohibition is imposed on discharges of solid high-acidiferous waste from old industrial plants, which is treated by chlorine. Member States facing technical and economic problems which make it difficult to comply with the implementation date of the discharge prohibition, are allowed a respite provided that a

---

[1]   Council Directive 94/31/EC, of 27 June 1994, amending Directive 91/689/EEC on hazardous waste (OJ L 168, 02.07.1994, p. 28).

[2]   Council Directive 92/112/EEC, of 15 December 1992, on procedures for harmonising the programmes for the reduction and eventual elimination of pollution caused by waste from the titanium dioxide industry (OJ L 409, 31.12.1992, p 11).

programme of efficient discharge reduction is submitted to the Commission on 15 June 1993.

Discharges in any kind of water, of low-acidiferous and neutralised waste from old industrial plants, which is treated by sulphate, are reduced from 31 December 1993 onwards, to a maximum of 800 kilos of sulphate per ton of titanium dioxide. A delay till 31 December 1994 can be obtained for reasons of economic and technical difficulties, provided that a programme of discharge reduction has been established. Moreover, the discharge of treated low-acidiferous and neutralised waste in any kind of water, is reduced to the values that depend on the minerals used.

The emission into the atmosphere of dust and SOx by old industrial plants using sulphate, are reduced from 31 December 1993 and 1 January 1995 onwards, respectively. Similar measures come into force concerning the emissions of dust and chlorine by old industrial plants using chlorine.

Waste from the titanium dioxide industry which is subject to the prohibition of discharge into water or the atmosphere, is either avoided or, if technically possible, re-used, or disposed of without endangering human health and without harming the environment.

Council Decision 93/98/EEC[1] — Control of transfrontier shipments of dangerous waste and its elimination

This Decision approves, on behalf of the Community, the Convention on the control of transfrontier shipments of dangerous waste and its elimination.

This Convention aims at contributing to environmental protection by imposing a more severe monitoring of transfrontier shipments of dangerous and other kinds of waste by means of an environmentally-friendly management. Therefore, procedures of monitoring the import, export and transit of waste have been stipulated.

Transfrontier shipments require the exporting country to notify the importing country and, if need be, the transit countries about any shipment of hazardous and other waste. The aforementioned notification includes the declarations and information appearing in Annexe V A.

Both the importing and transit countries acknowledge receipt of the notification, either approving, with or without reservations, or refusing to authorise the transfer. The shipment may only be authorised upon receipt of the approval, in writing, of both the importing and transit countries. In addition, the authorisa-

---

[1] Council Decision 93/98/EEC, of 1 February 1993, on the conclusion, on behalf of the Community, of the Convention on the control of transboundary movements of hazardous wastes and their disposal (Basel Convention) (OJ L 39, 16.02.1993, p. 1).

tion requires the confirmation of the existence of a contract between exporter and importer containing a statement of a environmentally-friendly management of the waste concerned.

A general procedure of notification may be used if transfrontier shipments of dangerous or other kinds of waste are carried out on a regular basis, using the same route.

The importer of the waste must acknowledge the receipt of the waste to both the exporter and the authorities of the exporting country. He must also inform both parties about the waste disposal in conformity with the stipulations agreed upon in the notification. Should the exporting country lack this information, it is required to inform the importing country as soon as possible.

The aforementioned procedure may also be used for transfrontier shipments of waste from a country which is a signatory of the Convention across one or several non-participating countries.

The exporting country has to make sure that the exporter re-enters the waste in the exporting country if the shipment of the waste is not allowed and no other measures for an environmentally-friendly disposal can be adopted. Therefore, the exporting and the transit countries do not object to the waste being re-entered, neither do they impede or prevent its repatriation.

Every transfrontier shipment of waste which does not comply with the Convention's stipulations, is considered illegal. When the exporter or the producer of the waste is responsible for the illegal action, the exporting country will see to it that the waste is re-entered by the exporter, producer or the country itself. If the waste is not repatriated, it must be disposed in accordance with the Convention's stipulations within 30 days upon the notification of the illegal action. When the importer or the waste disposal entity is responsible, the importing country has to ensure the waste disposal in an environmentally-friendly way by the importer, waste disposal entity or by itself within 30 days upon the discovery of the illegal action. If none of the aforementioned parties can be held responsible, the contracting Member States concerned co-operate to dispose of the waste in an environmentally-friendly way as soon as possible. Moreover, the contracting Member States adopt severe measures in order to prohibit and sanction the illicit shipments of dangerous waste.

The Basel Convention takes effect in the Community on 7 May 1994 in accordance with Article 25, paragraph 2 of the Convention[1].

---

[1] Council Information 94/C 211/01 concerning the entry into force for the European Community of the Convention on the control of transboundary movements of hazardous wastes and their disposal (Basel Convention) (OJ C 211, 02.08.1994, p. 1).

Council Regulation (EEC) No 259/93[1] — Supervision and control of shipments of waste

This Regulations aims at gearing the existing Community system of supervision and control of shipments of waste to the stipulations of the Basel Convention and to the stipulations of the fourth ACP-EEC Convention. Thus, Directive 84/631/EEC[2] concerning the supervision and control of the Community on transfrontier shipments of dangerous waste, is replaced.

This Regulation concerns shipments of waste within, into and out of the European Community.

Concerning waste for disposal, the forwarding party must notify the competent authorities of the importing country after which a copy of the notification must be sent to the competent authorities of both the forwarding country and, if this is the case, the transit countries as well as to the addressee. Notification must be done by means of the transfer note issued by the authorities of the forwarding country.

It is obligatory to draw up a contract between the forwarder and the receiver of the waste. This contract is required to include the stipulation that the forwarder will take back the waste if the shipment was not carried out on time. It must also include that the receiver is allowed six months upon receipt of the waste, to provide a document which proves its environmentally-friendly disposal.

Upon receipt of the notification, the competent authorities of destination acknowledge receipt of this notification to the forwarder and send a copy to all the other competent authorities. after that, the competent authorities of the importing country are allowed 30 days to decide whether the shipment will be consented, under certain conditions or not, or rejected. The shipment is authorised only when the competent authorities concerned have no objections.

The shipment may only be carried out upon receipt of the authorisation of the country of destination. The forwarder subsequently completes the document, a copy of which must be sent to the authorities concerned, three working days before the shipment takes place. This document goes along with the shipment. Within six months of receipt of the waste, the receiver is required to transmit a certificate on the disposal of the waste to the competent authorities.

---

[1] Council Regulation (EEC) No 259/93, of 1 February 1993, on the supervision and control of shipments of waste within, into and out of the European Community (OJ L 326, 13.12.1984, p. 31).

[2] Council Directive 84/631/EEC, of 6 December 1984, on the supervision and control within the European Community of the transfrontier shipment of hazardous waste (OJ L 326, 13.12.1984, p. 31). See also Community Legislation concerning the environment, Volume 6, Waste, first edition, p. 76 and xxxi.

Waste for reclamation, requires a similar procedure as the one for waste for disposal. However, the competent authorities concerned with the specific reclamation installations may decide not to object to any transfer of certain kinds of waste to a specific reclamation installation. This Decision may be limited in time and may be lifted at any time. This Decision requires the aforementioned authorities to inform the Commission, the competent authorities of the Member States and the Secretariat of the OECD, about the name and address of the installation concerned, the technologies used, the type of waste the Decision concerns and the period of time covered. Shipments to these installations must be notified and the competent forwarding and transit authorities may object to these shipments or impose transport conditions on them.

The shipment of waste between Member States involving a transit of the waste through one or several third countries requires the forwarder to transmit a notification to the competent authorities of those countries. The authorities of the importing country ask the authorities of the third country if it is willing to issue a written authorisation for the transit. The receiver of the shipment may not authorise the transfer without the authorisation of the third country.

Transfers of waste which do not involve transfrontier shipment to other Member States, are subject to the national system of supervision and control of that country. The organisation of this system must be notified to the Commission which in its turn will inform the other Member States about this system.

Forwarding waste for disposal is prohibited unless the waste is exported to member states of the EFTA which are also signatories of the Basel Convention. Exportation of waste to these countries is allowed, provided that they issue a written authorisation for its importation and provided that its importation is not prohibited. The exportation to EFTA countries is also prohibited if the authorities concerned with forwarding suppose that the waste will not be treated on an environmentally-friendly way in the EFTA country of destination.

The forwarder planning to ship waste to be disposed of, to an EFTA country is required to notify the competent authorities with forwarding by means of a transfer note. A copy of this notification is transmitted to all the other competent authorities concerned and to the addressee.

Upon receipt of the notification, the authorities concerned with forwarding must acknowledge receipt of this notification in writing. A copy of this acknowledgement will be sent to all the other authorities concerned. The aforementioned authorities are then allowed 70 days to decide whether they will approve, under certain conditions or not, of the shipment, or reject it. The shipment will only be consented to if there are no objections from the competent authorities concerned. In addition, copies of the authorisation from the EFTA country of destination are required as well as copies confirming the existence of a contract between the forwarder and the addressee. The authorities concerned with forwarding send a copy of their Decision to the other authorities concerned, to the customs office for exportation of the Community and to the addressee.

The forwarder is only allowed to carry out the shipment after receipt of the authorisation from the authorities concerned with forwarding. The forwarder completes the transfer note, a copy of which is transmitted to the authorities concerned, three working days before the shipment. The transport company is required to transmit a copy of the transfer note to the last customs office for exportation after which the waste leaves the Community. The customs office notifies the competent authorities as soon as the waste leaves the Community. The authorities concerned with forwarding are expected to receive an acknowledgement of receipt of the waste within 42 days upon the waste leaving the Community. They must notify the competent authorities from the importing country if no acknowledgement of receipt has been received within this delay. The same procedure must be complied with if no certificate of disposal was transmitted within a maximum delay of six months.

Forwarding authorities may well decide to transmit the notification as well as the copies of this notification to the addressee and the authorities concerned of the transit country instead of the forwarder. Notifications are not to be transmitted if the forwarding authorities object to the shipment of the waste. In this case, the forwarder must be informed about the objections.

Exportation of waste for reclamation is prohibited except to countries subject to the OECD Decision, to countries which are signatories of the Basel Convention, to countries, the Community signed bilateral, multilateral or regional agreements with and to countries, Member States signed bilateral agreements and arrangements with, before the present Regulation took effect. These agreements must ensure the environmentally-friendly disposal of waste. However, exportation of waste for reclamation to the aforementioned is not authorised if these countries prohibit its importation or if they did not consent to the particular importation of the waste. The exportation of waste is not to be carried out if the authorities concerned with forwarding assume that the waste will not be treated in an environmentally acceptable way.

Countries which are not subject to the OECD Decision are asked to confirm in writing if the waste mentioned in the green List of Annexe II, is subject to a control procedure on their territory or if some of the waste is considered hazardous.

Waste listed in Annexe II may only be used for reclamation operations in plants whose activities are authorised by the importing country. In addition, every transfer requires an export permit which must be obtained beforehand. A copy of the export permit must be transmitted to the authorities of the importing country immediately.

The exportation of waste listed in Annexe II is subject to supervision, If it is either subject to supervision or considered hazardous in the importing country.

The Commission or the exporting Member State notifies these cases to the committee after which the Commission and the importing country jointly agree upon the control procedures to be implemented: control procedures for Annexes III (orange List of waste) and IV (red List of waste) or control procedures for waste to be disposed of.

The procedure of notification and authorisation for internal shipments of waste to be reclaimed appearing in the orange List in Annexe III also applies to the exportation to or transit through countries which are subject to the OECD Decision.

The procedures for shipments of waste to be reclaimed within the Community also apply to the exportation and transit of waste mentioned on the red List of Annexe IV as well as waste to be reclaimed which is not yet registered in Annexes II, III and IV to countries subject to the OECD Decision. However, the approval of the competent authorities concerned must be notified before the shipment takes place. In addition, the transport company must deliver a copy of the transfer note to the customs office for exportation when the waste leaves the Community. Upon the waste leaving the Community, the customs office for exportation notifies the competent authorities which issued the authorisation. The addressee is required to acknowledge receipt of the waste to the forwarding authorities within 42 days upon its leaving the Community. The forwarding authorities notify the competent authorities of the importing country if no acknowledgement has been received within this delay.

Waste shipments to ACP countries are prohibited. However, a Member State that has upgraded waste from an ACP country, is allowed to ship the reclaimed waste back to the ACP country of origin.

Importing waste to be disposed of in the Community is prohibited except for waste EFTA countries and other countries which are signatories of the Basel Convention. Waste to be disposed of in the Community may also be imported from countries, the Community or its Member States signed bilateral agreements or arrangements with. These agreements and arrangements must be in conformity with Community Legislation.

Importation of waste for disposal requires the importer to send a notification to the competent authorities of the importing country. A copy of this notification must be sent to both the addressee and the competent authorities of the transit countries. In this case the transfer note is delivered by the competent authorities of the importing country.

The importing authorities acknowledge receipt of the notification to the importer and send a copy to the transit authorities of the Community. Subsequently, the competent authorities of the importing country are allowed 70 days to decide whether they approve, under certain conditions or not, of the transfer or reject it. The shipment will only be authorised if none of the competent authorities concerned object to it.

The shipment is only to be carried out after receipt of the authorisation of the importing authorities. The importer completes the transfer note and transmits a copy to all the authorities concerned three days before the shipment takes place. A copy of the transfer note is delivered to the customs office for importation in the Community. The addressee is required to send a certificate of disposal to the forwarder and the competent authorities within six months upon receipt of the waste.

Importation of waste to be reclaimed into the Community is prohibited except from the countries whose waste for disposal is allowed into the Community.

Importing waste for reclamation appearing in Annexe III, from countries under the OECD Decision, is subject to the same procedures of shipments of waste to be reclaimed within the Community. These procedures also apply to waste listed in Annexe IV and waste which is not yet registered in Annexes II, III or IV except that the competent authorities must transmit the authorisation in writing before the shipment takes place.

The procedures of notification and authorisation for the importation of waste for disposal also apply to the importation of the types of waste listed in Annexes III and IV or which have not yet been registered in Annexes II, III or IV, from countries to which the OECD Decision does not apply.

If the Community functions as a transit area for waste coming from and going to a non-member state, a transfer note is required for both waste for disposal and waste for regeneration. The transfer note is transmitted to the last competent transit authorities in the Community. The aforementioned authorities must acknowledge receipt of the notification and are allowed 60 days to consent to, under certain conditions or not, or reject the transfer. A copy of the Decision must be sent to all the other competent authorities concerned and to the customs offices for both importation and exportation.

The forwarder completes the transfer note upon receipt of the authorisation and transmits a copy of the document to all the competent authorities concerned, three days before the shipment takes place. The customs office of exportation notifies to the last competent authority of transit when the waste leaves the Community. In addition, the forwarder must certify the arrival of the waste at its destination within 40 days.

Shipments of waste which do not meet the requirements of the present Regulation are considered illegal. All competent authorities must co-operate to eliminate or reclaim this illegal waste in an ecologically-acceptable way. Moreover, the Member States institute legal proceedings in order to prohibit and sanction illegal transfers.

A financial warranty has been instituted to cover transport costs and costs for disposal or regeneration. This warranty is refunded when the arrival of the waste at its destination has been proved.

Council and Commission Decision 94/1/ECSC, EC[1] — The European Economic Area

The contracting parties agree to preserve, protect and improve the quality of the environment, to contribute to the protection of public health and to ensure an economical and rational use of natural resources. Therefore, a whole range of Community Directives concerning the environment apply to the entire European Economic Area. These measures, however, do not obstruct the implementation or establishment of reinforced measures of protection, compatible with the present agreement.

Their actions concerning the environment are based upon the principles of preventing and remedying environmental threats, preferably at source, and on the principle of "the polluter pays". The contracting parties are required to insert the measures concerning environmental protection into their other policies.

Commission Directive 94/3/EC[2] — The framework for waste

This Directive establishes the List of the waste which constitutes the categories of Annexe I to Directive 75/442/EEC[3] on waste.

---

[1] Decision 94/1/EC, ECSC of the Council and the Commission, of 13 December 1993, on the conclusion of the agreement on the European Economic Area between the European Communities, their Member States and the Republic of Austria, the Republic of Finland, the Republic of Iceland, the Principality of Liechtenstein, the Kingdom of Norway, the Kingdom of Sweden and the Swiss Confederation (OJ L 1, 03.01.1994, p. 1).

[2] Commission Decision 94/3/EC, of 20 December 1993, establishing a List of wastes pursuant to Article 1 (a) of Council Directive 75/442/EEC on waste (OJ L 5, 07.01.1994, p. 15).

[3] Council Directive 75/442/EEC, of 15 July 1975, on waste (OJ L 194, 25.07.1975, p. 39). Also see Community Legislation concerning the environment, Volume 6, Waste, first edition, p 14 and xxvi

Legislation concerning Waste

DIRECTIVE 91/689/EEC[1]
of 12 December 1991
on hazardous waste

THE COUNCIL OF THE EUROPEAN COMMUNITIES,

Having regard to the Treaty establishing the European Economic Community, and in particluar Article 103s thereof,

Having regard to the proposal from the Commission[2],

Having regard to the opinion of the European Parliament[3],

Having regard to the opinion of the Economic and Social Committee[4],

Whereas Council Directive 78/319/EEC of 20 March 1978 on toxic and dangerous waste[5], established Community rules on the disposal of dangerous waste; whereas in order to take account of experience gained in the implementation of that Directive by the Member States, it is necessary to amend the rules and to replace Directive 78/319/EEC by this Directive;

Whereas the Council resolution of 7 May 1990 on waste policy[6] and the action programme of the European Communities on the environment, which was the subject of the resolution of the Council of the European Communities and of the representatives of the Government of the Member States, meeting within the Council, of 19 October 1987 on the continuation and implementation of a European Community policy and action programme on the environment (1987 to 1992)[7], envisage Community measures to improve the conditions under which hazardous wastes are disposed of and managed;

Whereas the general rules applying to waste management which are laid down by Council Directive 75/442/EEC of 15 July 1975 on waste[8], as amended by Directive 91/156/EEC[9], also apply to the management of hazardous waste;

---

[1] OJ No L 377, 31. 12. 1991, p. 20.
[2] OJ No C 295, 19. 11. 1988, p. 8, and OJ No C 42, 22. 2. 1990, p. 19.
[3] OJ No C 158, 26. 6. 1989, p. 238.
[4] OJ No C 56, 6. 3. 1989, p. 2.
[5] OJ No L 84, 31. 3. 1978, p. 43.
[6] OJ No C 122, 18. 5. 1990, p. 2.
[7] OJ No C 328, 7. 12. 1987, p. 1.
[8] OJ No L 194, 25. 7. 1975, p. 39.
[9] OJ No L 78, 26. 3. 1991, p. 32.

Whereas the correct management of hazardous waste necessitates additional, more stringent rules to take account of the special nature of such waste;

Whereas it is necessary, in order to improve the effectiveness of the management of hazardous waste in the Community, to use a precise and uniform definition of hazardous waste based on experience;

Whereas it is necessary to ensure that disposal and recovery of hazardous waste is monitored in the fullest manner possible;

Whereas it must be possible rapidly to adapt the provisions of this Directive to scientific and technical progress; whereas the Committee set up by Directive 75/442/EEC must also empowered to adapt the provisions of this Directive to such progress,

HAS ADOPTED THIS DIRECTIVE:

Article 1

1.   The object of this Directive, drawn up pursuant to Article 2 (2) of Directive 75/442/EEC, is to approximate the laws of the Member States on the controlled management of hazardous waste.

2.   Subject ot this Directive, Directive 75/442/EEC shall apply to hazardous waste.

3.   The definition of 'waste' and of the other terms used in this Directive shall be those in Directive 75/442/EEC.

4.   For the purpose of this Directive 'hazardous waste' means:

—   wastes featuring on a list to be drawn up in accordance with the procedure laid down in Article 18 of Directive 75/442/EEC on the basis of Annexes I and II to this Directive, not later than six months before the date of implementation of this Directive. These wastes must have one or more of the properties listed in Annex III. The list shall take into account the origin and composition of the waste and, where necessary, limit values of concentration. This list shall be periodically reviewed and if necessary by the same procedure,

—   any other waste which is considered by a Member State to display any of the properties listed in Annex III. Such cases shall be notified to the Commission and reviewed in accordance with the procedure laid down in Article 18 of Directive 75/442/EEC with a view to adaptation of the list.

5.   Domestic waste shall be exempted from the provisions of this Directive. The Council shall establish, upon a proposal from the Commission, specific rules taking into consideration the particular nature of domestic waste not later than the end of 1992.

Article 2

1.   Member States shall take the necessary measures to require that on every site where tipping (discharge) of hazardous waste takes place the waste is recorded and identified.

2.   Member States shall take the necessary measures to require that establishment and undertaking which dispose of, recover, collect or transport hazardous waste do not mix different categories of hazardous waste or mix hazardous waste with non-hazardous waste.

3.   By way of derogation from paragraph 2, the mixing of hazardous waste with other hazardous waste or with other waste, substances or materials may be permitted only where the conditions laid down in Article 4 of Directive 75/442/EEC are complied with and in particular for the purpose of improving safety during disposal or recovery. Such an operation shall be subject to the permit requirement imposed in Articles 9, 10 and 11 of Directive 75/442/EEC.

4.   Where waste is already mixed with other waste, substances or materials, separation must be effected, where technically and economically feasible, and where necessary in order to comply with Article 4 of Directive 75/442/EEC.

Article 3

1.   The derogation referred to in Article 11 (1) (a) of Directive 75/442/EEC from the permit requirement for establishments or undertakings which carry out their own waste disposal shall not apply to hazardous waste covered by this Directive.

—   In accordance with Article 11 (1) (b) of Directive 75/442/EEC, a Member State may waive Article 10 of that Directive for establishments or undertakings which recover waste covered by this Directive:

—   if the Member State adopts general rules listing the type and quantity of waste and laying down specific conditions (limit values for the content of hazardous substances in the waste, emission limit values, type of activity) and other necessary requirements for carrying out different forms of recovery, and

— if the types or quantities of waste and methods of recovery are such that the conditions laid down in Article 4 of Directive 75/442/EEC are complied with.

2. The establishments or undertankings referred to in paragraph 2 shall be registered with the competent authorities.

3. If a Member State intends to make use of the provisions of paragraph 2, the rules referred to in that paragraph shall be sent to the Commission not later than three months prior to their coming into force. The Commission shall consult the Member States. In the light of these consultations the Commission shall propose that the rules be finally agreed upon in accordance with the procedure laid down in Article 18 of Directive 75/442/EEC.

Article 4

1. Article 13 of Directive 75/442/EEC shall also apply to producers of hazardous waste.

2. Article 14 of Directive 75/442/EEC shall also apply to producers of hazardous waste and to all establishments and undertakings transporting hazardous waste.

3. The records referred to in Article 14 of Directive 75/442/EEC must be preserved for at least three years except in the case of establishments and undertakings transporting hazardous waste which must keep such records for at least 12 months. Documentary evidence that the management operations have been carried out must be supplied at the request of the competent authorities or of a previous holder.

Article 5

1. Member States shall take the necessary measures to ensure that, in the course of collection, transport and temporary storage, waste is properly packaged and labelled in accordance with the international and Community standards in force.

2. In the case of hazardous waste, inspections concerning collection and transport operations made on the basis of Article 13 of Directive 75/442/EEC shall cover more particularly the origin and destination of such waste.

3. Where hazardous waste is transferred, it shall be accompanied by an identification form containing the details specified in Section A of Annex I to Council Directive 84/631/EEC of 6 December 1984 on the supervision and

control within the European Community of the transfrontier shipment of hazardous waste[1], as last amended by Directive 86/279/EEC[2].

Article 6

1.   As provided in Article 7 of Directive 75/442/EEC, the competent authorities shall draw up, either separately or in the framework of their general waste management plans, plans for the management of hazardous waste and shall make these plans public.

2.   The Commission shall compare these plans, and in particular the methods of disposal and recovery. It shall make this information available to the competent authorities of the Member States which ask for it.

Article 7

In cases of emergency or grave danger, Member States shall take all necessary steps, including, where appropriate, temporary derogations from this Directive, to ensure that hazardous waste is so dealt with as not to constitute a threat to the population or the environment. The Member State shall inform the Commission of any such derogations.

Article 8

1.   In the context of the report provided for in Article 16 (1) of Directive 75/442/EEC, and on the basis of a questionnaire drawn up in accordance with that Article, the Member States shall send the Commission a report on the implementation of this Directive.

2.   In addition to the consolidated report referred to in Article 16 (2) of Directive 75/442/EEC, the Commission shall report to the European Parliament and the Council every three years on the implementation of this Directive.

3.   In addition, by 12 December 1994, the Member States shall send the Commission the following information for every establishment or undertaking which carries out disposal and/or recovery of hazardous waste principally on behalf of third parties and which is likely to form part of the integrated network referred to in Article of Directive 75/442/EEC:

---

[1] OJ No L 326, 13. 12. 1984, p. 31.
[2] OJ No L 181, 4. 7. 1986, p. 13.

— name and address,

— the method used to treat waste,

— the types and quantities of waste which can be treated.

Once a year, Member States shall inform the Commission of any changes in this information.

The Commission shall make this information available on request to the competent authorities in the Member States.

The format in which this information will be supplied to the Commission shall be agreed upon in accordance with the procedure laid down in Article 18 of Directive 75/442/EEC.

Article 9

The amendments necessary for adapting the Annexes to this Directive to scientific and technical progress and for revising the list of wastes referred to in Article 1 (4) shall be adopted in accordance with the procedure laid down in Article 18 of Directive 74/442/EEC.

Article 10

1. The Member States shall bring into force the laws, regulations and administrative provisions necessary to comply with this Directive before 12 December 1993. They shall forthwith inform the Comission thereof.

2. When Member States adopt these measures, they shall contain a reference to this Directive or shall be accompanied by such reference on the occasion of their official publication. The methods of making such a reference shall be laid down by the Member States.

3. Member States shall communicate to the Commission the texts of the main provisions of national law which they adopt in the field governed by this Directive.

Article 11

Directive 78/319/EEC is hereby repealed with effect from 12 December 1993.

Article 12

This Directive is addressed to the Member States.

Done at Brussels, 12 December 1991.

For the Council

The President

J.G.M. ALDERS

ANNEX I

CATEGORIES OR GENERIC TYPES OF HAZARDOUS WASTE LISTED ACCORDING TO THEIR NATURE OR THE ACTIVITY WHICH GENERATED THEM[1] (WASTE MAY BE LIQUID, SLUDGE OR SOLID IN FORM)

ANNEX I.A.

Wastes displaying any of the properties listed in Annex III and which consist of:

1) anatomical substances; hospital and other clinical wastes;

2) pharmaceuticals, medicines and veterinary compounds;

3) wood preservatives;

4) biocides and phyto-pharmaceutical substances;

5) residue from substances employed as solvents;

6) halogenated organic substances not employed as solvents excluding inert polymerized materials;

7) tempering salts containing cyanides;

8) mineral oils and oily substances (e.g. cutting sludges, etc.);

9) oil/water, hydrocarbon/water mixtures, emulsions;

10) substances containing PCBs and/or PCTs (e.g. dielectrics etc.);

11) tarry materials arising from refining, distillation and any pyrolytic treatment (e.g. still bottoms, etc.);

12) inks, dyes, pigments, paints, lacquers, varnishes;

13) resins, latex, plasticizers, glues/adhesives;

14) chemical substances arising from research and development or teaching activities which are not identified and/or are new and whose effects on man and/or the environment are not known (e.g. laboratory residues, etc.);

15) pyrotechnics and other explosive materials;

16) photographic chemicals and processing materials;

---

[1] Certain duplications of entries found in Annex II are intentional.

17) any material contaminated with any congener of polychlorinated dibenzo-furan;

18) any material contaminated with any congener of polychlorinated dibenzo-p-dioxin.

ANNEX I.B.

Wastes which contain any of the constituents listed in Annex II and having any of the properties listed in Annex III and consisting of:

19) animal or vegetable soaps, fats, waxes;

20) non-halogenated organic substances not employed as solvents;

21) inorganic substances without metals or metal compounds;

22) ashes and/or cinders;

23) soil, sand, clay including dredging spoils;

24) non-cyanidic tempering salts;

25) metallic dust, powder;

26) spent catalyst materials;

27) liquids or sludges containing metals or metal compounds;

28) residue from pollution control operations (e.g. baghouse dusts, etc.) except (29), (30) and (33);

29) scrubber sludges;

30) sludges from water purification plants;

31) decarbonization residue;

32) ion-exchange column residue;

33) sewage sludges, untreated or unsuitable for use in agriculture;

34) residue from cleaning of tanks and/or equipment;

35) contaminated equipment;

36) contaminated containers (e.g. packaging, gas cylinders, etc.) whose contents included one or more of the constituents listed in Annex II;

37) batteries and other electrical cells;

38) vegetable oils;

39) materials resulting from selective waste collections from households and which exhibit any of the characteristics listed in Annex III;

40) any other wastes which contain any of the constituents listed in Annex II and any of the properties listed in Annex III.

ANNEX II

CONSTITUENTS OF THE WASTES IN ANNEX I.B. WHICH RENDER THEM HAZARDOUS WHEN THEY HAVE THE PROPERTIES DESCRIBED IN ANNEX III[1]

Wastes having as constituents:

C1   beryllium; beryllium compounds;

C2   vanadium compounds;

C3   chromium (VI) compounds;

C4   cobalt compounds;

C5   nickel compounds;

C6   copper compounds;

C7   zinc compounds;

C8   arsenic; arsenic compounds;

C9   selenium; selenium compounds;

C10   silver compounds;

C11   cadmium; cadmium compounds;

C12   tin compounds;

C13   antimony; antimony compounds;

C14   tellurium; tellurium compounds;

C15   barium compounds; excluding barium sulfate;

C16   mercury; mercury compounds;

---

[1] Certain duplications of generic types of hazardous wastes listed in Annex I are intentional.

C17   thallium; thallium compounds;

C18   lead; lead compounds;

C19   inorganic sulphides;

C20   inorganic fluorine compounds, excluding calcium fluoride;

C21   inorganic cyanides;

C22   the following alkaline or alkaline earth metals: lithium, sodium, potassium, calcium, magnesium in uncombined form;

C23   acidic solutions or acids in solid form;

C24   basic solutions or bases in solid form;

C25   asbestos (dust and fibres);

C26   phosphorus: phosphorus compounds, excluding mineral phosphates;

C27   metal carbonyls;

C28   peroxides;

C29   chlorates;

C30   perchlorates;

C31   azides;

C32   PCBs and/or PCTs;

C33   pharmaceutical or veterinary coumpounds;

C34   biocides and phyto-pharmaceutical substances (e.g. pesticides, etc.);

C35   infectious substances;

C36   creosotes;

C37   isocyanates; thiocyanates;

C38   organic cyanides (e.g. nitriles, etc.);

C39   phenols; phenol compounds;

C40   halogenated solvents;

C41   organic solvents, excluding halogenated solvents;

C42   organohalogen compounds, excluding inert polymerized materials and other substances referred to in this Annex;

C43   aromatic compounds; polycyclic and heterocyclic organic compounds;

C44   aliphatic amines;

C45   aromatic amines

C46   ethers;

C47   substances of an explosive character, excluding those listed elsewhere in this Annex;

C48   sulphur organic compounds;

C49   any congener of polychlorinated dibenzo-furan;

C50   any congener of polychlorinated dibenzo-p-dioxin;

C51   hydrocarbons and their oxygen; nitrogen and/or sulphur compounds not otherwise taken into account in this Annex.

Annex III

PROPERTIES OF WASTES WHICH RENDER THEM HAZARDOUS

H1 'Explosive': substances and preparations which may explode under the effect of flame or which are more sensitive to shocks or friction than dinitrobenzene.

H2 'Oxidizing': substances and preparations which exhibit highly exothermic reactions when in contact with other substances, particularly flammable substances.

H3-A 'Highly flammable':

— liquid substances and preparations having a flash point below 21 °C (including extremely flammable liquids), or

— substances and preparations which may become hot and finally catch fire in contact with air at ambient temperature without any application of energy, or

— solid substances and preparations which may readily catch fire after brief contact with a source of ignition and which continue to burn or to be consumed after removal of the source of ignition, or

— gaseous substances and preparations which are flammable in air at normal pressure, or

— substances and preparations which, in contact with water or damp air, evolve highly flammable gases in dangerous quantities.

H3-B 'Flammable': liquid substances and preparations having a flash point equal to or greater than 21 °C and less than or equal to 55 °C.

H4 'Irritant': non-corrosive substances and preparations which, through immediate, prolonged or repeated contact with the skin or mucous membrane, can cause inflammation.

H5 'harmful': substances and preparations which, if they are inhaled or ingested or if they penetrate the skin, may involve limited health risks.

H6 'Toxic': substances and preparations (including very toxic substances and preparations) which, if they are inhaled or ingested or if they penetrate the skin, may involve serious, acute or chronic health risks and even death.

H7 'Carcinogenic': substances and preparations which, if they are inhaled or ingested or if they penetrate the skin, may induce cancer or increase its incidence.

H8   'Corrosive': substances and preparations which may destroy living tissue on contacts.

H9   'Infectious': substances containing viable micro-organisms or their toxins which are known or reliably believed to cause disease in man or other living organisms.

H10   'Teratogenic': substances and preparations which, if they are inhaled or ingested or if they penetrate the skin, may induce non-hereditary congenital malformations or increase their incidence.

H11   'Mutagenic': substances and preparations which, if they are inhaled or ingested or if they penetrate the skin, may induce hereditary genetic defects or increase their incidence.

H12   Substances and preparations which release toxic or very toxic gases in contact with water, air or an acid.

H13   Substances and preparations capable by any means, after disposal, of yielding another substance, e.g. a leachate, which possesses any of the characteristics listed above.

H14   'Ecotoxic': substances and preparations which present or may present immediate or delayed risks for one or more sectors of the environment.

Notes

1)   Attribution of the hazard properties 'toxic' (and 'very toxic'), 'harmful', 'corrosive' and 'irritant' is made on the basis of the criteria laid down by Annex VI, part I A and part II B, of Council Directive 67/548/EEC of 27 June 1967 of the approximation of laws, regulations and administrative provisions relating to the classification, packaging and labelling of dangerous substances[1], in the version as amended by Council Directive 79/831/EEC[2].

2)   With regard to attribution of the properties 'carcinogenic', 'teratogenic' and 'mutagenic', and reflecting the most recent findings, additional criteria are contained in the Guide to the classification and labelling of dangerous substances and preparations of Annex VI (part II D) to Directive 67/548/EEC in the version as amended by Commission Directive 83/467/EEC [3].

---

[1]   OJ No L 196, 16. 8. 1967, p. 1.
[2]   OJ No L 259, 15. 10. 1979, p. 10.
[3]   OJ No L 257, 16. 9. 1983, p. 1.

15

Test methods

The test methods serve to give specific meaning to the definitions given in Annex III.

The methods to be used are those described in Annex V to Directive 67/548/EEC, in the version as amended by Commission Directive 84/449/EEC [1], or by subsequent Commission Directives adapting Directive 67/548/EEC to technical progress. These methods are themselves based on the work and recommendations of the competent international bodies, in particular the OECD.

---

[1]   OJ No L 251, 19. 9. 1984, p. 1.

COUNCIL DIRECTIVE 94/31/EC[1]
of 27 June 1994
amending Directive 91/689/EEC
on hazardous waste

THE COUNCIL OF THE EUROPEAN UNION,

Having regard to the Treaty establishing the European Community, and in particular Article 130s (1) thereof,

Having regard to the proposal from the Commission[2],

Having regard to the opinion of the Economic and Social Committee[3],

Acting in accordance with the procedure laid down in Article 189 c of the Treaty,

Whereas it has become apparent, through the work of the committee provided for in Article 18 of Council Directive 75/442/EEC[4] that it has not been possible, within the time limits fixed by Directive 91/689/EEC[5], to draw up a binding list of hazardous waste, but whereas the implementation of Directive 91/689/EEC depends on the Commission's establishing such a list;

Whereas it is necessary to ensure the implementation of Directive 91/689/EEC within the shortest possible time;

Whereas a Community list of hazardous waste must still be established in accordance with Article 1 (4) of Directive 91/689/EEC;

Whereas the repeal of Council Directive 78/319/EEC of 20 March 1978 on toxic and dangerous waste[6] must therefore be postponed,

HAS ADOPTED THIS DIRECTIVE:

---

[1]   OJ No L 168, 2. 7; 1994, p; 28.
[2]   OJ No C 271, 7. 10. 1993, p. 16.
[3]   OJ No C 34, 2. 2. 1994, p. 7.
[4]   OJ No L 194, 25. 7. 1975, p. 39.
      Directive last amended by Directive 91/156/EEC
      (OJ No L 78, 26. 3. 1991, p. 32).
[5]   OJ No L 377, 31. 12. 1991, p. 20.
[6]   OJ No L 84, 31. 3. 1978, p. 43.
      Directive last amended by Directive 91/692/EEC
      (OJ No L 377, 31. 12. 1991, p. 48).

Article 1

Directive 91/689/EEC is hereby amended as follows:

1)   The following shall be substituted for Article 10 (1):

'Article 10

1. Member States shall bring into force the laws, regulations and administrative provisions necessary for them to comply with this Directive by 27 June 1995. They shall immediately inform the Commission thereof.'

2)   The following shall be substituted for Article 11:

'Annex 11

Directive 78/319/EEC shall be repealed with effect from 27 June 1995.'

Article 2

This Directive is addressed to the Member States.

Done at Luxembourg, 27 June 1994.

For the Council

The President

C. SIMITIS

DIRECTIVE 92/112/EEC[1] of 15 December 1992 on procedures for harmonizing the programmes for the reduction and eventual elimination of pollution caused by waste from the titanium dioxide industry

THE COUNCIL OF THE EUROPEAN COMMUNITIES,

Having regard to the Treaty establishing the European Economic Community, and in particular Article 100a thereof,

Having regard to the proposal from the Commission[2],

In cooperation with the European Parliament[3],

Having regard to the opinion of the Economic and Social Committee[4],

Whereas Council Directive 89/428/EEC of 21 June 1989 on procedures for harmonizing the programmes for the reduction and eventual elimination of pollution caused by waste from the titanium dioxide industry[5] was annulled by the Court of Justice in its judgment of 11 June 1991 on the grounds that it lacked an appropriate legal basis[6];

Whereas, if Member States have taken the necessary measures to comply with the said Directive, it is not necessary for them to adopt new measures to meet this Directive, provided the measures already taken comply with the latter;

Whereas the legal void caused by the annulment of the said Directive may have adverse effects on the environment and on conditions of competition in the titanium dioxide production sector; whereas it is necessary to restore the material situation created by the said Directive;

Whereas the objective of this Directive is to approximate national rules relating to titanium dioxide production conditions in order to eliminate the existing distortions of competition between the various producers in the industry and to ensure a high level of environmental protection;

---

[1]   OJ No L 409, 7. 12. 1991, p. 5.
[2]   OJ No C 317, 7. 12. 1991, p. 5.
[3]   OJ No C 94, 13. 4. 1992, p. 158, and OJ No C 305, 23. 11. 1992.
[4]   OJ No C 98, 21. 4. 1992, p. 9.
[5]   OJ No L 201, 14. 7. 1989, p. 56.
[6]   Judgment of 11 June 1991, Case C-300/89, Commission v. Council (not yet published).

Whereas Council Directive 78/176/EEC of 20 February 1978 on waste from the titanium dioxide industry[1], and in particular Article 9 thereof, requires the Member States to draw up programmes for the progressive reduction and eventual elimination of pollution caused by waste from industrial establishments in existence on 20 February 1978;

Whereas these programmes set general targets for the reduction of pollution caused by liquid, solid and gaseous wastes to be achieved by 1 July 1987; whereas these programmes were to be submitted to the Commission so that it could present suitable proposals to the Council for their harmonization with regard to the reduction and eventual elimination of this pollution and the improvement of the conditions of competition in the titanium dioxide industry;

Whereas, in order to protect the aquatic environment, dumping of waste and discharges of certain wastes, in particular of solid and strong acid wastes, should be prohibited and discharges of other wastes, in particular of weak acid and neutralized wastes, should be progressively reduced;

Whereas existing industrial establishments should employ the appropriate systems for treating the wastes in order to meet the requisite targets by the set dates;

Whereas installation of those systems can give rise to major technico-economic difficulties in the case of weak acid waste and neutralized waste from certain establishments; whereas Member States should therefore be able to defer application of these provisions, on condition that a programme of effective reduction of pollution is drawn up and submitted to the Commission; whereas where Member States experience such difficulties, the Commission should be able to extend the relevant time limits;

Whereas, in respect of discharges of certain wastes, Member States should be able to make use of quality objectives in such a way that the results are equivalent in all respects to those obtained through limit values; whereas such equivalence should be demonstrated in a programme to be presented to the Commission;

Whereas, without prejudice to the obligations placed on Member States by Council Directive 80/779/EEC of 15 July 1980 on air quality limit values and guide values for sulphur dioxide and suspended particulates[2], and Council Directive 84/360/EEC of 28 June 1984 on the combating of air pollution from industrial plants[3], it is expedient to protect the quality of the air by fixing

---

[1] OJ No L 54, 25. 2. 1978, p. 19;
      Directive as last amended by Directive 83/29/EEC
      (OJ No L 32, 3. 2. 1983, p. 28).

appropriate emission standards in respect of gaseous discharges from the titanium dioxide industry;

Whereas, in order to verify the effective application of the measures, Member States should undertake monitoring in relation to the actual production of each establishment;

Whereas all waste from the titanium dioxide industry should be avoided or reused where technically and economically feasible and whereas such waste should be reused or disposed of without endangering human health or the environment,

HAS ADOPTED THIS DIRECTIVE:

Article 1

This Directive lays down, as required by Article 9 (3) of Directive 78/176/EEC, procedures for harmonizing the programmes for the reduction and eventual elimination of pollution from existing industrial establishments and is intended to improve the conditions of competition in the titanium dioxide industry.

Article 2

1. For the purposes of this Directive:

   a) where the sulphate process is used:

   — *solid waste shall mean*:

   - insoluble ore residues not broken down by sulphuric acid during the manufacturing proces,

   - copperas, i. e. crystalline ferrous sulphate ($FeSO_47H_2O$),

   — *strong acid waste shall mean*:

   - the mother liquors arising from the filtration phase following hydrolysis of the titanyl sulphate solution. If these mother liquors are associated with weak acid wastes which overall contain more than 0,5 % free sulphuric acid and various heavy metals[1], the liquors and waste taken together shall be considered strong acid waste,

---

[2] OJ No L 229, 30. 8. 1980, p. 30;
   Directive as last amended by Directive 89/427/EEC
   (OJ No L 201, 14. 7. 1989, p. 53).

[3] OJ No L 188, 16. 7. 1989, p. 20.

— *treatment waste shall mean*:

- filtration salts, sludges and liquid waste arising from the treatment (concentration or neutralization) of strong acid waste and containing various heavy metals, but not including neutralized and filtered or decanted waste containing only traces of heavy metals and which, before any dilution, has a pH value above 5,5,

— *weak acid waste shall mean*:

- wash waters, cooling waters, condensates and other sludges and liquid wastes, other than those included in the above definitions, containing 0,5 % or less free sulphuric acid,

— *neutralized waste shall mean*:

- any liquid which has a pH value over 5,5, contains only traces of heavy metals, and is obtained directly by filtration or decantation from strong or weak acid waste after its treatment to reduce its acidity and its heavy metal content,

— *dust shall mean*:

- all kinds of dust from production plants and in particular ore and pigment dust,

— SO_x *shall mean*:

- gaseous sulphur dioxide and trioxide released in the various stages of the manufacturing and internal waste treatment processes, including acid droplets;

b) where the chlorine process is used:

— *solid waste shall mean*:

- insoluble ore residues not broken down by the chlorine during the manufacturing process,

- metal chlorides and metal hydroxides (filtration substances), arising in solid form from the manufacture of titanium tetrachloride,

- coke residues arising from the manufacture of titanium tetrachloride,

— *strong acid waste shall mean*:

- waste containing more than 0,5 % free hydrochloric acid and various heavy metals[1];

---

[1] Strong acid waste which has been diluted until it contains 0,5 % or less free sulphuric acid shall also be covered by this difinition.

— *treatment waste shall mean*:

- filtration salts, sludges and liquid waste arising from the treatment (concentration or neutralization) of strong acid waste and containing various heavy metals, but not including neutralized and filtered or decanted waste containing only traces of heavy metals and which, before any dilution, has a pH value over 5,5,

— *weak acid waste shall mean*:

- wash waters, cooling waters, condensates and other sludges and liquid wastes, other than those included in the above definitions, containing 0,5 % or less free hydrochloric acid,

— *neutralized waste shall mean*:

- any liquid which has a pH value over 5,5, contains only traces of heavy metals, and is obtained directly by filtration or decantation from strong or weak acid waste after its treatment to reduce its acidity and its heavy metal content,

— *dust shall mean*:

- all kinds of dust from production plants and in particular ore, pigment and coke dust,

— *chlorine shall mean*:

- gaseous chlorine released in the various stages of the manufacturing process;

c) where the sulphate process or the chlorine process is used

— *dumping shall mean*:

- any deliberate disposal into inland surface waters, internal coastal waters, territorial waters or the high seas of substances and materials by or from ships or aircraft[1]

2. The terms defined in Directive 78/176/EEC shall have the same meaning for the purposes of this Directive.

---

[1] Strong acid waste which has been diluted until it contains 0,5 % or less free sulphuric acid shall also be covered by this definition.

[1] '*Ships and aircraft*' shall mean waterborne vessels and airborne craft of any type whatsoever. This expression shall include air-cushion craft, floating craft, whether self-propelled or not, and fixed or floating platforms.

Article 3

The dumping of any solid waste, strong acid waste, treatment waste, weak acid waste, or neutralized waste, as referred to in Article 2 shall be prohibited with effect from 15 June 1993.

Article 4

Member States shall take the necessary measures to ensure that discharges of waste into inland surface waters, internal coastal waters, territorial waters and the high sea are prohibited:

   a)   as regards solid waste, strong acid waste and treatment waste from existing industrial establishments using the sulphate process:

—   by 15 June 1993 in all the abovementioned waters;

   b)   as regards solid waste and strong acid waste from existing industrial establishments using the chlorine process:

—   by 15 June 1993 in all the abovementioned waters.

Article 5

In the case of Member States which have serious technical and economic difficulties in complying with the date of application referred to in Article 4, the Commission may grant an extension, provided that a programme for the effective reduction of discharges of such waste is submitted to the Commission by 15 June 1993. That programme must result in a definitive ban on such discharges by 30 June 1993.

No later than three months after adoption of this Directive, the Commission shall be informed of any such cases and shall be consulted thereon. The Commission shall inform the other Member States.

Article 6

Member States shall take the necessary measures to ensure that discharges of waste are reduced in accordance with the following provisions:

   a)   from existing industrial establishments using the sulphate process:

—   weak acid waste and neutralized waste shall be reduced by 31 December 1993 in all waters to a value of not more than 800 kg of total sulphate per tonne of titanium dioxide produced (i. e. corresponding to the SO4 ions contained in the free sulphuric acid and in the metallic sulphates);

b) from existing industrial establishments using the chlorine process:

— weak acid waste, treatment waste and neutralized waste shall be reduced by 15 June 1993 in all waters to the following values of total chloride per tonne of titanium dioxide produced (i. e. corresponding to the C1 ions contained in the free hydrochloric acid and in the metallic chlorides):

- 130 kg using neutral rutile,

- 228 kg using synthetic rutile,

- 450 kg using slag.

In the case of an establishment using more than one type or ore, the values shall apply in proportion to the quantity of these ores used.

Article 7

Except where inland surface waters are concerned, Member States may defer the date of application referred to in point (a) of Article 6 until 31 December 1994 at the latest if serious technico-economic difficulties so require and provided that a programme of effective reduction of discharges of such waste is submitted to the Commission by 15 June 1993. Such a programme shall enable the following limit value per tonne of titanium dioxide produced to be reached by the date shown:

— weak acid waste and neutralized waste: 1 200 kg - 15 June 1993,

— weak acid waste and neutralized waste: 800 kg - 31 December 1994.

Three months at the latest following adoption of this Directive the Commission shall be informed of such cases, which shall be the subject of consultation with the Commission. The Commission shall inform the other Member States.

Article 8

1.   As regards the requirements of Article 6, Member States may choose to make use of quality objectives coupled with appropriate limit values applied in such a way that the effects in terms of protecting the environment and avoiding distortions of competition are equivalent to that of the limit values laid down in this Directive.

2.   If a Member State chooses to make use of quality objectives, it shall present to the Commission a programme[1] demonstrating that the measures achieve an effect which, in terms of protecting the environment and avoiding distortion of competition, is equivalent to that of the limit values by the dates when these limit values are applied in accordance with Article 6.

This programme shall be submitted to the Commission at least six months before the Member State proposes to apply the quality objectives.

This programme shall be assessed by the Commission in accordance with the procedures laid down in Article 10 of Directive 78/176/EEC.

The Commission shall inform the other Member States.

Article 9

1.   Member States shall take the necessary measures to ensure that discharges into the atmosphere are reduced in accordance with the following provisions:

a) in the case of existing industrial establishments using the sulphate process:

i) as regards dust, discharges shall be reduced by 31 December 1993 to a value of not more than 50 mg/nm^3 [2] from major sources and not more than 150 mg/nm^3 [2] from any other source [3];

ii) as regards SO_x, discharges arising from digestion and calcination steps in the manufacture of titanium dioxide shall be reduced by 1 January 1995 to a value of not more than 10 kg of SO_2 equivalent per tonne of titanium dioxide produced;

---

[1] Such information shall be provided under Article 14 of Directive 78/176/EEC or separately should circumstances so require.

[2] Cubic metre at a temperature of 273 K and a pressure of 101,3 kPa.

[3] Member States shall inform the Commission of those minor sources not included in their measurements.

iii) Member States shall require means to be installed for preventing the emission of acid droplets;

iv) plants for the concentration of waste acid shall not discharge more than 500 mg/nm^3 SO$_x$ calculated as SO$_2$ equivalent[3];

v) plants for the roasting of salts generated by the treatment of waste shall be equipped with the best available technology not entailing excessive costs in order to reduce SO$_x$ emissions;

b) in the case of existing industrial establishments using the chlorine process:

i) as regards dust, discharges shall be reduced by 15 June 1993 to a value of not more than 50 mg/nm^3 [1] for major sources and not more than 150 mg/nm^3 [2] from any other source [3];

ii) as regards chlorine, discharges shall be reduced by 15 June 1993 to a daily average concentration of not more than 5 mg/nm^3 [4] and not more than 40 mg/ng^3 at any time.

2. This Directive shall not prejudice Directive 80/779/EEC.

3. The procedure for monitoring the reference measurements for discharges of SO$_x$ into the atmosphere is set out in the Annex.

Article 10

Member States shall monitor the values and reductions specified in Articles 6, 8 and 9 in relation to the actual production of each establishment.

Article 11

Member States shall take the measures necessary to ensure that all waste from the titanium dioxide industry, and in particular waste subject to prohibition on discharge or dumping into water or on discharge into the atmosphere is:

— avoided or reused where technically and economically feasible,

---

[1] For new concentration processes the Commission can agree to a different value if the Member States can demonstrate the non-availability of techniques to achieve this standard.

[2] Cubic meter at a temperature of 273 K and a pressure of 101,3 kPa.

[3] Member States shall inform the Commission of those minor sources not included in their measurements.

[4] It is considered that these values correspond to a maximum of six grammes per tonne of titanium dioxide produced.

—   reused or disposed of without endangering human health or harming the environment.

The same shall apply to waste arising from the reuse or treatment of the above-mentioned waste.

Article 12

1.   Member States which have not yet taken the necessary measures to comply with this Directive shall bring them into force not later than 15 June 1993. They shall inform the Commission forthwith of the national provisions adopted to comply with this Directive.

When Member States adopt these provisions, they shall contain a reference to this Directive or shall be accompanied by such reference at the time of their official publication. The procedure for such reference shall be adopted by Member States.

2.   Member States shall communicate to the Commission the provisions of national law which they adopt in the field governed by this Directive.

Article 13

This Directive is addressed to the Member States.

Done at Brussels, 15 December 1992.

For the Council

The President

M. HOWARD

ANNEX

Procedure for monitoring the reference measurements for gaseous SO_x emissions

For the purposes of calculating the quantities of SO_2 and SO_3 and acid droplets expressed as SO_2 equivalent, discharged by specific installations, account must be taken of the volume of gas discharged over the duration of the specific operations in question and of the average SO_2/SO_3 content measured over the same period. The SO_2/SO_3 flow rate and content must be determined under the same temperature and humidity conditions.

DECISION 93/98/EEC[1]
of 1 February 1993
on the conclusion, on behalf of the Community, of the Convention on the control of transboundary movements of hazardous wastes and their disposal (Basel Convention)

THE COUNCIL OF THE EUROPEAN COMMUNITIES,

Having regard to the Treaty establishing the European Economic Community, and in particular Article 130s thereof,

Having regard to the proposal from the Commission,

Having regard to the opinion of the European Parliament[2],

Having regard to the opinion of the Economic and Social[3],

Whereas, by virtue of a Council Decision of 28 October 1988, the Commission participated on behalf of the Community, in consultation with the representatives of the Member States, in the negotiation in the ad hoc working group meetings under the auspices of the United Nations Environment Programme (UNEP) with a view to preparing a Global Convention on the Control of Transboundary Movements of Hazardous Waste;

Whereas, as a result of those negotiations, on 22 March 1989 the Basel Convention on the control of transboundary movements of hazardous wastes and their disposal was adopted and then signed by the Community on the basis of the mandate conferred by a Council Decision of 21 March 1989;

Whereas the Convention aims to help protect the environment in the area of waste through more stringent control of transboundary movements of hazardous wastes and other waste and through ecologically sound management thereof; whereas, in this respect, it determines procedures for controls on imports, exports and transit;

Whereas the Council, by adopting Regulation (EEC) No 259/93 of 1 February 1993 on the supervision and control of shipments of waste, within, into and out of the European Community[4], has established rules to curtail and to control

---

[1] OJ No L 39, 16. 2; 1993, p. 1.
[2] OJ No C 72, 18. 3. 1991, p. 67.
[3] OJ No C 31, 6. 2. 1991, p. 27.

such movements; whereas these rules are designed, inter alia, to make the existing Community system for the supervision and control of waste movements comply with the requirements of the Basel Convention and the Fourth ACP-EEC Convention;

Whereas, pursuant to its Articles 22 and 23, the Basel Convention is open for ratification, acceptance or approval and accession by States and for formal confirmation or approval by political and/or economic integration organizations,

HAS DECIDED AS FOLLOWS:

Article 1

The Convention on the control of transboundary movements of hazardous wastes and their disposal, as adopted in Basel on 22 March 1989, is hereby approved on behalf of the European Economic Community.

The text of the Convention is attached to this Decision.

Article 2

1. The President of the Council shall, on behalf of the Community, deposit the instrument of approval with the Secretary-General of the United Nations, as provided for by Article 22 of the Convention[1].

2. The President shall deposit at the same time the declaration of competence annexed to this Decision in conformity with Article 22 (3) of this Convention.

---

[4] OJ No L 30, 6. 2. 1993, p. 1.
[1] The date of entry into force for the Community of the Convention will be published in the Official Journal of the European Communities by the General Secretariat of the Council.

Article 3

This Decision shall be published in the *Official Journal of the European Communities.*

Done at Brussels, 1 February 1993.

For the Council

The President

N. HELVEG PETERSEN

BASEL CONVENTION
on the control of transboundary movements of hazardous wastes and their disposal

PREAMBLE

THE PARTIES TO THIS CONVENTION,

AWARE of the risk of damage to human health and the environment caused by hazardous wastes and other wastes and the transboundary movement thereof,

MINDFUL of the growing threat to human health and the environment posed by the increased generation and complexity, and the transboundary movement of hazardous wastes and other wastes,

MINDFUL ALSO that the most effective way of protecting human health and the environment from the dangers posed by such wastes is the reduction of their generation to a minimum in terms of quantity and/or hazard potential,

CONVINCED that States should take necessary measures to ensure that the management of hazardous wastes and other wastes including their transboundary movement and disposal is consistent with the protection of human health and the environment whatever the place of their disposal,

NOTING that States should ensure that the generator should carry out duties with regard to the transport and disposal of hazardous wastes and other wastes in a manner that is consistent with the protection of the environment, whatever the place of disposal,

FULLY RECOGNIZING that any State has the sovereign right to ban the entry or disposal of foreign hazardous wastes and other wastes in its territory,

RECOGNIZING ALSO the increasing desire for the prohibition of transboundary movements of hazardous wastes and their disposal in other States, especially developing countries,

CONVINCED that hazardous wastes and other wastes should, as far as is compatible with environmentally sound and efficient management, be disposed of in the State where they were generated,

AWARE ALSO that transboundary movements of such wastes from the State of their generation to any other State should be permitted only when conducted under conditions which do not endanger human health and the environment, and under conditions in conformity with the provisions of this Convention,

CONSIDERING that enhanced control of transboundary movement of hazardous wastes and other wastes will act as an incentive for their environmentally sound management and for the reduction of the volume of such transboundary movement,

CONVINCED that States should take measures for the proper exchange of information on and control of the transboundary movement of hazardous wastes and other wastes from and to those States,

NOTING that a number of international and regional agreements have addressed the issue of protection and preservation of the environment with regard to the transit of dangerous goods.

TAKING INTO ACCOUNT the Declaration of the United Nations Conference on the Human Environment (Stockholm, 1972), the Cairo Guidelines and Principles for the Environmentally Sound Management of Hazardous Wastes adopted by the Governing Council of the United Nations Environment Programme (UNEP) by decision 14/30 of 17 June 1987, the recommendations of the United Nations Committee of Experts on the Transport of Dangerous Goods (formulated in 1957 and updated biennially), relevant recommendations, declarations, instruments and regulations adopted within the United Nations system and the work and studies done within other international and regional organizations,

MINDFUL of the spirit, principles, aims and functions of the World Charter for Nature adopted by the General Assembly of the United Nations at its 37th session (1982) as the rule of ethics in respect of the protection of the human environment and the conservation of natural resources,

AFFIRMING that States are responsible for the fulfilment of their international obligations concerning the protection of human health and protection and preservation of the environment, and are liable in accordance with international law,

RECOGNIZING that in the case of a material breach of the provisions of this Convention or any protocol thereto the relevant international law of treaties shall apply,

AWARE of the need to continue the development and implementation of environmentally sound low-waste technologies, recycling options, good housekeeping and management systems with a view to reducing to a minimum the generation of hazardous wastes and other wastes,

AWARE ALSO of the growing international concern about the need for stringent control of transboundary movement of hazardous wastes and other wastes, and of the need as far as possible to reduce such movement to a minimum,

CONCERNED about the problem of illegal transboundary traffic in hazardous wastes and other wastes,

TAKING INTO ACCOUNT ALSO the limited capabilities of the developing countries to manage hazardous wastes and other wastes,

RECOGNIZING the need to promote the transfer of technology for the sound management of hazardous wastes and other wastes produced locally, particularly to the developing countries in accordance with the spirit of the Cairo Guidelines and decision 14/16 of the Governing Council of UNEP on promotion of the transfer of environmental protection technology,

RECOGNIZING ALSO that hazardous wastes and other wastes should be transported in accordance with relevant international conventions and recommendations,

CONVINCED ALSO that the transboundary movement of hazardous wastes and other wastes should be permitted only when the transport and the ultimate disposal of such wastes is environmentally sound,

DETERMINED to protect, by strict control, human health and the environment against the adverse effects which may result from the generation and management of hazardous wastes and other wastes,

HAVE AGREED AS FOLLOWS:

Article 1   Scope of the Convention

1.   The following wastes that are subject to transboundary movement shall be 'hazardous wastes' for the purposes of this Convention:

a)   wastes that belong to any category contained in Annex I, unless they do not possess any of the characteristics contained in Annex III; and

b)   wastes that are not covered under paragraph (a) but are defined as, or are considered to be, hazardous wastes by the domestic legislation of the Party of export, import or transit.

2.   Wastes that belong to any category contained in Annex II that are subject to transboundary movement shall be 'other wastes' for the purposes of this Convention.

3.   Wastes which, as a result of being radioactive, are subject to other international control systems, including international instruments, applying specifically to radioactive materials, are excluded from the scope of this Convention.

4.   Wastes which derive from the normal operations of a ship, the discharge of which is covered by another international instrument, are excluded from the scope of this Convention.

Article 2   Definitions

For the purposes of this Convention:

1.   wastes are substances or objects which are disposed of or are intended to be disposed of or are required to be disposed of by the provisions of national law;

2.   management means the collection, transport and disposal of hazardous wastes or other wastes, including after-care of disposal sites;

3.   transboundary movement means any movement of hazardous wastes or other wastes from an area under the national jurisdiction of one State to or through an area under the national jurisdiction of another State or to or through an area not under the national jurisdiction of any State, provided at least two States are involved in the movement;

4.   disposal means any operation specified in Annex IV to this Convention;

5.   approved site or facility means a site or facility for the disposal of hazardous wastes or other wastes which is authorized or permitted to operate for this purpose by a relevant authority of the State where the site or facility is located;

6.   competent authority means one governmental authority designated by a Party to be responsible, within such geographical areas as the Party may think fit, for receiving the notification of a transboundary movement of hazardous wastes or other wastes, and any information related to it, and for responding to such a notification, as provided in Article 6;

7.   focal point means the entity of a Party referred to in Article 5 responsible for receiving and submitting information as provided for in Articles 13 and 16;

8.   environmentally sound management of hazardous wastes or other wastes means taking all practicable steps to ensure that hazardous wastes or other wastes are managed in a manner which will protect human health and the environment against the adverse effects which may result from such wastes;

9.   area under the national jurisdiction of a State means any land, marine area or airspace within which a State exercises administrative and regulatory responsibility in accordance with international law in regard to the protection of human health or the environment;

10.   State of export means a Party from which a transboundary movement of hazardous wastes or other wastes is planned to be initiated or is initiated;

11.   State of import means a Party to which a transboundary movement of hazardous wastes or other wastes is planned or takes place for the purpose of disposal therein or for the purpose of loading prior to disposal in an area not under the national jurisdiction of any State;

12.   State of transit means any State, other than the State of export or import, through which a movement of hazardous wastes or other wastes is planned or takes place;

13.   States concerned means Parties which are States of export or import, or transit States, whether or not parties;

14.   person means any natural or legal person;

15.   exporter means any person under the jurisdiction of the State of export who arranges for hazardous wastes or other wastes to be exported;

16.   importer means any person under the jurisdiction of the State of import who arranges for hazardous wastes or other wastes to be imported;

17.   carrier means any person who carries out the transport of hazardous wastes or other wastes;

18.   generator means any person whose activity produces hazardous wastes or other wastes or, if that person is not known, the person who is in possession and/or control of those wastes;

19.   disposer means any person to whom hazardous wastes or other wastes are shipped and who carries out the disposal of such wastes;

20.   political and/or economic integration organization means an organization constituted by sovereign States to which its member States have transferred competence in respect of matters governed by this Convention and

which has been duly authorized, in accordance with its internal procedures, to sign, ratify, accept, approve, formally confirm or accede to it;

21.　illegal traffic means any transboundary movement of hazardous wastes or other wastes as specified in Article 9.

Article 3　　　*National definitions of hazardous wastes*

1.　Each Party shall, within six months of becoming a Party to this Convention, inform the Secretariat of the Convention of the wastes, other than those listed in Annexes I and II, considered or defined as hazardous under its national legislation and of any requirements concerning transboundary movement procedures applicable to such wastes.

2.　Each Party shall subsequently inform the Secretariat of any significant changes to the information it has provided pursuant to paragraph 1.

3.　The Secretariat shall forthwith inform all Parties of the information it has received pursuant to paragraphs 1 and 2.

4.　Parties shall be responsible for making the information transmitted to them by the Secretariat under paragraph 3 available to their exporters.

Article 4　　　*General obligations*

1.
   a)　Parties exercising their right to prohibit the import of hazardous wastes or other wastes for disposal shall inform the other Parties of their decision pursuant to Article 13.

   b)　Parties shall prohibit or shall not permit the export of hazardous wastes and other wastes to the Parties which have prohibited the import of such wastes, when notified pursuant to subparagraph (a).

   c)　Parties shall prohibit or shall not permit the export of hazardous wastes and other wastes if the State of import does not consent in writing to the specific import, in the case where that State of import has not prohibited the import of such wastes.

2.　Each Pary shall take the appropriate measures to:

   a)　ensure that the generation of hazardous wastes and other wastes within it is reduced to a minimum, taking into account social, technological and economic aspects;

b) ensure the availability of adequate disposal facilities, for the environmentally sound management of hazardous wastes and other wastes, that shall be located, to the extent possible, within it, whatever the place of their disposal;

c) ensure that persons involved in the management of hazardous wastes or other wastes within it take such steps as are necessary to prevent pollution due to hazardous wastes and other wastes arising from such management and, if such pollution occurs, to minimize the consequences thereof for human health and the environment;

d) ensure that the transboundary movement of hazardous wastes and other wastes is reduced to the minimum consistent with the environmentally sound and efficient management of such wastes, and is conducted in a manner which will protect human health and the environment against the adverse effects which may result from such movement;

e) not allow the export of hazardous wastes or other wastes to a State or group of States belonging to an economic and/or political integration organization that are Parties, particularly developing countries, which have prohibited by their legislation all imports, or if it has reason to believe that the wastes in question will not be managed in an environmentally sound manner, according to criteria to be decided on by the Parties at their first meeting.

f) require that information about a proposed transboundary movement of hazardous wastes and other wastes be provided to the States concerned, according to Annex V. A, to state clearly the effects of the proposed movement on human health and the environment;

g) prevent the import of hazardous wastes and other wastes if it has reason to believe that the wastes in question will not be managed in an environmentally sound manner;

h) cooperate in activities with other Parties and interested organizations, directly and through the Secretariat, including the dissemination of information on the transboundary movement of hazardous wastes and other wastes, in order to improve the environmentally sound management of such wastes and to achieve the prevention of illegal traffic.

3. The Parties consider that illegal traffic in hazardous wastes or other wastes is criminal.

4. Each Party shall take appropriate legal, administrative and other measures to implement and enforce the provisions of this Convention, including measures to prevent and punish conduct in contravention of the Convention.

5.   A Party shall not permit hazardous wastes or other wastes to be exported to a non-party or to be imported from a non-party.

6.   The Parties agree not to allow the export of hazardous wastes or other wastes for disposal within the area south of 60o south latitude, whether or not such wastes are subject to transboundary movement.

7.   Furthermore, each Party shall:

    a)   prohibit all persons under its national jurisdiction from transporting or disposing of hazardous wastes or other wastes unless such persons are authorized or allowed to perform such types of operations;

    b)   require that hazardous wastes and other wastes that are to be the subject of a transboundary movement be packaged, labelled, and transported in conformity with generally accepted and recognized international rules and standards in the field of packaging, labelling, and transport, and that due account is taken of relevant internationally recognized practices;

    c)   require that hazardous wastes and other wastes be accompanied by a movement document from the point at which a transboundary movement commences to the point of disposal.

8.   Each Party shall require that hazardous wastes or other wastes, to be exported, are managed in an environmentally sound manner in the State of import or elsewhere. Technical guidelines for the environmentally sound management of wastes subject to this Convention shall be decided by the Parties at their first meeting.

9.   Parties shall take the appropriate measures to ensure that the transboundary movement of hazardous wastes and other wastes only be allowed if:

    a)   the State of export does not have the technical capacity and the necessary facilities, capacity or suitable disposal sites in order to dispose of the wastes in question in an environmentally sound and efficient manner; or

    b)   the wastes in question are required as a raw material for recycling or recovery industries in the State of import; or

    c)   the transboundary movement in question is in accordance with other criteria to be decided by the Parties, provided those criteria do not differ from the objectives of this Convention.

10.   The obligation under this Convention of States in which hazardous wastes and other wastes are generated to require that those wastes are managed

in an environmentally sound manner may not under any circumstances be transferred to the States of import or transit.

11. Nothing in this Convention shall prevent a Party from imposing additional requirements that are consistent with the provisions of this Convention, and are in accordance with the rules of international law, in order better to protect human health and the environment.

12. Nothing in this Convention shall affect in any way the sovereignty of States over their territorial sea established in accordance with international law, and the sovereign rights and the jurisdiction which States have in their exclusive economic zones and their continental shelves in accordance with international law, and the exercise by ships and aircraft of all States of navigational rights and freedoms as provided for in international law and as reflected in relevant international instruments.

13. Parties shall undertake to review periodically the possibilities for the reduction of the amount and/or the pollution potential of hazardous wastes and other wastes which are exported to other States, in particular to developing countries.

Article 5   Designation of competent authorities and focal point

To facilitate the implementation of this Convention, the Parties shall:

1. designate or establish one or more competent authorities and one focal point. One competent authority shall be designated to receive the notification in case of a State of transit;

2. inform the Secretariat, within three months of the date of the entry into force of this Convention for them, which agencies they have designated as their focal point and their competent authorities;

3. inform the Secretariat, within one month of the date of decision, of any changes regarding the designation made by them under paragraph 2.

Article 6   *Transboundary movement between Parties*

1.   The State of export shall notify, or shall require the generator or exporter to notify, in writing, through the channel of the competent authority of the State of export, the competent authority of the States concerned of any proposed transboundary movement of hazardous wastes or other wastes. Such notification shall contain the declaration and information specified in Annex V. A, written in a language acceptable to the State of import. Only one notification need be sent to each State concerned.

2.   The State of import shall respond to the notifier in writing, consenting to the movement with or without conditions, denying permission for the movement, or requesting additional information. A copy of the final response of the State of import shall be sent to the competent authorities of the States concerned which are Parties.

3.   The State of export shall not allow the generator or exporter to commence the transboundary movement until it has received written confirmation that:

    a)   the notifier has received the written consent of the State of import; and

    b)   the notifier has received from the State of import confirmation of the existence of a contract between the exporter and the disposer specifying environmentally sound management of the wastes in question.

4.   Each State of transit which is a Party shall promptly acknowledge to the notifier receipt of the notification. It may subsequently respond to the notifier in writing, within 60 days, consenting to the movement with or without conditions, denying permission for the movement, or requesting additional information. The State of export shall not allow the transboundary movement to commence until it has received the written consent of the State of transit. However, if at any time a Party decides not to require prior written consent, either generally or under specific conditions, for transit transboundary movements of hazardous wastes or other wastes, or modifies its requirements in this respect, it shall forthwith inform the other Parties of its decision pursuant to Article 13. In this latter case, if no response is received by the State of export within 60 days of the receipt of a given notification by the State of transit, the State of export may allow the export to proceed through the State of transit.

5.   In the case of a transboundary movement of wastes where the wastes are legally defined as or considered to be hazardous wastes only:

    a)   by the State of export, the requirements of paragraph 9 of this Article that apply to the importer or disposer and the State of import shall apply mutatis mutandis to the exporter and State of export, respectively:

b) by the State of import, or by the States of import and transit which are Parties, the requirements of paragraphs 1, 3, 4 and 6 of this Article that apply to the exporter and State of export shall apply mutatis mutandis to the importer or disposer and State of import, respectively; or

c) by any State of transit which is a Party, the provisions of paragraph 4 shall apply to such State.

6. The State of export may, subject to the written consent of the States concerned, allow the generator or the exporter to use a general notification where hazardous wastes or other wastes having the same physical and chemical characteristics are shipped regularly to the same disposer via the same customs office of exit of the State of export via the same customs office of entry of the State of import, and, in the case of transit, via the same customs office of entry and exit of the State or States of transit.

7. The States concerned may make their written consent to the use of the general notification referred to in paragraph 6 subject to the supply of certain information, such as the exact quantities or periodical lists of hazardous wastes or other wastes to be shipped.

8. The general notification and written consent referred to in paragraphs 6 and 7 may cover multiple shipments of hazardous wastes or other wastes during a maximum period of 12 months.

9. The Parties shall require that each person who takes charge of a transboundary movement of hazardous wastes or other wastes sign the movement document either upon delivery or receipt of the wastes in question. They shall also require that the disposer inform both the exporter and the competent authority of the State of export of receipt by the disposer of the wastes in question and, in due course, of the completion of disposal as specified in the notification. If no such information is received within the State of export, the competent authority of the State of export or the exporter shall so notify the State of import.

10. The notification and response required by this Article shall be transmitted to the competent authority of the Parties concerned or to such governmental authority as may be appropriate in the case of non-Parties.

11. Any transboundary movement of hazardous wastes or other wastes shall be covered by insurance, bond or other guarantee as may be required by the State of import or any State of transit which is a Party.

Article 7 Transboundary movement from a party through States which are not Parties

Article 6 (2) of the Convention shall apply mutatis mutandis to transboundary movement of hazardous wastes or other wastes from a Party through a State or States which are not parties.

Article 8 Duty to re-import

When a transboundary movement of hazardous wastes or other wastes to which the consent of the States concerned has been given, subject to the provisions of this Convention, cannot be completed in accordance with the terms of the contract, the State of export shall ensure that the wastes in question are taken back into the State of export, by the exporter, if alternative arrangements cannot be made for their disposal in an environmentally sound manner, within 90 days from the time that the importing State informed the State of export and the Secretariat, or such other period of time as the States concerned agree. To this end, the State of export and any Party of transit shall not oppose, hinder or prevent the return of those wastes to the State of export.

Article 9 Illegal traffic

1.   For the purpose of this Convention, any transboundary movement of hazardous wastes or other wastes:

   a)   without notification pursuant to the provisions of this Convention to all States concerned; or

   b)   without the consent pursuant to the provisions of this Convention of a State concerned; or

   c)   with consent obtained from States concerned through falsification, misrepresentation or fraud; or

   d)   that does not conform in a material way with the documents; or

   e)   that results in deliberate disposal (e.g. dumping) of hazardous wastes or other wastes in contravention of this Convention and of general principles of international law, shall be deemed to be illegal traffic.

2.   In case of a transboundary movement of hazardous wastes or other wastes deemed to be illegal traffic as the result of conduct on the part of the exporter or generator, the State of export shall ensure that the wastes in question are:

a) taken back by the exporter or the generator or, if necessary, by itself into the State of export; or, if impracticable,

b) are otherwise disposed of in accordance with the provisions of this Convention, within 30 days from the time the State of export has been informed about the illegal traffic or such other period of time as States concerned may agree. To this end the Parties concerned shall not oppose, hinder or prevent the return of those wastes to the State of export.

3.   In the case of a transboundary movement of hazardous wastes or other wastes deemed to be illegal traffic as the result of conduct on the part of the importer or disposer, the State of import shall ensure that the wastes in question are disposed of in an environmentally sound manner by the importer or disposer or, if necessary, by itself within 30 days from the time the illegal traffic has come to the attention of the State of import or such other period of time as the States concerned may agree. To this end, the Parties concerned shall cooperate, as necessary, in the disposal of the wastes in an environmentally sound manner.

4.   In cases where the responsibility for the illegal traffic cannot be assigned either to the exporter or generator or to the importer or disposer, the Parties concerned or other Parties, as appropriate, shall ensure, through cooperation, that the wastes in question are disposed of as soon as possible in an environmentally sound manner either in the State of export or the State of import or elsewhere as appropriate.

5.   Each Party shall introduce appropriate national/domestic legislation to prevent and punish illegal traffic. The Parties shall cooperate with a view to achieving the objects of this Article.

Article 10   International cooperation

1.   The Parties shall cooperate with each other in order to improve and achieve environmentally sound management of hazardous wastes and other wastes.

2.   To this end, the Parties shall:

a) upon request, make available information, whether on a bilateral or multilateral basis, with a view to promoting the environmentally sound management of ardous wastes and other wastes, including harmonization of technical standards and practices for the adequate management of hazardous wastes and other wastes;

b) cooperate in monitoring the effects of the management of hazardous wastes on human health and the environment;

c) cooperate, subject to their national laws, regulations and policies, in the development and implementation of new environmentally sound low-waste technologies and the improvement of existing technologies with a view to eliminating, as far as practicable, the generation of hazardous wastes and other wastes and achieving more effective and efficient methods of ensuring their management in an environmentally sound manner, including the study of the economic, social and environmental effects of the adoption of such new or improved technologies;

d) cooperate actively, subject to their national laws, regulations and policies, in the transfer of technology and management systems related to the environmentally sound management of hazardous wastes and other wastes. They shall also cooperate in developing the technical capacity among Parties, especially those which may need and request technical assistance in this field;

e) cooperate in developing appropriate technical guidelines and/or codes of practice.

3.   The Parties shall employ appropriate means to cooperate in order to assist developing countries in the implementation of subparagraphs (a) to (d) of Article 4 (2).

4.   Taking into account the needs of developing countries, cooperation between Parties and the competent international organizations is encouraged to promote, inter alia, public awareness, the development of sound management of hazardous wastes and other wastes and the adoption of new low-waste technologies.

Article 11   *Bilateral, multilateral and regional agreements*

1.   Notwithstanding the provisions of Article 4 (5), Parties may enter into bilateral, multilateral, or regional agreements or arrangements regarding transboundary movement of hazardous wastes or other wastes with Parties or nonparties provided that such agreements or arrangements do not derogate from the environmentally sound management of hazardous wastes and other wastes as required by this Convention. These agreements or arrangements shall stipulate provisions which are not less environmentally sound than those provided for by this Convention in particular taking into account the interests of developing countries.

2.   Parties shall notify the Secretariat of any bilateral, multilateral or regional agreements or arrangements referred to in paragraph 1 and those

which they have entered into prior to the entry into force of this Convention for them, for the purpose of controlling transboundary movements of hazardous wastes and other wastes which take place entirely among the Parties to such agreements. The provisions of this Convention shall not affect transboundary movements which take place pursuant to such agreements provided that such agreements are compatible with the environmentally sound management of hazardous wastes and other wastes as required by this Convention.

Article 12   *Consultations on liability*

The Parties shall cooperate with a view to adopting, as soon as practicable, a protocol setting out appropriate rules and procedures in the field of liability and compensation for damage resulting from the transboundary movement and disposal of hazardous wastes and other wastes.

Article 13   *Transmission of information*

1. The Parties shall, whenever it comes to their knowledge, ensure that, in the case of an accident occuring during the transboundary movement of hazardous wastes or other wastes or their disposal, which are likely to present risks to human health and the environment in other States, those States are immediately informed.

2. The Parties shall inform each other, through the Secretariat, of:

   a) changes regarding the designation of competent authorities and/or focal points, pursuant to Article 5;

   b) changes in their national definition of hazardous wastes, pursuant to Article 3;

   and, as soon as possible,

   c) decisions made by them not to consent totally or partially to the import of hazardous wastes or other wastes for disposal within the area under their national jurisdiction;

   d) decisions taken by them to limit or ban the export of hazardous wastes or other wastes;

   e) any other information required pursuant to paragraph 4 of this Article.

3. The Parties, consistent with national laws and regulations, shall transmit, through the Secretariat, to the Conference of the Parties established pursuant to Article 15, before the end of each calendar year, a report on the previous calendar year, containing the following information:

a) competent authorities and focal points that have been designated by them pursuant to Article 5;

b) information regarding transboundary movements of hazardous wastes or other wastes in which they have been involved, including:

    i) the amount of hazardous wastes and other wastes exported, their category, characteristics, destination, any transit country and disposal method as stated on the response to notification;

    ii) the amount of hazardous wastes and other wastes imported, their category, characteristics, origin, and disposal methods;

    iii) disposals which did not proceed as intended;

    iv) efforts to achieve a reduction of the amount of hazardous wastes or other wastes subject to transboundary movement;

c) information on the measures adopted by them in implementation of this Convention;

d) information on available qualified statistics which have been compiled by them on the effects on human health and the environment of the generation, transportation and disposal of hazardous wastes or other wastes;

e) information concerning bilateral, multilateral and regional agreements and arrangements entered into pursuant to Article 11 of this Convention;

f) information on accidents occurring during the transboundary movement and disposal of hazardous wastes and other wastes and on the measures undertaken to deal with them;

g) information on disposal options operated within the area of their national jurisdiction;

h) information on measures undertaken for development of technologies for the reduction and/or elimination of production of hazardous wastes and other wastes; and

i) such other matters as the Conference of the Parties shall deem relevant.

4.   The Parties, consistent with national laws and regulations, shall ensure that copies of each notification concerning any given transboundary movement of hazardous wastes or other wastes, and the response to it, are sent to the Secretariat when a Party considers that its environment may be affected by that transboundary movement has requested that this should be done.

Article 14   *Financial aspects*

1.   The Parties agree that, according to the specific needs of different regions and subregions, regional or subregional centres for training and technology transfers regarding the management of hazardous wastes and other wastes and the minimization of their generation should be established. The Parties shall decide on the establishment of appropriate funding mechanisms of a voluntary nature.

2.   The Parties shall consider the establishment of a revolving fund to assist on an interim basis in case of emergency situations to minimize damage from accidents arising from transboundary movements of hazardous wastes and other wastes or during the disposal of those wastes.

Article 15   *Conference of the Parties*

1.   A Conference of the Parties is hereby established. The first meeting of the Conference of the Parties shall be convened by the Executive Director of UNEP not later than one year after the entry into force of this Convention. Thereafter, ordinary meetings of the Conference of the Parties shall be held at regular intervals to be determined by the Conference at its first meeting.

2.   Extraordinary meetings of the Conference of the Parties shall be held at such other times as may be deemed necessary by the Conference, or at the written request of any Party, provided that, within six months of the request being communicated to them by the Secretariat, it is supported by at least one-third of the Parties.

3.   The Conference of the Parties shall by consensus agree upon and adopt rules of procedure for itself and for any subsidiary body it may establish as well as financial rules to determine in particular the financial participation of the Parties under this Convention.

4.   The Parties at their first meeting shall consider any additional measures needed to assist them in fulfilling their responsibilities with respect to the protection and the preservation of the marine environment in the context of this Convention.

5.   The Conference of the Parties shall keep under continuous review and evaluation the effective implementation of this Convention, and, in addition, shall:

    a)   promote the harmonization of appropriate policies, strategies and measures for minimizing harm to human health and the environment by hazardous wastes and other wastes;

b) consider and adopt, as required, amendments to this Convention and its Annexes, taking into consideration, inter alia, available scientific, technical, economic and environmental information;

c) consider and undertake any additional action that may be required for the achievement of the purposes of this Convention in the light of experience gained in its operation and in the operation of the agreements and arrangements envisaged in Article 11;

d) consider and adopt protocols as required; and

e) establish such subsidiary bodies as are deemed necessary for the implementation of this Convention.

6. The United Nations, its specialized agencies, as well as any State not party to this Convention, may be represented as observers at meetings of the Conference of the Parties. Any other body or agency, whether national or international, governmental or non-governmental, qualified in fields relating to hazardous wastes or other wastes which has informed the Secretariat of its wish to be represented as an observer at a meeting of the Conference of the Parties, may be admitted unless at least one-third of the Parties present object. The admission and participation of observers shall be subject to the rules of procedure adopted by the Conference of the Parties.

7. The Conference of the Parties shall undertake three years after the entry into force of this Convention, and at least every six years thereafter, an evaluation of its effectiveness and, if deemed necessary, to consider the adoption of a complete or partial ban of transboundary movements of hazardous wastes and other wastes in the light of the latest scientific, environmental, technical and economic information.

Article 16   Secretariat

1. The functions of the Secretariat shall be:

a) to arrange for and service meetings provided for in Articles 15 and 17;

b) to prepare and transmit reports based upon information received in accordance with Articles 3, 4, 6, 11 and 13 as well as upon information derived from meetings of subsidiary bodies established pursuant to Article 15 as well as upon, as appropriate, information provided by relevant intergovernmental and non-governmental entities;

c) to prepare reports on its activities carried out in implementation of its functions under this Convention and present them to the Conference of the Parties;

d) to ensure the necessary coordination with relevant international bodies, and in particular to enter into such administrative and contractual arrangements as may be required for the effective discharge of its functions;

e) to communicate with focal points and competent authorities established by the Parties in accordance with Article 5 of this Convention;

f) to compile information concerning authorized national sites and facilities of Parties available for the disposal of their hazardous wastes and other wastes and to circulate this information among Parties;

g) to receive and convey information from and to Parties on:

- sources of technical assistance and training,

- available technical and scientific know-how,

- sources of advice and expertise,

and

- availability of resources,

- with a view to assisting them, upon request, in such areas as:

- the handling of the notification system of this Convention,

- the management of hazardous wastes and other wastes,

- environmentally sound technologies relating to hazardous wastes and other wastes, such as low- and non-waste technology,

- the assessment of disposal capabilities and sites,

- the monitoring of hazardous wastes and other wastes,

and

- emergency responses;

h) to provide Parties, upon request, with information on consultants or consulting firms having the necessary technical competence in the field, which can assist them to examine a notification for a transboundary movement, the concurrence of a shipment of hazardous wastes or other wastes with the relevant notification, and/or the fact that the proposed disposal facilities for hazardous wastes or other wastes are environmentally sound, when they have reason to believe that the wastes in question will not be managed in an environmentally sound manner. Any such examination would not be at the expense of the Secretariat;

i) to assist Parties upon request in their identification of cases of illegal traffic and to circulate immediately to the Parties concerned any information it has received regarding illegal traffic;

j) to cooperate with Parties and with relevant and competent international organizations and agencies in the provision of experts and equipment for the purpose of rapid assistance to States in the event of an emergency situation; and

k) to perform such other functions relevant to the purposes of this Convention as may be determined by the Conference of the Parties.

2. The secretariat functions will be carried out on an interim basis by UNEP until the completion of the first meeting of the Conference of the Parties held pursuant to Article 15.

3. At is first meeting, the Conference of the Parties shall designate the Secretariat from among those existing competent intergovernmental organizations which have signified their willingness to carry out the secretariat functions under this Convention. At this meeting, the Conference of the Parties shall also evaluate the implementation by the interim Secretariat of the functions assigned to it, in particular under paragraph 1, and decide upon the structures appropriate for those functions.

Article 17   Amendment of the Convention

1. Any Party may propose amendments to this Convention and any Party to a Protocol may propose amendments to that Protocol. Such amendments shall take due account, inter alia, of relevant scientific and technical considerations.

2. Amendments to this Convention shall be adopted at a meeting of the Conference of the Parties. Amendments to any Protocol shall be adopted at a meeting of the Parties to the Protocol in question. The text of any proposed amendment to this Convention or to any Protocol, except as may otherwise be provided in such Protocol, shall be communicated to the Parties by the Secretariat at least six months before the meeting at which it is proposed for adoption. The Secretariat shall also communicate proposed amendments to the Signatories to this Convention for information.

3. The Parties shall make every effort to reach agreement on any proposed amendment to this Convention by consensus. If all efforts at consensus have been exhausted, and no agreement reached, the amendment shall as a last resort be adopted by a three-fourths majority vote of the Parties present and voting at the meeting, and shall be submitted by the Depositary to all Parties for ratification, approval, formal confirmation or acceptance.

4.   The procedure mentioned in paragraph 3 above shall apply to amendments to any Protocol, except that a two-thirds majority of the Parties to that Protocol present and voting at the meeting shall suffice for their adoption.

5.   Instruments of ratification, approval, formal confirmation or acceptance of amendments shall be deposited with the Depositary. Amendmends adopted in accordance with paragraphs 3 or 4 above shall enter into force between Parties having accepted them on the 90th day after the receipt by the Depositary of their instrument of ratification, approval, formal confirmation or acceptance by at least three-fourths of the Parties who accepted the amendments to the Protocol concerned, except as may otherwise be provided in such Protocol. The amendments shall enter into force for any other Party on the 90th day after that Party deposits its instrument of ratification, approval, formal confirmation or acceptance of the amendments.

6.   For the purpose of this Article, 'Parties present and voting_ means Parties present and casting an affirmative or negative vote.

Article 18   Adoption and amendment of Annexes

1.   The Annexes to this Convention or to any Protocol shall form an integral part of this Convention or of such Protocol, as the case may be and, unless expressly provided otherwise, a reference to this Convention or its Protocols constitutes at the same time a reference to any Annexes thereto. Such Annexes shall be restricted to scientific, technical and administrative matters.

2.   Except as may be otherwise provided in any protocol with respect to its Annexes, the following procedure shall apply to the proposal, adoption and entry into force of additional Annexes to this Convention or of Annexes to a protocol:

   a)   Annexes to this Convention and its Protocols shall be proposed and adopted according to the procedure laid down in Article 17 (2), (3) and (4);

   b)   any Party that is unable to accept an additional Annex to this Convention or an Annex to any Protocol to which it is party shall so notify the Depositary, in writing, within six months from the date of the communication of the adoption by the Depositary. The Depositary shall without delay notify all Parties of any such notification received. A Party may at any time substitute an acceptance for a previous declaration of objection and the Annexes shall thereupon enter into force for that Party;

c) on the expiry of six months from the date of the circulation of the communication by the Depositary, the Annex shall become effective for all Parties to this Convention or to any Protocol concerned, which have not submitted a notification in accordance with the provision of subparagraph (b).

3.   The proposal, adoption and entry into force of amendments to Annexes to this Convention or to any Protocol shall be subject to the same procedure as for the proposal, adoption and entry into force of Annexes to the Convention or Annexes to a Protocol. Annexes and amendments thereto shall take due account, inter alia, of relevant scientific and technical considerations.

4.   If an additional Annex or an amendment to an Annex involves an amendment to this Convention or to any Protocol, the additional Annex or amended Annex shall not enter into force until such time as the amendment to this Convention or to the Protocol enters into force.

Article 19   Verification

Any Party which has reason to believe that another Party is acting or has acted in breach of its obligations under this Convention may inform the Secretariat thereof, and in such an event, shall simultaneously and immediately inform, directly or through the Secretariat, the Party against whom the allegations are made. All relevant information should be submitted by the Secretariat to the Parties.

Article 20   Settlement of disputes

1.   In case of a dispute between Parties as to the interpretation or application of, or compliance with, this Convention or any Protocol thereto, they shall seek a settlement of the dispute through negotiation or any other peaceful means of their own choice.

2.   If the Parties concerned cannot settle their dispute through the means mentioned in the preceding paragraph, the dispute, if the parties to the dispute agree, shall be submitted to the International Court of Justice or to arbitration under the conditions set out in Annex VI on arbitration. However, failure to reach common agreement on submission of the dispute to the International Court of Justice or to arbitration shall not absolve the Parties from the responsibility of continuing to seek to resolve it by the means referred to in paragraph 1.

3.   When ratifying, accepting, approving, formally confirming or acceding to this Convention, or at any time thereafter, a State or political and/or

economic integration organization may declare that it recognizes as compulsory ipso facto and without special agreement, in relation to any Party accepting the same obligation:

a) submission of the dispute to the International Court of Justice; and/or

b) arbitration in accordance with the procedures set out in Annex VI.

Such declaration shall be notified in writing to the Secretariat which shall communicate it to the Parties.

Article 21   Signature

This Convention shall be open for signature by States, by Namibia, represented by the United Nations Council for Namibia, and by political and/or economic integration organizations, in Basel on 22 March 1989, at the Federal Department of Foreign Affairs of Switzerland in Berne from 23 March to 30 June 1989 and at United Nations Headquarters in New York from 1 July 1989 to 22 March 1990.

Article 22   Ratification, acceptance, formal confirmation of approval

1.   This Convention shall be subject to ratification, acceptance or approval by States and by Namibia, represented by the United Nations Council for Namibia, and to formal confirmation or approval by political and/or economic integration organizations. Instruments of ratification, acceptance, formal confirmation, or approval shall be deposited with the Depositary.

2.   Any organization referred to in paragraph 1 above which becomes a Party to this Convention without any of its member States being a Party shall be bound by all the obligations under the Convention. In the case of such organizations, one or more of whose member States is a Party to the Convention, the organization and its member States shall decide on their respective responsibilities for the performance of their obligations under the Convention. In such cases, the organization and the member States shall not be entitled to exercise rights under the Convention concurrently.

3.   In their instruments of formal confirmation or approval, the organizations referred to in paragraph 1 above shall declare the extent of their competence with respect to the matters governed by the Convention. These organizations shall also inform the Depositary, who will inform the Parties of any substantial modification in the extent of their competence.

Article 23   Accession

1.   This Convention shall be open for accession by States, by Namibia, represented by the United Nations Council for Namibia, and by political and/or economic integration organizations from the day after the date on which the Convention is closed for signature. The instruments of accession shall be deposited with the Depositary.

2.   In their instruments of accession, the organizations referred to in paragraph 1 shall declare the extent of their competence with respect to the matters governed by the Convention. These organizations shall also inform the Depositary of any substantial modification in the extent of their competence.

3.   The provisions of Article 22 (2) shall apply to political and/or economic integration organizations which accede to this Convention.

Article 24   Right to vote

1.   Except as provided for in paragraph 2 each Contracting Party to this Convention shall have one vote.

2.   Political and/or economic integration organizations, in matters within their competence, in accordance with Articles 22 (3) and 23 (2) shall exercise their right to vote with a number of votes equal to the number of their member States which are Parties to the Convention or the relevant Protocol. Such organizations shall not exercise their right to vote if their member States exercise theirs, and vice versa.

Article 25   Entry into force

1.   This Convention shall enter into force on the 90th day after the date of deposit of the 20th instrument of ratification, acceptance, formal confirmation, approval or accession.

2.   For each State or political and/or economic integration organization which ratifies, accepts, approves or formally confirms this Convention or accedes thereto after the date of the deposit of the 20th instrument of ratification, acceptance, approval, formal confirmation or accession, it shall enter into force on the 19th day after the date of deposit by such State or political and/or economic integration organization of its instrument of ratification, acceptance, approval, formal confirmation or accession.

3.   For the purposes of paragraphs 1 and 2, any instrument deposited by a political and/or economic integration organization shall not be counted as additional to those deposited by member States of such organization.

Article 26   Reservations and declarations

1.   No reservation or exception may be made to this Convention.

2.   Paragraph 1 of this Article does not preclude a State or political and/or economic integration organization, when signing, ratifying, accepting, approving, formally confirming or acceding to this Convention, from making declarations or statements, however phrased or named, with a view, inter alia, to the harmonization of its law and regulations with the provisions of this Convention, provided that such declarations or statements do not purport to exclude or to modify the legal effects of the provisions of the Convention in their application to that State.

Article 27   Withdrawal

1.   At any time after three years from the date on which this Convention has entered into force for a Party, that Party may withdraw from the Convention by giving written notification to the Depositary.

2.   Withdrawal shall be effective one year from receipt of notification by the Depositary, or on such later date as may be specified in the notification.

Article 28   Depository

The Secretary-General of the United Nations shall be the Depository of this Convention and of any Protocol thereto.

Article 29   Authentic texts

The original Arabic, Chinese, English, French, Russian and Spanish texts of this Convention are equally authentic.

In witness whereof the undersigned, being duly authorized to that effect, have signed this Convention.

Done at Basel on the twenty-second day of March 1989.

ANNEX I

CATEGORIES OF WASTES TO BE CONTROLLED

Waste streams

Y1   Clinical wastes from medical care in hospitals, medical centres and clinics.

Y2   Wastes from the production and preparation of pharmaceutical products.

Y3   Waste pharmaceuticals, drugs and medicines.

Y4   Wastes from the production, formulation and use of biocides and phytopharmaceuticals.

Y5   Wastes from the manufacture, formulation and use of wood preserving chemicals.

Y6   Wastes from the production, formulation and use of organic solvents.

Y7   Wastes from heat treatment and tempering operations containing cyanides.

Y8   Waste mineral oils unfit for their originally intended use.

Y9   Waste oils/water, hydrocarbons/water mixtures, emulsions.

Y10   Waste substances and articles containing or contaminated with polychlorinated biphenyls (PCBs) and/or polychlorinated terphenyls (PCTs) and/or polybrominated biphenyls (PBBs).

Y11   Waste tarry residues arising from refining, distillation and any pyrolytic treatment.

Y12   Wastes from production, formulation and use of inks, dyes, pigments, paints, lacquers, varnish.

Y13   Wastes from production, formulation and use of resins, latex, plasticizers, glues/adhesives.

Y14   Waste chemical substances arising from research and development or teaching activities which are not identified and/or are new and whose effects on man and/or the environment are not known.

Y15   Waste of an explosive nature not subject to other legislation.

Y16   Wastes from production, formulation and use of photographic chemicals and processing materials.

Y17   Wastes resulting from surface treatment of metals and plastics.

Y18   Residues arising from industrial waste disposal operations.

Wastes having as constituents:

Y19   Metal carbonyls.

Y20   Beryllium; beryllium compounds.

Y21   Hexavalent chromium compounds.

Y22   Copper compounds.

Y23   Zinc compounds.

Y24   Arsenic; arsenic compounds.

Y25   Selenium; selenium compounds.

Y26   Cadmium; cadmium compounds.

Y27   Antimony; antimony compounds.

Y28   Tellurium; tellurium compounds.

Y29   Mercury; mercury compounds.

Y30   Thallium; thallium compounds.

Y31   Lead; lead compounds.

Y32   Inorganic fluorine compounds excluding calcium fluoride.

Y33   Inorganic cyanides.

Y34   Acidic solutions or acids in solid form.

Y35   Basic solutions or bases in solid form.

Y36   Asbestos (dust and fibres).

Y37   Organic phosphorous compounds.

Y38   Organic cyanides.

Y39   Phenols; phenol compounds including chlorphenols.

Y40   Ethers.

Y41   Halogenated organic solvents.

Y42   Organic solvents excluding halogenated solvents.

Y43   Any congenor of polychlorinated dibenzo-furan.

Y44   Any congenor of polychlorinated dibenzo-p-dioxin.

Y45   Organohalogen compounds other than substances referred to in this Annex (eg. Y39, Y41, Y42, Y43, Y44).

ANNEX II

CATEGORIES OF WASTES REQUIRING SPECIAL CONSIDERATION

Y46   Wastes collected from households.

Y47   Residues arising from the incineration of househould wastes.

ANNEX III

LIST OF HAZARDOUS CHARACTERISTICS

UN class (1)	Code	Characteristics
1	H1	*Explosive* An explosive substance or waste is a solid or liquid substance or waste (or mixture of substances or wastes) which is in itself capable by chemical reaction of producing gas at such a temperature and pressure and at such a speed as to cause damage to the surroundings.
3	H3	*Flammable liquids* The word 'flammable' has the same meaning as 'inflammable'. Flammable liquids are liquids, or mixtures of liquids, or liquids containing solids in solution or suspension (for example, paints, varnishes, lacquers, etc., but not including substances or wastes otherwise classified on account of their dangerous characteristics) which give off a flammable vapour at temperatures of not more than 60,5 °C, closed-cup test, or not more than 65,6 °C, open-cup test. (Since the results of open-cup tests and of closed-cup tests are not strictly comparable and even individual results by the same test are often variable, regulations varying from the above figures to make allowance for such differences would be within the spirit of this definition.)
4.1	H4.1	*Flammable solids* Solids, or waste solids, other than those classed as explosives, which under conditions encountered in transport are readily combustible, or may cause or contribute to fire through friction.
4.2	H4.2	*Substances or wastes liable to spontaneous combustion* Substances or wastes which are liable to spontaneous heating under normal conditions encountered in transport, or to heating up on contact with air, and being then liable to catch fire.
4.3	H4.3	*Substances or wastes which, in contact with water emit flammable gases* Substances or wastes which, by interaction with water, are liable to become spontaneously flammable or to give off flammable gases in dangerous quantities.
5.1	H5.1	*Oxidizing* Substances or wastes which, while in themselves not necessarily combustible, may, generally by yielding oxygen cause, or contribute to, the combustion of other materials.

UN class (1)	Code	Characteristics
5.2	H5.2	*Organic peroxides* Organic substances or wastes which contain the bivalent -O-O-structure are thermally unstable substances which may undergo exothermic self-accelerating decomposition.
6.1	H6.1	*Poisonous (acute)* Substances or wastes liable either to cause death or serious injury or to harm human health if swallowed or inhaled or by skin contact.
6.2	H6.2	*Infectious substances* Substances or wastes containing viable micro-organisms or their toxins which are known or suspected to cause disease in animals or humans.
8	H8	*Corrosives* Substances or wastes which, by chemical action, will cause severe damage when in contact with living tissue, or, in the case of leakage, will materially damage, or even destroy, other goods or the means of transport; they may also cause other hazards.
9	H10	*Liberation of toxic gases in contact with air or water* Substances or wastes which, by interaction with air or water, are liable to give off toxic gases in dangerous quantities.
9	H11	*Toxic (delayed or chronic)* Substances or wastes which, if they are inhaled or ingested or if they penetrate the skin, may involve delayed or chronic effects, including carcinogenicity.
9	H12	*Ecotoxic* Substances or wastes which if released present or may present immediate or delayed adverse impacts to the environment by means of bioaccumulation and/or toxic effects upon biotic systems.
9	H13	Capable, by any means, after disposal, of yielding another material, e.g., leachate, which possesses any of the characteristics listed above.

(1) Corresponds to the hazard classification system included in the United Nations recommendations on the transport of dangerous goods (ST/SG/AC. 10/1/Rev. 5, United Nations, New York, 1988).

Tests

The potential hazards posed by certain types of wastes are not yet fully documented; tests to define quantitatively these hazards do not exist. Further research is necessary in order to develop means to characterize potential hazards posed to man and/or the environment by these wastes. Standardized tests have been derived with respect to pure substances and materials. Many countries have developed national tests which can be applied to materials listed in Annex I, in order to decide if these materials exhibit any of the characteristics listed in this Annex.

ANNEX IV

DISPOSAL OPERATIONS

A.   Operations which do not lead to the possibility of resource recovery, recycling, reclamation, direct reuse or alternative uses.

Section A encompasses all such disposal operations which occur in practice.

D1   Deposit into or onto land, (e.g., landfill, etc.).

D2   Land treatment, (e.g., biodegradation of liquid or sludgy discards in soils, etc.).

D3   Deep injection, (e.g., injection of pumpable discards into wells, salt domes or naturally occurring repositories, etc.).

D4   Surface impoundment, (e.g., placement of liquid or sludge discards into pits, ponds or lagoons, etc.).

D5   Specially engineered landfill, (e.g., placement into lined discrete cells which are capped and isolated from one another and the environment, etc.).

D6   Release into a water body except seas/oceans.

D7   Release into seas/oceans including sea-bed insertion.

D8   Biological treatment not specified elsewhere in this Annex which results in final compounds or mixtures which are discarded by means of any of the operations in Section A.

D9   Physico-chemical treatment not specified elsewhere in this Annex which results in final compounds or mixtures which are discarded by means of any of the operations in Section A, (e.g., evaporation, drying, calcination, neutralization, precipitation, etc.).

D10   Incineration on land.

D11   Incineration at sea.

D12   Permanent storage (e.g., emplacement of containers in a mine, etc.).

D13   Blending or mixing prior to submission to any of the operations in Section A.

D14   Repackaging prior to submission to any of the operations in Section A.

D15   Storage pending any of the operations in Section A.

B.   Operations which may lead to resource recovery, recycling, reclamation, direct reuse or alternative uses

Section B encompasses all such operations with respect to materials legally defined as or considered to be hazardous wastes and which otherwise would have been destined for operations included in Section A.

R1   Use as a fuel (other than in direct incineration) or other means to generate energy.

R2   Solvent reclamation/regeneration.

R3   Recycling/reclamation of organic substances which are not used as solvents.

R4   Recycling/reclamation of metals and metal compounds.

R5   Recycling/reclamation of other inorganic materials.

R6   Regeneration of acids or bases.

R7   Recovery of components used for pollution abatement.

R8   Recovery of components from catalysts.

R9   Used oil re-refining or other reuses of previously used oil.

R10   Land treatment resulting in benefit to agriculture or ecological improvement.

R11   Uses of residual materials obtained from any of the operations numbered R1 to R10.

R12   Exchange of wastes for submission to any of the operations numbered R1 to R11.

R13   Accumulation of material intended for any operation in Section B.

ANNEX V.A

INFORMATION TO BE PROVIDED ON NOTIFICATION

1) Reason for waste export.

2) Exporter of the waste[1].

3) Generator(s) of the waste and site of generation[1].

4) Disposer of the waste and actual site of disposal[1].

5) Intended carrier(s) of the waste or their agents, if known[1].

6) Country of export of the waste
Competent authority[2].

7) Expected countries of transit
Competent authority[2].

8) Country of import of the waste
Competent authority[2].

9) General or single notification.

10) Projected date(s) of shipment(s) and period of time over which waste is to be exported and proposed itinerary (including point of entry and exit)[3].

11) Means of transport envisaged (road, rail, sea, air, inland waters).

12) Information relating to insurance[4].

13) Designation and physical description of the waste including Y number and UN number and its composition[5] and information on any special handling requirements including emergency provisions in case of accidents.

14) Type of packaging envisaged (e.g. bulk, drummed, tanker).

15) Estimated quantity in weight/volume[6].

16) Process by which the waste is generated[7].

17) For wastes listed in Annex I, classifications from Annex III: hazardous characteristics, H number, and UN class.

18) Method of disposal as per Annex IV.

19) Declaration by the generator and exporter that the information is correct.

20) Information transmitted (including technical description of the plant) to the exporter or generator from the disposer of the waste upon which the

latter has based his assessment that there was no reason to believe that the wastes will not be managed in an environmentally sound manner in accordance with the laws and regulations of the country of import.

21)   Information concerning the contract between the exporter and disposer.

Notes

(1)   Full name and address, telephone, telex or telefax number and the name, address, telephone, telex or telefax number of the person to be contacted.

(2)   Full name and address, telephone, telex or telefax number.

(3)   In the case of a general notification covering several shipments, either the expected dates of each shipment or, if this is not known, the expected frequency of the shipments will be required.

(4)   Information to be provided on relevant insurance requirements and how they are met by exporter, carrier and disposer.

(5)   The nature and the concentration of the most hazardous components, in terms of toxicity and other dangers presented by the waste both in handling and in relation to the proposed disposal method.

(6)   In the case of a general notification covering several shipments, both the estimated total quantity and the estimated quantities for each individual shipment will be required.

(7)   In so far as this is necessary to assess the hazard and determine the appropriateness of the proposed disposal operation.

ANNEX V.B

INFORMATION TO BE PROVIDED ON THE MOVEMENT DOCUMENT

1) Exporter of the waste[1].

2) Generator(s) of the waste and site of generation[1].

3) Disposer of the waste and actual site of disposa[1].

4) Carrier(s) of the waste[1] or his agent(s).

5) Subject of general or single notification.

6) The date the transboundary movement started and date(s) and signature on receipt by each person who takes charge of the waste.

7) Means of transport (road, rail, inland waterway, sea, air) including countries of export, transit and import, also point of entry and exit where these have been designated.

8) General description of the waste (physical state, proper UN shipping name and class, UN number, Y number and H number as applicable).

9) Information on special handling requirements including emergency provision in case of accidents.

10) Type and number of packages.

11) Quantity in weight/volume.

12) Declaration by the generator or exporter that the information is correct.

13) Declaration by the generator or exporter indicating no objection from the competent authorities of all States concerned which are Parties.

14) Certification by disposer of receipt at designated disposal facility and indication of method of disposal and of the approximate date of disposal.

Notes

The information required on the movement document shall where possible be integrated in one document with that required under transport rules. Where this is not possible the information should complement rather than duplicate that required under the transport rules. The movement document shall carry instructions as to who is to provide information and fill out any form.

[1] Full name and address, telephone, telex or telefax number and the name, address, telephone, telex or telefax number of the person to be contacted in case of emergency.

ANNEX VI

ARBITRATION

Article 1

Unless the agreement referred to in Article 20 of the Convention provides otherwise, the arbitration procedure shall be conducted in accordance with Articles 2 to 10 below.

Article 2

The claimant Party shall notify the Secretariat that the Parties have agreed to submit the dispute to arbitration pursuant to paragraph 2 or 3 of Article 20 and include, in particular, the Articles of the Convention the interpretation or application of which are at issue. The Secretariat shall forward the information thus received to all Parties to the Convention.

Article 3

The arbitral tribunal shall consist of three members. Each of the Parties to the dispute shall appoint an arbitrator, and the two arbitrators so appointed shall designate by common agreement the third arbitrator, who shall be the chairman of the tribunal. The latter shall not be a national of one of the Parties to the dispute, nor have his usual place of residence in the territory of one of these Parties, nor be employed by any of them, nor have dealt with the case in any other capacity.

Article 4

1.   If the chairman of the arbitral tribunal has not been designated within two months of the appointment of the second arbitrator, the Secretary-General of the United Nations shall, at the request of either Party, designate him within a further two months' period.

2.   If one of the Parties to the dispute does not appoint an arbitrator within two months of the receipt of the request, the other Party may inform the Secretary-General of the United Nations who shall designate the chairman of the arbitral tribunal within a further two months' period. Upon designation, the chairman of the arbitral tribunal shall request the Party which has not appointed an arbitrator to do so within two months. After such period, he shall

inform the Secretary-General of the United Nations, who shall make this appointment within a further two months' period.

Article 5

1.   The arbitral tribunal shall render its decision in accordance with international law and in accordance with the provisions of this Convention.

2.   Any arbitral tribunal constituted under the provisions of this Annex shall draw up its own rules of procedure.

Article 6

1.   The decisions of the arbitral tribunal both on procedure and on substance, shall be taken by majority vote of its members.

2.   The tribunal may take all appropriate measures in order to establish the facts. It may, at the request of one of the Parties, recommend essential interim measures of protection.

3.   The Parties to the dispute shall provide all facilities necessary for the effective conduct of the proceedings.

4.   The absence or default of a Party in the dispute shall not constitute an impediment to the proceedings.

Article 7

The tribunal may hear and determine counter-claims arising directly out of the subject-matter of the dispute.

Article 8

Unless the arbitral tribunal determines otherwise because of the particular circumstances of the case, the expenses of the tribunal, including the remuneration of its members, shall be borne by the Parties to the dispute in equal shares. The tribunal shall keep a record of all its expenses, and shall furnish a final statement thereof to the Parties.

Article 9

Any Party that has an interest of a legal nature in the subject-matter of the dispute which may be affected by the decision in the case, may intervene in the proceedings with the consent of the tribunal.

Article 10

1.   The tribunal shall render its award within five months of the date on which it is established unless it finds it necessary to extend the time limit for a period which should not exceed five months.

2.   The award of the arbitral tribunal shall be accompanied by a statement of reasons. It shall be final and binding upon the Parties to the dispute.

3.   Any dispute which may arise between the Parties concerning the interpretation or execution of the award may be submitted by either party to the arbitral tribunal which made the award or, if the latter cannot be seized thereof, to another tribunal constituted for this purpose in the same manner as the first.

CONVENTION DE BALE
sur le contrôle des mouvements transfrontières de déchets dangereux et de leur élimination

PREAMBULE

LES PARTIES A LA PRESENTE CONVENTION,

CONSCIENTES des dommages que les déchets dangereux et d'autres déchets ainsi que les mouvements transfrontières de ces déchets risquent de causer à la santé humaine et à l'environnement,

AYANT PRESENTE A L'ESPRIT la menace croissante que représentent pour la santé humaine et l'environnement la complexité grandissante et le développement de la production de déchets dangereux et d'autres déchets et leurs mouvements transfrontières,

AYANT EGALEMENT PRESENT A L'ESPRIT le fait que la manière la plus efficace de protéger la santé humaine et l'environnement des dangers que représentent ces déchets consiste à réduire leur production au minimum du point de vue de la quantité et/ou du danger potentiel,

CONVAINCUES que les Etats devraient prendre les mesures nécessaires pour faire en sorte que la gestion des déchets dangereux et d'autres déchets, y compris leurs mouvements transfrontières et leur élimination, soit compatible avec la protection de la santé humaine et de l'environnement, quel que soit le lieu où ces déchets sont éliminés,

NOTANT que les Etats devraient veiller à ce que le producteur s'acquitte des obligations ayant trait au transport et à l'élimination des déchets dangereux et d'autres déchets d'une manière qui soit compatible avec la protection de l'environnement, quel que soit le lieu où ils sont éliminés,

RECONNAISSANT PLEINEMENT que tout Etat possède le droit souverain d'interdire l'entrée ou l'élimination de déchets dangereux et d'autres déchets d'origine étrangère sur son territoire,

RECONNAISSANT EGALEMENT le sentiment croissant favorable à l'interdiction des mouvements transfrontières de déchets dangereux et de leur élimination dans d'autres Etats, en particulier dans les pays en développement,

CONVAINCUES que les déchets dangereux et autres déchets devraient, dans toute la mesure où cela est compatible avec une gestion écologiquement rationnelle et efficace, être éliminés dans l'Etat où ils ont été produits,

CONSCIENTES EGALEMENT que les mouvements transfrontières de ces déchets de l'Etat de leur production vers tout autre Etat ne devraient être autorisés que lorsqu'ils sont réalisés dans des conditions ne présentant aucun danger pour la santé humaine et l'environnement et conformes aux dispositions de la présente convention,

CONSIDERANT que le contrôle accru des mouvements transfrontières de déchets dangereux et d'autres déchets encouragera une gestion écologiquement rationnelle de ces déchets et une réduction du volume des mouvements transfrontières correspondants,

CONVAINCUES que les Etats devraient prendre des mesures pour assurer un échange approprié d'informations et un contrôle effectif des mouvements transfrontières de déchets dangereux et d'autres déchets en provenance et à destination de ces Etats,

NOTANT qu'un certain nombre d'accords internationaux et régionaux ont porté sur la question de la protection et de la préservation de l'environnement lorsqu'il y a transit de marchandises dangereuses,

TENANT COMPTE de la déclaration de la conférence des Nations unies sur l'environnement (Stockholm, 1972), des lignes directrices et principes du Caire concernant la gestion écologiquement rationnelle des déchets dangereux, adoptés par le conseil d'administration du Programme des Nations unies pour l'environnement (PNUE) par sa décision 14/30 du 17 juin 1987, des recommandations du comité d'experts des Nations unies en matière de transport des marchandises dangereuses (formulées en 1957 et mises à jour tous les deux ans), des recommandations, déclarations, instruments et règlements pertinents adoptés dans le cadre du système des Nations unies ainsi que des travaux et études effectués par d'autres organisations internationales et régionales,

CONSCIENTES de l'esprit, des principes, des buts et des fonctions de la Charte mondiale de la nature adoptée par l'Assemblée générale des Nations unies à sa trente-septième session (1982) en tant que règle d'éthique concernant la protection de l'environnement humain et la conservation des ressources naturelles,

AFFIRMANT que les Etats sont tenus de s'acquitter de leurs obligations internationales concernant la protection de la santé humaine ainsi que la protection et la sauvegarde de l'environnement et sont responsables à cet égard conformément au droit international,

74

RECONNAISSANT que, dans le cas d'une violation substantielle des dispositions de la présente convention ou de tout protocole y relatif, les dispositions pertinentes du droit international des traités s'appliqueront,

CONSCIENTES de la nécessité de continuer à mettre au point et à appliquer des techniques peu polluantes et écologiquement rationnelles, des mesures de recyclage et des systèmes appropriés de maintenance et de gestion en vue de réduire au minimum la production de déchets dangereux et d'autres déchets,

CONSCIENTES EGALEMENT du fait que la communauté internationale est de plus en plus préoccupée par la nécessité de contrôler rigoureusement les mouvements transfrontières de déchets dangereux et d'autres déchets et par la nécessité de réduire dans la mesure du possible ces mouvements au minimum,

PREOCCUPEES par le problème du trafic transfrontière illicite de déchets dangereux et d'autres déchets,

TENANT COMPTE AUSSI de ce que les pays en développement n'ont que des capacités limitées de gestion des déchets dangereux et d'autres déchets,

RECONNAISSANT qu'il est nécessaire de promouvoir le transfert, surtout vers les pays en développement, de techniques destinées à assurer une gestion rationnelle des déchets dangereux et d'autres déchets produits localement, dans l'esprit des lignes directrices du Caire et de la décision 14/16 du conseil d'administration du PNUE sur la promotion du transfert des techniques de protection de l'environnement,

RECONNAISSANT EGALEMENT que les déchets dangereux et d'autres déchets devraient être transportés conformément aux conventions et recommandations internationales pertinentes,

CONVAINCUES EGALEMENT que les mouvements transfrontières de déchets dangereux et d'autres déchets ne devraient être autorisés que si le transport et l'élimination finale de ces déchets sont écologiquement rationnels,

DETERMINEES à protéger par un contrôle strict la santé humaine et l'environnement contre les effets nocifs qui peuvent résulter de la production et de la gestion des déchets dangereux et d'autres déchets,

SONT CONVENUES DE CE QUI SUIT:

Article premier Champ d'application de la convention

1.   Les déchets ci-après, qui font l'objet de mouvements transfrontières, seront considérés comme des «déchets dangereux» aux fins de la présente convention:

a) les déchets qui appartiennent à l'une des catégories figurant à l'annexe I, à moins qu'ils ne possèdent aucune des caractéristiques indiquées à l'annexe III

et

b) les déchets auxquels les dispositions du point a) ne s'appliquent pas, mais qui sont définis ou considérés comme dangereux par la législation interne de la partie d'exportation, d'importation ou de transit.

2.   Les déchets qui appartiennent à l'une des catégories figurant à l'annexe II et font l'objet de mouvements transfrontières seront considérés comme «d'autres déchets» aux fins de la présente convention.

3.   Les déchets qui, en raison de leur radioactivité, sont soumis à d'autres systèmes de contrôle internationaux, y compris des instruments internationaux, s'appliquant spécifiquement aux matières radioactives, sont exclus du champ d'application de la présente convention.

4.   Les déchets provenant de l'exploitation normale d'un navire et dont le rejet fait l'objet d'un autre instrument international sont exclus du champ d'application de la présente convention.

Article 2   Définitions

Aux fins de la présente convention entend par:

1) «déchets»: des substances ou objets qu'on élimine, qu'on a l'intention d'éliminer ou qu'on est tenu d'éliminer en vertu des dispositions du droit national;

2) «gestion»: la collecte, le transport et l'élimination des déchets dangereux ou d'autres déchets, y compris la surveillance des sites d'élimination;

3) «mouvement transfrontière»: tout mouvement de déchets dangereux ou d'autres déchets en provenance d'une zone relevant de la compétence nationale d'un Etat et à destination d'une zone relevant de la compétence nationale d'un autre Etat, ou en transit par cette zone, ou d'une zone ne relevant de la compétence nationale d'aucun Etat, ou en transit

par cette zone, pour autant que deux Etats au moins soient concernés par le mouvement;

4)   «élimination»: toute opération prévue à l'annexe IV de la présente convention;

5)   «site ou installation agréé»: un site ou une installation où l'élimination des déchets dangereux ou d'autres déchets a lieu en vertu d'une autorisation ou d'un permis d'exploitation délivré par une autorité compétente de l'Etat où le site ou l'installation se trouve;

6)   «autorité compétente»: l'autorité gouvernementale désignée par une partie pour recevoir, dans la zone géographique que la partie peut déterminer, la notification d'un mouvement transfrontière de déchets dangereux ou d'autres déchets ainsi que tous les renseignements qui s'y rapportent et pour prendre position au sujet de cette notification comme le prévoit l'article 6;

7)   «correspondant»: l'organisme d'une partie mentionné à l'article 5 et chargé de recevoir et de communiquer les renseignements prévus aux articles 13 et 16;

8)   «gestion écologiquement rationnelle des déchets dangereux ou d'autres déchets»: toutes mesures pratiques permettant d'assurer que les déchets dangereux ou d'autres déchets sont gérés d'une manière qui garantisse la protection de la santé humaine et de l'environnement contre les effets nuisibles que peuvent avoir ces déchets;

9)   «zone relevant de la compétence nationale d'un Etat»: toute zone terrestre, maritime ou aérienne à l'intérieur de laquelle un Etat exerce conformément au droit international des compétences administratives et réglementaires en matière de protection de la santé humaine ou de l'environnement;

10)   «Etat d'exportation»: toute partie d'où est prévu le déclenchement ou où est déclenché un mouvement transfrontière de déchets dangereux ou d'autres déchets;

11)   «Etat d'importation»: toute partie vers laquelle est prévu ou a lieu un mouvement transfrontière de déchets dangereux ou d'autres déchets pour qu'ils y soient éliminés ou aux fins de chargement avant élimination dans une zone qui ne relève de la compétence nationale d'aucun Etat;

12)   «Etat de transit»: tout Etat, autre que l'Etat d'exportation ou d'importation, à travers lequel un mouvement transfrontière de déchets dangereux ou d'autres déchets est prévu ou a lieu;

13)   «Etats concernés»: les parties qui sont Etats d'exportation ou d'importation et les Etats de transit, qu'ils soient ou non parties;

14) «personne»: toute personne physique ou morale;

15) «exportateur»: toute personne qui relève de la juridiction de l'Etat d'exportation et qui procède à l'exportation de déchets dangereux ou d'autres déchets;

16) «importateur»: toute personne qui relève de la juridiction de l'Etat d'importation et qui procède à l'importation de déchets dangereux ou d'autres déchets;

17) «transporteur»: toute personne qui transporte des déchets dangereux ou d'autres déchets;

18) «producteur»: toute personne dont l'activité produit des déchets dangereux ou d'autres déchets ou, si cette personne est inconnue, la personne qui est en possession de ces déchets et/ou qui les contrôle;

19) «éliminateur»: toute personne à qui sont expédiés des déchets dangereux ou d'autres déchets et qui effectue l'élimination desdits déchets;

20) «organisation d'intégration politique ou économique»: toute organisation constituée d'Etats souverains à laquelle les Etats membres ont donné compétence dans les domaines régis par la présente convention et qui a été dûment autorisée, selon ses procédures internes, à signer, ratifier, accepter, approuver ou confirmer formellement la convention ou à y adhérer;

21) «trafic illicite»: tout mouvement de déchets dangereux ou d'autres déchets tel que précisé dans l'article 9.

Article 3   *Définitions nationales des déchets dangereux*

1.   Chacune des parties informe le Secrétariat de la convention, dans un délai de six mois après être devenue partie à la convention, des déchets, autres que ceux indiqués dans les annexes I et II, qui sont considérés ou définis comme dangereux par sa législation nationale, ainsi que de toute autre disposition concernant les procédures en matière de mouvement transfrontière applicables à ces déchets.

2.   Chacune des parties informe par la suite le Secrétariat de toute modification importante aux renseignements communiqués par elle en application du paragraphe 1.

3.   Le Secrétariat informe immédiatement toutes les parties des renseignements qu'il a reçus en application des paragraphes 1 et 2.

4.   Les parties sont tenues de mettre à la disposition de leurs exportateurs les renseignements qui leur sont communiqués par le Secrétariat en application du paragraphe 3.

Article 4   *Obligations générales*

1.

   a) Les parties exerçant leur droit d'interdire l'importation de déchets dangereux ou d'autres déchets en vue de leur élimination en informent les autres parties conformément aux dispositions de l'article 13.

   b) Les parties interdisent ou ne permettent pas l'exportation de déchets dangereux ou d'autres déchets vers les parties qui ont interdit l'importation de tels déchets, lorsque cette interdiction a été notifiée conformément aux dispositions du point a).

   c) Les parties interdisent ou ne permettent pas l'exportation de déchets dangereux ou d'autres déchets si l'Etat d'importation ne donne pas par écrit son accord spécifique pour l'importation de ces déchets, dans le cas où cet Etat d'importation n'a pas interdit l'importation de ces déchets.

2.   Chaque partie prend les dispositions voulues pour:

   a) veiller à ce que la production de déchets dangereux ou d'autres déchets à l'intérieur du pays soit réduite au minimum, compte tenu des considérations sociales, techniques et économiques;

   b) assurer la mise en place d'installations adéquates d'élimination, qui devront, dans la mesure du possible, être situées à l'intérieur du pays, en vue d'une gestion écologiquement rationnelle des déchets dangereux ou d'autres déchets en quelque lieu qu'ils soient éliminés;

   c) veiller à ce que les personnes qui s'occupent de la gestion des déchets dangereux ou d'autres déchets à l'intérieur du pays prennent les mesures nécessaires pour prévenir la pollution résultant de cette gestion et, si une telle pollution se produit, pour en réduire au minimum les conséquences pour la santé humaine et l'environnement;

   d) veiller à ce que les mouvements transfrontières de déchets dangereux ou d'autres déchets soient réduits à un minimum compatible avec une gestion efficace et écologiquement rationnelle desdits déchets et qu'ils s'effectuent de manière à protéger la santé humaine et l'environnement contre les effets nocifs qui pourraient en résulter;

   e) interdire les exportations de déchets dangereux ou d'autres déchets à destination des Etats ou groupes d'Etats appartenant à des organisations d'intégration politique ou économique qui sont parties, particulièrement les pays en développement, qui ont interdit par leur législation toute importation, ou si elle a des raisons de croire que les déchets en question n'y seront pas gérés selon des méthodes écologiquement rationnelles telles que définies par les critères que retiendront les parties à leur première réunion;

f) exiger que les renseignements sur les mouvements transfrontières proposés de déchets dangereux ou d'autres déchets soient communiqués aux Etats concernés, conformément à l'annexe V A, pour qu'ils puissent évaluer les conséquences pour la santé humaine et l'environnement des mouvements envisagés;

g) empêcher les importations de déchets dangereux ou d'autres déchets si elle a des raisons de croire que les déchets en question ne seront pas gérés selon des méthodes écologiquement rationnelles;

h) coopérer avec les autres parties et les autres organisations intéressées, directement et par l'intermédiaire du Secrétariat, à des activités portant notamment sur la diffusion de renseignements sur les mouvements transfrontières de déchets dangereux ou d'autres déchets, afin d'améliorer la gestion écologiquement rationnelle desdits déchets et d'empêcher le trafic illicite.

3. Les parties considèrent que le trafic illicite de déchets dangereux ou d'autres déchets constitue une infraction pénale.

4. Chaque partie prend les mesures juridiques, administratives et autres qui sont nécessaires pour mettre en œuvre et faire respecter les dispositions de la présente convention, y compris les mesures voulues pour prévenir et réprimer tout comportement en contravention de la convention.

5. Les parties n'autorisent pas les exportations de déchets dangereux ou d'autres déchets vers un Etat non partie ou l'importation de tels déchets en provenance d'un Etat non partie.

6. Les parties conviennent d'interdire l'exportation de déchets dangereux ou d'autres déchets en vue de leur élimination dans la zone située au sud du soixantième parallèle de l'hémisphère Sud, que ces déchets fassent ou non l'objet d'un mouvement transfrontière.

7. En outre, chaque partie:

a) interdit à toute personne relevant de sa compétence nationale de transporter ou d'éliminer des déchets dangereux ou d'autres déchets, à moins que la personne en question ne soit autorisée ou habilitée à procéder à ce type d'opération;

b) exige que les déchets dangereux et autres déchets qui doivent faire l'objet d'un mouvement transfrontière soient emballés, étiquetés et transportés conformément aux règles et normes internationales généralement acceptées et reconnues en matière d'emballage, d'étiquetage et de transport, et qu'il soit dûment tenu compte des pratiques internationalement admises en la matière;

c) exige que les déchets dangereux et autres déchets soient accompagnés d'un document de mouvement depuis le lieu d'origine du mouvement jusqu'au lieu d'élimination.

8. Chaque partie exige que les déchets dangereux ou autres déchets dont l'exportation est prévue soient gérés selon des méthodes écologiquement rationnelles dans l'État d'importation ou ailleurs. À leur première réunion, les parties arrêteront des directives techniques pour la gestion écologiquement rationnelle des déchets entrant dans le cadre de la présente convention.

9. Les parties prennent les mesures requises pour que les mouvements transfrontières de déchets dangereux et d'autres déchets ne soient autorisés que:

a) si l'Etat d'exportation ne dispose pas des moyens techniques et des installations nécessaires ou des sites d'élimination voulus pour éliminer les déchets en question selon des méthodes écologiquement rationnelles et efficaces

ou

b) si les déchets en question constituent une matière brute nécessaire pour les industries de recyclage ou de récupération de l'Etat d'importation

ou

c) si le mouvement transfrontière en question est conforme à d'autres critères qui seront fixés par les parties pour autant que ceux-ci ne soient pas en contradiction avec les objectifs de la présente convention.

10. L'obligation, aux termes de la présente convention, des Etats producteurs de déchets dangereux et d'autres déchets d'exiger que les déchets soient traités selon des méthodes écologiquement rationnelles ne peut en aucun cas être transférée à l'Etat d'importation ou de transit.

11. Rien dans la présente convention n'empêche une partie d'imposer, pour mieux protéger la santé humaine et l'environnement, des conditions supplémentaires qui soient compatibles avec les dispositions de la présente convention et conformes aux règles du droit international.

12. Aucune disposition de la présente convention ne portera atteinte de quelque façon que ce soit à la souveraineté des Etats sur leurs eaux territoriales établie conformément au droit international, ni aux droits souverains et à la juridiction qu'exercent les Etats dans leur zone économique exclusive et sur

leur plateau continental conformément au droit international, ni à l'exercice par les navires et les aéronefs de tous les Etats des droits et de la liberté de navigation tels qu'ils sont régis par le droit international et qu'ils ressortent des instruments internationaux pertinents.

13.   Les parties s'engagent à examiner périodiquement les possibilités de réduire le volume et/ou le potentiel de pollution des déchets dangereux et d'autres déchets qui sont exportés vers d'autres Etats, en particulier vers les pays en développement.

Article 5   *Désignation des autorités compétentes et du correspondant*

Pour faciliter l'application de la présente convention, les parties:

1)   désignent ou créent une ou plusieurs autorités compétentes et un correspondant. Une autorité compétente est désignée pour recevoir les notifications dans le cas d'un Etat de transit;

2)   informent le Secrétariat, dans un délai de trois mois à compter de l'entrée en vigueur de la convention à leur égard, des organes qu'elles ont désignés comme correspondant et autorités compétentes;

3)   informent le Secrétariat de toute modification apportée aux désignations qu'elles ont faites en application du paragraphe 2, dans un délai d'un mois à compter de la date où la modification a été décidée.

Article 6   *Mouvements transfrontières entre parties*

1.   L'Etat d'exportation informe par écrit, par l'intermédiaire de l'autorité compétente de l'Etat d'exportation, l'autorité compétente des Etats concernés de tout mouvement transfrontière de déchets dangereux ou d'autres déchets envisagé, ou exige du producteur ou de l'exportateur qu'il le fasse. Ces notifications doivent contenir les déclarations et renseignements spécifiés à l'annexe V A, rédigés dans une langue acceptable pour l'Etat d'importation. Une seule notification est envoyée à chacun des Etats concernés.

2.   L'Etat d'importation accuse par écrit réception de la notification à celui qui l'a donnée en consentant au mouvement avec ou sans réserve, ou en refusant l'autorisation de procéder au mouvement, ou en demandant un complément d'information. Une copie de la réponse définitive de l'Etat d'importation est envoyée aux autorités compétentes des Etats concernés qui sont parties.

3.   L'Etat d'exportation n'autorise pas le producteur ou l'exportateur à déclencher le mouvement transfrontière avant d'avoir reçu confirmation écrite que:

a) l'auteur de la notification a reçu le consentement écrit de l'Etat d'importation

et que

b) l'auteur de la notification a reçu de l'Etat d'importation confirmation de l'existence d'un contrat entre l'exportateur et l'éliminateur spécifiant une gestion écologiquement rationnelle des déchets considérés.

4.   Chaque Etat de transit qui est partie accuse sans délai réception de la notification à celui qui l'a donnée. Il peut ultérieurement prendre position par réponse écrite à l'auteur de la notification dans un délai de soixante jours en consentant au mouvement avec ou sans réserve, ou en refusant l'autorisation de procéder au mouvement, ou en demandant un complément d'information. L'Etat d'exportation n'autorise pas le déclenchement du mouvement transfrontière avant d'avoir reçu le consentement écrit de l'Etat de transit. Cependant, si, à quelque moment que ce soit, une partie décide de ne pas demander un accord préalable écrit, en général ou dans des conditions particulières, pour ce qui concerne des mouvements transfrontières de transit de déchets dangereux ou d'autres déchets, ou si elle modifie ses exigences à cet égard, elle informe immédiatement les autres parties de sa décision conformément aux dispositions de l'article 13. Dans ce dernier cas, si l'Etat d'exportation ne reçoit aucune réponse dans un délai de soixante jours à compter de la réception de la notification donnée par l'Etat de transit, l'Etat d'exportation peut permettre que cette exportation se fasse à travers l'Etat de transit.

5.   Lorsque, dans un mouvement transfrontière de déchets, ces déchets ne sont juridiquement définis ou considérés comme dangereux que:

a) par l'Etat d'exportation, les dispositions du paragraphe 9 du présent article qui s'appliquent à l'importateur ou à l'éliminateur et à l'Etat d'importation s'appliqueront mutatis mutandis à l'exportateur et à l'Etat d'exportation, respectivement;

b) par l'Etat d'importation ou par les Etats d'importation et de transit qui sont parties, les dispositions des paragraphes 1, 3, 4 et 6 du présent article qui s'appliquent à l'exportateur et à l'Etat d'exportation s'appliqueront mutatis mutandis à l'importateur ou à l'éliminateur et à l'Etat d'importation, respectivement;

c) pour tout Etat de transit qui est partie, les dispositions du paragraphe 4 s'appliqueront audit Etat.

6.   L'Etat d'exportation peut, sous réserve du consentement écrit des Etats concernés, autoriser le producteur ou l'exportateur à utiliser une procédure de notification générale lorsque des déchets dangereux ou d'autres déchets ayant les mêmes caractéristiques physiques et chimiques sont régulièrement expédiés au même éliminateur par le même poste douanier de sortie de l'Etat d'exportation, le même poste douanier d'entrée du pays d'importation et, en cas de transit, par les mêmes postes douaniers d'entrée et de sortie du ou des Etats de transit.

7.   Les Etats concernés peuvent subordonner leur consentement écrit à l'emploi de la procédure de notification générale visée au paragraphe 6 pour la communication de certains renseignements, tels que la quantité exacte des déchets dangereux ou d'autres déchets à expédier ou la liste périodique de ces déchets.

8.   La notification générale et le consentement écrit visés aux paragraphes 6 et 7 peuvent porter sur des expéditions multiples de déchets dangereux ou d'autres déchets au cours d'une période maximale de douze mois.

9.   Les parties exigent de toute personne prenant en charge un mouvement transfrontière de déchets dangereux ou d'autres déchets qu'elle signe le document de mouvement à la livraison ou à la réception des déchets en question. Elles exigent aussi de l'éliminateur qu'il informe l'exportateur et l'autorité compétente de l'Etat d'exportation de la réception des déchets en question et, en temps voulu, de l'achèvement des opérations d'élimination selon les modalités indiquées dans la notification. Si cette information n'est pas reçue par l'Etat d'exportation, l'autorité compétente de cet Etat ou l'exportateur en informe l'Etat d'importation.

10. La notification et la réponse exigées aux termes du présent article sont communiquées à l'autorité compétente des parties concernées ou à l'organisme gouvernemental compétent dans le cas des Etats non parties.

11. Les Etats d'importation ou de transit qui sont parties peuvent exiger comme condition d'entrée que tout mouvement transfrontière de déchets dangereux ou d'autres déchets soit couvert par une assurance, un cautionnement ou d'autres garanties.

Article 7 Mouvements transfrontières en provenance d'une partie à travers le territoire d'Etats qui ne sont pas parties

Les dispositions du paragraphe 1 de l'article 6 de la convention s'appliquent mutatis mutandis aux mouvements transfrontières de déchets dangereux ou d'autres déchets en provenance d'une partie à travers un ou plusieurs Etats qui ne sont pas parties.

Article 8 Obligation de réimporter

Lorsqu'un mouvement transfrontière de déchets dangereux ou d'autres déchets auquel les Etats concernés ont consenti, sous réserve des dispositions de la présente convention, ne peut être mené à terme conformément aux clauses du contrat, l'Etat d'exportation veille, si d'autres dispositions ne peuvent être prises pour éliminer les déchets selon des méthodes écologiquement rationnelles dans un délai de quatre-vingt-dix jours à compter du moment où l'Etat concerné a informé l'Etat d'exportation et le Secrétariat, ou toute autre période convenue par les Etats concernés, à ce que l'exportateur réintroduise ces déchets dans l'Etat d'exportation. À cette fin, l'Etat d'exportation et toute partie de transit ne s'opposent pas à la réintroduction de ces déchets dans l'Etat d'exportation, ni ne l'entravent ou ne l'empêchent.

Article 9 Trafic illicite

1.   Aux fins de la présente convention, est réputé constituer un trafic illicite tout mouvement transfrontière de déchets dangereux ou d'autres déchets:

a) effectué sans qu'une notification ait été donnée à tous les Etats concernés conformément aux dispositions de la présente convention

   ou

b) effectué sans le consentement que doit donner l'Etat intéressé conformément aux dispositions de la présente convention

   ou

c) effectué avec le consentement des Etats intéressés obtenu par falsification, fausse déclaration ou fraude

   ou

d) qui n'est pas conforme matériellement aux documents

   ou

e) qui entraîne une élimination délibérée (par exemple, déversement) de déchets dangereux ou d'autres déchets, en violation des dispositions de la présente convention et des principes généraux du droit international.

2.   Au cas où un mouvement transfrontière de déchets dangereux ou d'autres déchets est considéré comme trafic illicite du fait du comportement de l'exportateur ou du producteur, l'Etat d'exportation veille à ce que les déchets dangereux en question soient:

a) repris par l'exportateur ou le producteur ou, s'il y a lieu, par lui-même sur son territoire ou, si cela est impossible,

b) éliminés d'une autre manière conformément aux dispositions de la présente convention, dans un délai de trente jours à compter du moment où l'Etat d'exportation a été informé du trafic illicite ou tout autre délai dont les Etats concernés pourraient convenir. À cette fin, les parties concernées ne s'opposent pas au retour de ces déchets dans l'Etat d'exportation ni ne l'entravent ou ne l'empêchent.

3.   Lorsqu'un mouvement transfrontière de déchets dangereux ou d'autres déchets est considéré comme trafic illicite par suite du comportement de l'importateur ou de l'éliminateur, l'Etat d'importation veille à ce que les déchets dangereux en question soient éliminés d'une manière écologiquement rationnelle par l'importateur ou l'éliminateur ou, s'il y a lieu, par lui-même dans un délai de trente jours à compter du moment où le trafic illicite a retenu l'attention de l'Etat d'importation ou tout autre délai dont les Etats concernés pourraient convenir. À cette fin, les parties concernées coopèrent, selon les besoins, pour éliminer les déchets selon des méthodes écologiquement rationnelles.

4.   Lorsque la responsabilité du trafic illicite ne peut être imputée ni à l'exportateur ou au producteur, ni à l'importateur ou à l'éliminateur, les parties concernées ou d'autres parties, le cas échéant, coopèrent pour veiller à ce que les déchets dangereux en question soient éliminés le plus tôt possible selon des méthodes écologiquement rationnelles dans l'Etat d'exportation, dans l'Etat d'importation ou ailleurs, s'il y a lieu.

5.   Chaque partie adopte les lois nationales/internes voulues pour interdire et réprimer sévèrement le trafic illicite. Les parties coopèrent en vue de parvenir aux objectifs énoncés dans le présent article.

Article 10   *Coopération internationale*

1.   Les parties coopèrent entre elles afin d'améliorer et d'assurer la gestion écologiquement rationnelle des déchets dangereux et d'autres déchets.

2.   À cette fin, les parties:

a) communiquent sur demande des renseignements, sur base bilatérale ou multilatérale, en vue d'encourager la gestion écologiquement rationnelle des déchets dangereux et d'autres déchets, y compris par l'harmonisation des normes et pratiques techniques visant à une bonne gestion des déchets dangereux et d'autres déchets;

b) coopèrent en vue de surveiller les effets de la gestion des déchets dangereux sur la santé humaine et l'environnement;

c) coopèrent, sous réserve des dispositions de leurs lois, réglementations et politiques nationales, à la mise au point et à l'application de nouvelles techniques écologiquement rationnelles produisant peu de déchets et à l'amélioration des techniques existantes en vue d'éliminer, dans la mesure du possible, la production de déchets dangereux et d'autres déchets et d'élaborer des méthodes plus efficaces pour en assurer la gestion d'une manière écologiquement rationnelle, notamment en étudiant les conséquences économiques, sociales et environnementales de l'adoption de ces innovations ou perfectionnements techniques;

d) coopèrent activement, sous réserve des dispositions de leurs lois, réglementations et politiques nationales, au transfert des techniques relatives à la gestion écologiquement rationnelle des déchets dangereux et d'autres déchets et des systèmes d'organisation de cette gestion. Elles coopèrent aussi pour favoriser le développement des moyens techniques des parties et notamment de celles qui auraient besoin d'une aide technique dans ce domaine et en feraient la demande;

e) coopèrent à la mise au point de directives techniques et/ou de codes de bonne pratique appropriés.

3.   Les parties utiliseront les moyens appropriés pour coopérer afin d'aider les pays en développement à appliquer les dispositions contenues dans les points a), b), c) et d) du paragraphe 2 de l'article 4.

4.   Compte tenu du besoin des pays en développement, la coopération entre les parties et les organisations internationales compétentes est encouragée, afin de promouvoir, entre autres, la sensibilisation du public, le développement d'une gestion rationnelle de déchets dangereux et d'autres déchets et l'adoption de nouvelles techniques peu polluantes.

Article 11   Accords bilatéraux, multilatéraux et régionaux

1.   Nonobstant les dispositions de l'article 4 paragraphe 5, les parties peuvent conclure des accords ou arrangements bilatéraux, multilatéraux ou régionaux touchant les mouvements transfrontières de déchets dangereux ou d'autres déchets avec des parties ou des non parties à condition que de tels accords ou arrangements ne dérogent pas à la gestion écologiquement rationnelle des déchets dangereux et d'autres déchets prescrite dans la présente convention. Ces accords ou arrangements doivent énoncer des dispositions qui ne sont pas moins écologiquement rationnelles que celles prévues dans la présente convention, compte tenu notamment des intérêts des pays en développement.

2.   Les parties notifient au Secrétariat tout accord ou arrangement bilatéral, multilatéral ou régional visé au paragraphe 1, ainsi que ceux qu'ils ont conclus avant l'entrée en vigueur à leur égard de la présente convention aux fins de contrôler les mouvements transfrontières de déchets dangereux et d'autres déchets qui se déroulent entièrement entre les parties auxdits accords. Les dispositions de la présente convention sont sans effet sur les mouvements transfrontières conformes à de tels accords à condition que ceux-ci soient compatibles avec la gestion écologiquement rationnelle des déchets dangereux et d'autres déchets tel que prescrit dans la présente convention.

Article 12   Consultations sur les questions de responsabilité

Les parties coopèrent en vue d'adopter le plus tôt possible un protocole établissant les procédures appropriées en ce qui concerne la responsabilité et l'indemnisation en cas de dommages résultant d'un mouvement transfrontière de déchets dangereux et d'autres déchets.

Article 13   Communication de renseignements

1.   Les parties veillent à ce que, chaque fois qu'ils en ont connaissance, en cas d'accident survenu au cours du mouvement transfrontière de déchets dangereux ou d'autres déchets ou de leur élimination susceptible de présenter des risques pour la santé humaine et l'environnement d'autres Etats, ceux-ci soient immédiatement informés.

2.   Les parties s'informent mutuellement par l'intermédiaire du Secrétariat:

   a)   des changements concernant la désignation des autorités compétentes et/ou des correspondants, conformément à l'article 5;

b) des changements dans la définition nationale des déchets dangereux, conformément à l'article 3;

et, dès que possible,

c) des décisions prises par elles de ne pas autoriser, en totalité ou en partie, l'importation de déchets dangereux ou d'autres déchets pour élimination dans une zone relevant de leur compétence nationale;

d) des décisions prises par elles pour limiter ou interdire les exportations de déchets dangereux ou d'autres déchets;

e) de tout autre renseignement demandé conformément au paragraphe 4 du présent article.

3.   Les parties, conformément aux lois et réglementations nationales, transmettent à la conférence des parties instituée en application de l'article 15, par l'intermédiaire du Secrétariat, et avant la fin de chaque année civile, un rapport sur l'année civile précédente contenant les renseignements suivants:

a) les autorités compétentes et les correspondants qui ont été désignés par elles, conformément à l'article 5;

b) des renseignements sur les mouvements transfrontières de déchets dangereux ou d'autres déchets auxquel elles ont participé, et notamment:

   i) la quantité de déchets dangereux et d'autres déchets exportée, la catégorie à laquelle ils appartiennent et leurs caractéristiques, leur destination, le pays éventuel de transit et la méthode d'élimination utilisée comme spécifiée dans leur prise de position;

   ii) la quantité de déchets dangereux et d'autres déchets importée, la catégorie à laquelle ils appartiennent et leurs caractéristiques, leur origine et la méthode d'élimination utilisée;

   iii) les éliminations auxquelles il n'a pas été procédé comme prévu;

   iv) les efforts entrepris pour parvenir à réduire le volume de déchets dangereux ou d'autres déchets faisant l'objet de mouvements transfrontières;

c) des renseignements sur les mesures adoptées par elles en vue de l'application de la présente convention;

d) des renseignements sur les données statistiques pertinentes qu'elles ont compilées touchant les effets de la production, du transport et de l'élimination des déchets dangereux ou d'autres déchets sur la santé humaine et l'environnement;

e) des renseignements sur les accords et arrangements bilatéraux, multila-téraux et régionaux conclus en application de l'article 11 de la présente convention;

f) des renseignements sur les accidents survenus durant les mouvements transfrontières et l'élimination de déchets dangereux et d'autres déchets et sur les mesures prises pour y faire face;

g) des renseignements sur les diverses méthodes d'élimination utilisées dans la zone relevant de leur compétence nationale;

h) des renseignements sur les mesures prises pour la mise au point de tech-niques tendant à réduire et/ou à éliminer la production de déchets dan-gereux et d'autres déchets;

i) tous autres renseignements sur les questions que la conférence des parties peut juger utiles.

4. Les parties, conformément aux lois et réglementations nationales, veillent à ce qu'une copie de chaque notification concernant un mouvement transfrontière donné de déchets dangereux ou d'autres déchets et de chaque prise de position y relative soit envoyée au Secrétariat lorsqu'une partie dont l'environnement risque d'être affecté par ledit mouvement transfrontière l'a demandé.

Article 14   *Questions financières*

1. Les parties conviennent de créer, en fonction des besoins particuliers de différentes régions et sous-régions, des centres régionaux ou sous-régionaux de formation et de transfert de technologie pour la gestion des déchets dange-reux et d'autres déchets et la réduction de leur production. Les parties décide-ront de l'institution de mécanismes appropriés de financement de caractère volontaire.

2. Les parties envisageront la création d'un fonds renouvelable pour aider à titre provisoire à faire face aux situations d'urgence afin de limiter au minimum les dommages entraînés par des accidents découlant du mouvement transfrontière ou de l'élimination des déchets dangereux et d'autres déchets.

Article 15   Conférence des parties

1.   Il est institué une conférence des parties. La première session de la conférence des parties sera convoquée par le directeur exécutif du PNUE un an au plus tard après l'entrée en vigueur de la présente convention. Par la suite, les sessions ordinaires de la conférence des parties auront lieu régulièrement, selon la fréquence déterminée par la conférence à sa première session.

2.   Des sessions extraordinaires de la conférence des parties pourront avoir lieu à tout autre moment si la conférence le juge nécessaire, ou à la demande écrite d'une partie, sous réserve que cette demande soit appuyée par un tiers au moins des parties dans les six mois suivant sa communication auxdites parties par le Secrétariat.

3.   La conférence des parties arrêtera et adoptera par consensus son propre règlement intérieur et celui de tout organe subsidiaire qu'elle pourra créer, ainsi que le règlement financier qui fixera en particulier la participation financière des parties au titre de la présente convention.

4.   À leur première réunion, les parties examineront toutes mesures supplémentaires qui seraient nécessaires pour les aider à s'acquitter de leurs responsabilités en ce qui concerne la protection et la sauvegarde du milieu marin dans le cadre de la présente convention.

5.   La conférence des parties examine en permanence l'application de la présente convention et, en outre:

a)   encourage l'harmonisation des politiques, stratégies et mesures néces- saires pour réduire au minimum les dommages causés à la santé humaine et à l'environnement par les déchets dangereux et autres déchets;

b)   examine et adopte, selon qu'il convient, les amendements à la présente convention et à ses annexes, compte tenu notamment des informations scientifiques, techniques, économiques et écologiques disponibles;

c)   examine et prend toute autre mesure nécessaire à la poursuite des objec- tifs de la présente convention en fonction des enseignements tirés de son application ainsi que de l'application des accords et arrangements envisagés à l'article 11;

d)   examine et adopte des protocoles en tant que de besoin;

e)   crée les organes subsidiaires jugés nécessaires à l'application de la pré- sente convention.

6. L'Organisation des Nations unies et ses institutions spécialisées, de même que toute Etat non partie à la présente convention, peuvent se faire représenter en qualité d'observateurs aux sessions de la conférence des parties. Tout autre organe ou organisme national ou international, gouvernemental ou non gouvernemental, qualifié dans les domaines liés aux déchets dangereux ou autres déchets qui a informé le Secrétariat de son désir de se faire représenter en qualité d'observateur à une session de la conférence des parties peut être admis à y prendre part, à moins qu'un tiers au moins des parties présentes n'y fasse objection. L'admission et la participation des observateurs sont subordonnées au respect du règlement intérieur adopté par la conférence des parties.

7. Trois ans après l'entrée en vigueur de la présente convention, et par la suite au moins tous les six ans, la conférence des parties entreprend une évaluation de son efficacité et, si elle le juge nécessaire, envisage l'adoption d'une interdiction totale ou partielle des mouvements transfrontières de déchets dangereux et d'autres déchets à la lumière des informations scientifiques, environnementales, techniques et économiques les plus récentes.

Article 16 *Secrétariat*

1. Les fonctions du Secrétariat sont les suivantes:

a) organiser les réunions prévues aux articles 15 et 17 et en assurer le service;

b) établir et transmettre des rapports fondés sur les renseignements reçus conformément aux articles 3, 4, 6, 11 et 13 ainsi que sur les renseignements obtenus à l'occasion des réunions des organes subsidiaires créés en vertu de l'article 15 et, le cas échéant, sur les renseignements fournis par les organismes intergouvernementaux ou non gouvernementaux compétents;

c) établir des rapports sur les activités menées dans l'exercice des fonctions qui lui sont assignées en vertu de la présente convention et les présenter à la conférence des parties;

d) assurer la coordination nécessaire avec les organismes internationaux compétents, et en particulier conclure les arrangements administratifs et contractuels qui pourraient lui être nécessaires pour s'acquitter efficacement de ses fonctions;

e) communiquer avec les correspondants et autorités compétentes désignés par les parties conformément à l'article 5 de la présente convention;

f) recueillir des renseignements sur les installations et les sites nationaux agréés disponibles pour l'élimination de leurs déchets dangereux et d'autres déchets et diffuser ces renseignements auprès des parties;

g) recevoir les renseignements en provenance des parties et communiquer à celles-ci des informations sur:

- les sources d'assistance technique et de formation,

- les compétences techniques et scientifiques disponibles,

- les sources de conseils et de services d'expert

et

- les ressources disponibles pour les aider, sur leur demande, dans des domaines tels que:

- l'administration du système de notification prévue par la présente convention,

- la gestion des déchets dangereux et d'autres déchets,

- les techniques écologiquement rationnelles se rapportant aux déchets dangereux et d'autres déchets telles que les techniques peu polluantes et sans déchets,

- l'évaluation des moyens et sites d'élimination,

- la surveillance des déchets dangereux et d'autres déchets

et

- les interventions en cas d'urgence;

h) communiquer aux parties, sur leur demande, les renseignements sur les consultants ou bureaux d'études ayant les compétences techniques requises en la matière qui pourront les aider à examiner une notification de mouvement transfrontière, à vérifier qu'une expédition de déchets dangereux et d'autres déchets est conforme à la notification pertinente et/ou que les installations proposées pour l'élimination des déchets dangereux ou d'autres déchets sont écologiquement rationnelles, lorsqu'elles ont des raisons de croire que les déchets en question ne feront pas l'objet d'une gestion écologiquement rationnelle. Tout examen de ce genre ne serait pas à la charge du Secrétariat;

i) aider les parties, sur leur demande, à déceler les cas de trafic illicite et à communiquer immédiatement aux parties concernées tous les renseignements qu'il aura reçus au sujet de trafic illicite;

j) coopérer avec les parties et avec les organisations et institutions internationales intéressées et compétentes pour fournir les experts et le matériel nécessaires à une aide rapide aux Etats en cas d'urgence;

k) s'acquitter des autres fonctions entrant dans le cadre de la présente convention que la conférence des parties peut décider de lui assigner.

2.   Les fonctions du Secrétariat seront provisoirement exercées par le PNUE, jusqu'à la fin de la première réunion de la conférence des parties tenue conformément à l'article 15.

3.   À sa première réunion, la conférence des parties désignera le Secrétariat parmi les organisations internationales compétentes existantes qui se sont proposées pour assurer les fonctions de Secrétariat prévus par la présente convention. À cette session, la conférence des parties évaluera aussi la façon dont le Secrétariat intérimaire se sera acquitté des fonctions qui lui étaient confiées, en particulier aux termes du paragraphe 1, et elle décidera des structures qui conviennent à l'exercice de ces fonctions.

Article 17   Amendements à la convention

1.   Toute partie peut proposer des amendements à la présente convention et toute partie à un protocole peut proposer des amendements à ce protocole. Ces amendements tiennent dûment compte, entre autres, des considérations scientifiques et techniques pertinentes.

2.   Les amendements à la présente convention sont adoptés lors des réunions de la conférence des parties. Les amendements à un protocole sont adoptés lors des réunions des parties au protocole considéré. Le texte de tout amendement proposé à la présente convention ou aux protocoles, sauf s'il en est disposé autrement dans lesdits protocoles, est communiqué par le Secrétariat aux parties six mois au moins avant la réunion à laquelle il est proposé pour adoption. Le Secrétariat communique aussi les amendements proposés aux signataires de la présente convention pour information.

3.   Les parties n'épargnent aucun effort pour parvenir, au sujet de tout amendement proposé à la présente convention, à un accord par consensus. Si tous les efforts en vue d'un consensus ont été épuisés et si un accord ne s'est pas dégagé, l'amendement est adopté en dernier recours par un vote à la majorité des trois quarts des parties présentes à la réunion et ayant exprimé leur vote, et soumis par le dépositaire à toutes les parties pour ratification, approbation, confirmation formelle ou acceptation.

4.   La procédure énoncée au paragraphe 3 s'applique à l'adoption des amendements aux protocoles, à ceci près que la majorité des deux tiers des parties aux protocoles considérés présentes à la réunion et ayant exprimé leur vote suffit.

5. Les instruments de ratification, d'approbation, de confirmation formelle ou d'acceptation des amendements sont déposés auprès du dépositaire. Les amendements adoptés conformément aux paragraphes 3 ou 4 entrent en vigueur entre les parties les ayant acceptés le quatre-vingt-dixième jour après que le dépositaire a reçu leur instrument par les trois quarts au moins des parties les ayant acceptés ou par les deux tiers au moins des parties au protocole considéré les ayant acceptés, sauf disposition contraire dudit protocole. Les amendements entrent en vigueur à l'égard de toute autre partie le quatre-vingt-dixième jour après le dépôt par ladite partie de son instrument de ratification, d'approbation, de confirmation formelle ou d'acceptation des amendements.

6. Aux fins du présent article, l'expression «parties présentes et ayant exprimé leur vote» s'entend des parties présentes qui ont émis un vote affirmatif ou négatif.

Article 18   Adoption et amendement des annexes

1. Les annexes à la présente convention ou à tout protocole y relatif font partie intégrante de la convention ou du protocole considéré et, sauf disposition contraire expresse, toute référence à la présente convention ou à ses protocoles est aussi une référence aux annexes à ces instruments. Lesdites annexes sont limitées aux questions scientifiques, techniques et administratives.

2. Sauf disposition contraire des protocoles au sujet de leurs annexes, la proposition, l'adoption et l'entrée en vigueur d'annexes supplémentaires à la présente convention ou aux protocoles y relatifs sont régies par la procédure suivante:

a) les annexes à la présente convention et à ses protocoles sont proposées et adoptées selon la procédure décrite aux paragraphes 2, 3 et 4 de l'article 17;

b) toute partie qui n'est pas en mesure d'accepter une annexe supplémentaire à la présente convention ou à l'un des protocoles auxquels elle est partie en donne par écrit notification au dépositaire dans les six mois qui suivent la date de communication de l'adoption par le dépositaire. Ce dernier informe sans délai toutes les parties de toute notification reçue. Une partie peut à tout moment accepter une annexe à laquelle elle avait déclaré précédemment faire objection, et cette annexe entre alors en vigueur à l'égard de cette partie;

c) à l'expiration d'un délai de six mois à compter de la date de l'envoi de la communication par le dépositaire, l'annexe prend effet à l'égard de toutes les parties à la présente convention ou à tout protocole considéré qui n'ont pas soumis de notification conformément au point b).

3.   La proposition, l'adoption et l'entrée en vigueur des amendements aux annexes à la présente convention ou à tout protocole y relatif sont soumises à la même procédure que la proposition, l'adoption et l'entrée en vigueur des annexes à la convention ou à tout protocole y relatif. Les annexes et les amendements y relatifs tiennent dûment compte, entre autres, des considérations scientifiques et techniques pertinentes.

4.   Si une annexe supplémentaire ou un amendement à une annexe nécessite un amendement à la convention ou à tout protocole y relatif, l'annexe supplémentaire ou l'annexe modifiée n'entre en vigueur que lorsque l'amendement à la convention ou à tout protocole y relatif entre lui-même en vigueur.

Article 19   *Vérification*

Toute partie qui a des raisons de croire qu'une autre partie agit ou a agi en violation des obligations découlant des dispositions de la présente convention peut en informer le Secrétariat, et dans ce cas elle informe simultanément et immédiatement, directement ou par l'intermédiaire du Secrétariat, la partie faisant l'objet des allégations. Tous les renseignements pertinents devraient être transmis aux parties par le Secrétariat.

Article 20   *Règlement des différends*

1.   Si un différend surgit entre les parties à propos de l'interprétation de l'application ou du respect de la présente convention ou de tout protocole y relatif, ces parties s'efforcent de le régler par voie de négociations ou par tout autre moyen pacifique de leur choix.

2.   Si les parties en causes ne peuvent régler leur différend par les moyens mentionnés au paragraphe précédent, ce différend, si les parties en conviennent ainsi, est soumis à la Cour internationale de justice ou à l'arbitrage dans les conditions définies dans l'annexe VI relative à l'arbitrage. Toutefois, si les parties ne parviennent pas à s'entendre en vue de soumettre le différend à la Cour internationale de justice ou à l'arbitrage, elles ne sont pas relevées de leur responsabilité de continuer à chercher à le résoudre selon les moyens mentionnés au paragraphe 1.

3.   Lorsqu'il ratifie, accepte, approuve ou confirme formellement la présente convention ou y adhère, ou à tout moment par la suite, tout Etat ou toute organisation d'intégration politique ou économique peut déclarer qu'il

reconnaît comme étant obligatoire ipso facto et sans accord spécial, à l'égard de toute partie acceptant la même obligation, la soumission du différend:

a) à la Cour internationale de justice

et/ou

b) à l'arbitrage conformément aux procédures énoncées dans l'annexe VI.

Cette déclaration est notifiée par écrit au Secrétariat qui la communique aux parties.

Article 21   Signature

La présente convention est ouverte à la signature des Etats, de la Namibie, représentée par le Conseil des Nations unies pour la Namibie, et des organisations d'intégration politique ou économique à Bâle le 22 mars 1989, au département fédéral des affaires étrangères de la Suisse, à Berne, du 23 mars 1989 au 30 juin 1989, et au siège de l'Organisation des Nations unies à New York du 1er juillet 1989 au 22 mars 1990.

Article 22   Ratification, acceptation, confirmation formelle ou approbation

1.   La présente convention est soumise à la ratification, à l'acceptation ou a l'approbation des Etats et de la Namibie, représentée par le Conseil des Nations unies pour la Namibie, ainsi qu'à la confirmation formelle ou à l'approbation des organisations d'intégration politique ou économique. Les instruments de ratification, d'acceptation formelle ou d'approbation seront déposés auprès du dépositaire.

2.   Toute organisation visée au paragraphe 1 qui devient partie à la présente convention et dont aucun Etat membre n'est lui-même partie est liée par toutes les obligations énoncées dans la convention. Lorsqu'un ou plusieurs Etats membres d'une de ces organisations sont parties à la convention, l'organisation et ses Etats membres conviennent de leurs responsabilités respectives en ce qui concerne l'exécution de leurs obligations en vertu de la convention. Dans de tels cas, l'organisation et les Etats membres ne sont pas habilités à exercer simultanément leurs droits au titre de la convention.

3.   Dans leurs instruments de confirmation formelle ou d'approbation, les organisations visées au paragraphe 1 indiquent l'étendue de leurs compétences dans les domaines régis par la convention. Ces organisations notifient également toute modification importante de l'étendue de leurs compétences au dépositaire qui en informe les parties.

Article 23   Adhésion

1.   La présente convention est ouverte à l'adhésion des Etats, de la Namibie, représentée par le Conseil des Nations unies pour la Namibie, et des organisations d'intégration politique ou économique à partir de la date à laquelle la convention n'est plus ouverte à la signature. Les instruments d'adhésion seront déposés auprès du dépositaire.

2.   Dans leurs instruments d'adhésion, les organisations visées au paragraphe 1 indiquent l'étendue de leurs compétences dans les domaines régis par la convention. Elles notifient également au dépositaire toute modification importante de l'étendue de leurs compétences.

3.   Les dispositions du paragraphe 2 de l'article 22 s'appliquent aux organisations d'intégration politique ou économique qui adhèrent à la présente convention.

Article 24   Droit de vote

1.   Sous réserve des dispositions du paragraphe 2, chaque partie à la convention dispose d'une voix.

2.   Les organisations d'intégration politique ou économique disposent, conformément au paragraphe 3 de l'article 22 et au paragraphe 2 de l'article 23 pour exercer leur droit de vote dans les domaines qui relèvent de leur compétence, d'un nombre de voix égal au nombre de leurs Etats membres qui sont parties à la convention ou aux protocoles pertinents. Ces organisations n'exercent pas leur droit de vote si leurs Etats membres exercent le leur, et inversement.

Article 25   Entrée en vigueur

1.   La présente convention entrera en vigueur le quatre-vingt-dixième jour suivant la date du dépôt du vingtième instrument de ratification, d'acceptation, de confirmation formelle, d'approbation ou d'adhésion.

2.   À l'égard de chacun des Etats ou des organisations d'intégration politique ou économique qui ratifie, accepte, approuve ou confirme formellement la présente convention ou y adhère, après la date du dépôt du vingtième instrument de ratification, d'acceptation, d'approbation, de confirmation formelle ou d'adhésion, la convention entrera en vigueur le dix-neuvième jour suivant la date du dépôt, par ledit Etat ou ladite organisation d'intégration politique ou économique, de son instrument de ratification, d'acceptation, d'approbation, de confirmation formelle ou d'adhésion.

3.   Aux fins des paragraphes 1 et 2, aucun des instruments déposés par une organisation d'intégration politique ou économique ne doit être considéré comme un instrument venant s'ajouter aux instruments déjà déposés par les Etats membres de ladite organisation.

Article 26   Réserves et déclarations

1.   Aucune réserve ou dérogation ne pourra être faite à la présente convention.

2.   Le paragraphe 1 du présent article n'empêche pas un Etat ou une organisation d'intégration politique ou économique, lorsqu'il signe, ratifie, accepte, approuve ou confirme formellement la présente convention ou y adhère, de faire des déclarations ou des exposés, quelle que soit l'appellation qui leur est donnée en vue, entre autres, d'harmoniser ses lois et règlements avec les dispositions de la présente convention, à condition que ces déclarations ou exposés ne visent pas à annuler ou à modifier les effets juridiques des dispositions de la convention dans leur application à cet Etat.

Article 27   Dénonciation

1.   Àpres l'expiration d'un délai de trois ans à compter de la date d'entrée en vigueur de la présente convention à l'égard d'une partie, ladite partie pourra à tout moment dénoncer la convention par notification écrite donnée au dépositaire.

2.   La dénonciation prendra effet un an après la réception de la notification par le dépositaire, ou à toute autre date ultérieure qui pourra être spécifiée dans la notification.

Article 28   *Dépositaire*

Le secrétaire général de l'Organisation des Nations unies sera le dépositaire de la présente convention et de tout protocole y relatif.

Article 29   *Textes faisant foi*

Les textes anglais, arabe, chinois, espagnol, français et russe originaux de la présente convention font également foi.

En foi de quoi les soussignés, à ce dûment habilités, ont signé la présente convention.

Fait à Bâle, le vingt-deux mars mil neuf cent quatre-vingt-neuf.

ANNEXE I

CATEGORIES DE DECHETS À CONTROLER

Flux de déchets

Y1   Déchets cliniques provenant de soins médicaux dispensés dans des hôpitaux, centres médicaux et cliniques

Y2   Déchets issus de la production et de la préparation de produits pharmaceutiques

Y3   Déchets de médicaments et produits pharmaceutiques

Y4   Déchets issus de la production, de la préparation et de l'utilisation de biocides et de produits phytopharmaceutiques

Y5   Déchets issus de la fabrication, de la préparation et de l'utilisation des produits de préservation du bois

Y6   Déchets issus de la production, de la préparation et de l'utilisation de solvants organiques

Y7   Déchets cyanurés de traitement thermiques et d'opérations de trempe

Y8   Déchets d'huiles minérales impropres à l'usage initialement prévu

Y9   Mélanges et émulsions huile/eau ou hydrocarbure/eau

Y10   Substances et articles contenant, ou contaminés par, des diphényles polychlorés (PCB), des terphényles polychlorés (PCT) ou des diphényles polybromés (PBB)

Y11   Résidus goudronneux de raffinage, de distillation ou de toute opération de pyrolyse

Y12   Déchets issus de la production, de la préparation et de l'utilisation d'encres, de colorants, de pigments, de peintures, de laques ou de vernis

Y13   Déchets issus de la production, de la préparation et de l'utilisation de résines, de latex, de plastifiants ou de colles et adhésifs

Y14 Déchets de substances chimiques non identifiées et/ou nouvelles qui proviennent d'activités de recherche, de développement ou d'enseignement, et dont les effets sur l'homme et/ou sur l'environnement ne sont pas connus

Y15 Déchets de caractère explosible non soumis à une législation différente

Y16 Déchets issus de la production, de la préparation et de l'utilisation de produits et matériels photographiques

Y17 Déchets de traitements de surface des métaux et matières plastiques

Y18 Résidus d'opérations d'élimination des déchets industriels

Déchets ayant comme constituants:

Y19 Métaux carbonyles

Y20 Béryllium, composés du béryllium

Y21 Composés du chrome hexavalent

Y22 Composés du cuivre

Y23 Composés du zinc

Y24 Arsenic, composés de l'arsenic

Y25 Sélénium, composés du sélénium

Y26 Cadmium, composés du cadmium

Y27 Antimoine, composés de l'antimoine

Y28 Tellure, composé du tellure

Y29 Mercure, composés du mercure

Y30 Thallium, composés du thallium

Y31 Plomb, composés du plomb

Y32 Composés inorganiques du fluor, à l'exclusion du fluorure de calcium

Y33   Cyanures inorganiques

Y34   Solutions acides ou acides sous forme solide

Y35   Solutions basiques ou bases sous forme solide

Y36   Amiante (poussières et fibres)

Y37   Composés organiques du phosphore

Y38   Cyanures organiques

Y39   Phénols, composés phénolés, y compris les chlorophénols

Y40   Ethers

Y41   Solvants organiques halogénés

Y42   Solvants organiques, sauf solvants halogénés

Y43   Tout produit de la famille des dibenzofurannes polychlorés

Y44   Tout produit de la famille des dibenzoparadioxines polychlorées

Y45   Composés organohalogénés autres que les matières figurant dans la présente annexe (par exemple Y39, Y41, Y42, Y43, Y44).

ANNEXE II

CATEGORIES DE DECHETS DEMANDANT UN EXAMEN SPECIAL

Y46   Déchets ménagers collectés

Y47   Résidus provenant de l'incinération des déchets ménagers

ANNEXE III

LISTE DES CARACTERISTIQUES DE DANGER

Classe ONU [1]	Code	Caractéristiques
1	H1	*Matières explosives* Une matière ou un déchet explosif est une matière (ou un mélange de matières) solide ou liquide qui peut elle-même, par réaction chimique, émettre des gaz à une température et à une pression et à une vitesse telle qu'il en résulte des dégâts dans la zone environnante
3	H3	*Matières inflammables* Les liquides inflammables sont les liquides, mélanges de liquides, ou liquides contenant des solides en solution ou suspension (peintures, vernis, laques, etc., par exemple, à l'exclusion cependant des matières ou déchets classés ailleurs en raison de leurs caractéristiques dangereuses), qui émettent des vapeurs inflammables à une température ne dépassant pas 60,5 °C en creuset fermé ou 65,6 °C en creuset ouvert. (Comme les résultats des essais en creuset ouvert et en creuset fermé ne sont pas strictement comparables entre eux et que même les résultats de plusieurs essais effectués selon la même méthode diffèrent souvent, les règlements qui s'écarteraient des chiffres ci-dessus pour tenir compte de ces différences demeureraient conformes à l'esprit de cette définition.)
4.1	H4.1	*Matières solides inflammables* Les solides ou déchets solides inflammables sont les matières solides autres que celles classées comme explosives, qui, dans les conditions rencontrées lors du transport, s'enflamment facilement ou peuvent causer un incendie sous l'effet du frottement, ou le favoriser
4.2	H4.2	*Matières spontanément inflammables* Matières ou déchets susceptibles de s'échauffer spontanément dans des conditions normales de transport, ou de s'échauffer au contact de l'air, et pouvant alors s'enflammer
4.3	H4.3	*Matières ou déchets qui, au contact de l'eau, émettent des gaz inflammables* Matières ou déchets qui, par réaction avec l'eau, sont susceptibles de s'enflammer spontanément ou d'émettre des gaz inflammables en quantités dangereuses
5.1	H5.1	*Matières comburantes* Matières ou déchets qui, sans être toujours combustibles eux-mêmes, peuvent, en général en cédant de l'oxygène, provoquer ou favoriser la combustion d'autres matières

Classe ONU [1]	Code	Caractéristiques
5.2	H5.2	*Peroxydes organiques* Matières organiques ou déchets qui, contenant la structure bivalente -O-O-, sont des matières thermiquement instables, qui peuvent subir une décomposition auto-accélérée exothermique
6.1	H6.1	*Matières toxiques (aiguës)* Matières ou déchets qui, par ingestion, inhalation ou pénétration cutanée, peuvent causer la mort ou une lésion grave ou nuire à la santé humaine
6.2	H6.2	*Matières infectieuses* Matières ou déchets contenant des micro-organismes viables ou leurs toxines, dont on sait, ou dont on a de bonnes raisons de croire, qu'ils causent la maladie chez les animaux ou chez l'homme
8	H8	*Matières corrosives* Matières ou déchets qui, par action chimique, causent des dommages graves aux tissus vivants qu'ils touchent, ou qui peuvent en cas de fuite endommager sérieusement, voire détruire, les autres marchandises transportées ou les engins de transport et qui peuvent aussi comporter d'autres risques
9	H10	*Matières libérant des gaz toxiques au contact de l'air ou de l'eau* Matières ou déchets qui, par réaction avec l'air ou l'eau, sont susceptibles d'émettre des gaz toxiques en quantités dangereuses
9	H11	*Matières toxiques (effets différés ou chroniques)* Matières ou déchets qui, par inhalation, ingestion ou pénétration cutanée peuvent entraîner des effets différés ou chroniques, ou produire le cancer
9	H12	*Matières écotoxiques* Matières ou déchets qui, s'ils sont rejetés, provoquent ou risquent de provoquer, par bio-accumulation et/ou effets toxiques sur les systèmes biologiques, des impacts nocifs immédiats ou différés sur l'environnement
9	H13	Matières susceptibles après élimination de donner lieu, par quelque moyen que se soit, à une autre substance, par exemple un produit de lixiviation, qui possède l'une des caractéristiques énumérées ci-dessus

[1]Cette numérotation correspond au système de classification de danger adopté dans les recommandations des Nations unies pour le transport des marchandises dangereuses (ST/SG/AC. 10/1/Rev.5, Nations unies, New York, 1988).

Epreuves

Les dangers que certains types de déchets sont susceptibles de présenter ne sont pas encore bien connus; il n'existe pas d'épreuves d'appréciation quantitative de ces dangers. Des recherches plus approfondies sont nécessaires afin d'élaborer les moyens de caractériser les dangers que ces types de déchets peuvent présenter pour l'homme ou l'environnement. Des épreuves normalisées ont été mises au point pour des substances et matières pures. De nombreux pays membres ont élaboré des tests nationaux que l'on peut appliquer aux matières destinées à être éliminées par les opérations figurant à l'annexe I à la convention en vue de décider si ces matières présentent une quelconque des caractéristiques énumérées dans la présente annexe.

ANNEXE IV

OPERATIONS D'ELIMINATION

A. Opérations ne débouchant pas sur une possibilité de récupération, de recyclage, de réutilisation, de réemploi direct, ou toute autre utilisation des déchets

La section A récapitule toutes ces opérations d'élimination telles qu'elles sont effectuées en pratique.

D1   Dépôt sur ou dans le sol (par exemple mise en décharge, etc.)

D2   Traitement en milieu terrestre (par exemple biodégradation de déchets liquides ou de boues dans les sols, etc.)

D3   Injection en profondeur (par exemple des déchets pompables dans des puits, des dômes de sel, ou des failles géologiques naturelles, etc.)

D4   Lagunage (par exemple déversement de déchets liquides ou de boues dans des puits, des étangs ou des bassins, etc.)

D5   Mise en décharge spécialement aménagée (par exemple placement dans des alvéoles étanches séparées, recouvertes et isolées les unes des autres et de l'environnement, etc.)

D6   Rejet dans le milieu aquatique sauf l'immersion en mer

D7   Immersion en mer, y compris enfouissement dans le sous-sol marin

D8   Traitement biologique non spécifié ailleurs dans la présente annexe, aboutissant à des composés ou à des mélanges qui sont éliminés selon l'un des procédés énumérés à la section A

D9   Traitement physico-chimique non spécifié ailleurs dans la présente annexe, aboutissant à des composés ou à des mélanges qui sont éliminés selon l'un des procédés énumérés à la section A (par exemple évaporation, séchage, calcination, neutralisation, précipitation, etc.)

D10   Incinération à terre

D11   Incinération en mer

D12   Stockage permanent (par exemple placement de conteneurs dans une mine, etc.)

D13   Regroupement préalablement à l'une des opérations de la section A

D14   Reconditionnement préalablement à l'une des opérations de la section A

D15   Stockage préalablement à l'une des opérations de la section A

B. Opérations débouchant sur une possibilité de récupération, de recyclage, de réutilisation, de réemploi direct, ou toute autre utilisation des déchets

La section B est censée récapituler toutes ces opérations, concernant des matières qui sont considérées ou légalement définies comme déchets dangereux et qui auraient sinon subi l'une des opérations énoncées à la section A.

R1   Utilisation comme combustible (autrement qu'en incinération directe) ou autre moyen de produire de l'énergie

R2   Récupération ou régénération des solvants

R3   Recyclage ou récupération de substances organiques qui ne sont pas utilisées comme solvants

R4   Recyclage ou récupération des métaux ou des composés métalliques

R5   Recyclage ou récupération d'autres matières inorganiques

R6   Régénération des acides ou des bases

R7   Récupération des produits servant à capter les polluants

R8   Récupération des produits provenant des catalyseurs

R9   Régénération ou autres réemplois des huiles usées

R10   Epandage sur le sol au profit de l'agriculture ou de l'écologie

R11   Utilisation de matériaux résiduels obtenus à partir de l'une des opérations numérotées R1 à R10

R12   Echange de déchets en vue de les soumettre à l'une des opérations numérotées R1 à R11

R13   Mise en réserve de matériaux en vue de les soumettre à l'une des opérations fgurant à la section B

ANNEXE V A

INFORMATIONS À FOURNIR LORS DE LA NOTIFICATION

1) Motif de l'exportation de déchets

2) Exportateur des déchets [1]

3) Producteur(s) des déchets et lieu de production [1]

4) Eliminateur des déchets et lieu effectif d'élimination [1]

5) Transporteur(s) prévu(s) des déchets ou leurs agents, lorsqu'ils sont connus [1]

6) Pays d'exportation des déchets
   Autorité compétente [2]

7) Pays de transit prévus
   Autorité compétente [2]

8) Pays d'importation des déchets
   Autorité compétente [2]

9) Notification générale ou notification unique

10) Date(s) prévue(s) du (des) transfert(s), durée de l'exportation des déchets et itinéraire prévu (notamment points d'entrée et de sortie) [3]

11) Moyen(s) de transport prévu(s) (route, rail, mer, air, voie de navigation intérieure, etc.)

12) Informations relatives à l'assurance [4]

13) Dénomination et description physique des déchets, y compris numéro Y et numéro ONU, composition de ceux-ci [5] et renseignements sur toute disposition particulière relative à la manipulation, notamment mesures d'urgence à prendre en cas d'accident

14) Type de conditionnement prévu (par exemple vrac, fûts, citernes)

15) Quantité estimée en poids/volume [6]

16) Processus dont proviennent les déchets [7]

17) Pour les déchets énumérés à l'annexe I, classification de l'annexe III: caractéristique de danger, numéro H, classe de l'ONU

18) Mode d'élimination selon l'annexe IV

19) Déclaration du producteur et de l'exportateur certifiant l'exactitude des informations

20) Informations (y compris la description technique de l'installation) communiquées à l'exportateur ou au producteur par l'élimination des déchets et sur lesquelles ce dernier s'est fondé pour estimer qu'il n'y a aucune raison de croire que les déchets ne seront pas gérés selon des méthodes écologiquement rationnelles conformément aux lois et règlements du pays importateur

21) Renseignements concernant le contrat conclu entre l'exportateur et l'éliminateur.

Notes

[1]   Nom et adresse complets, numéros de téléphone, de télex ou de télécopieur, ainsi que nom, adresse et numéro de téléphone, de télex ou de télécopieur de la personne à contacter.

[2]   Nom et adresse complets, numéros de téléphone, de télex ou de télécopieur.

[3]   En cas de notification générale couvrant plusieurs transferts, indiquer soit les dates prévues de chaque transport, soit, si celles-ci ne sont pas connues, la fréquence prévue des transports.

[4]   Informations à fournir sur les dispositions pertinentes relatives à l'assurance et sur la manière dont l'exportateur, le transporteur et l'éliminateur s'en acquittent.

[5]   Indiquer la nature et la concentration des composés les plus dangereux au regard de la toxicité et des autres dangers présentés par les déchets tant pour la manipulation que pour le mode d'élimination prévu.

[6]   En cas de notification générale couvrant plusieurs transferts, indiquer à la fois la quantité totale estimée et les quantités estimées pour chacun des transferts.

[7]   Dans la mesure où ce renseignement est nécessaire pour évaluer les risques et déterminer la validité de l'opération d'élimination proposée.

ANNEXE V B

INFORMATIONS À FOURNIR DANS LE DOCUMENT DE MOUVEMENT

1) Exportateur des déchets [1]

2) Producteur(s) des déchets et lieu de production [1]

3) Eliminateur des déchets et lieu effectif d'élimination [1]

4) Transporteur(s) des déchets [1] ou son (ses) agent(s)

5) Sujet à notification générale ou à notification unique

6) Date de début du mouvement transfrontière et date(s) et signature de la réception par chaque personne qui prend en charge les déchets

7) Moyen de transport (route, rail, voie de navigation intérieure, mer, air), y compris pays d'exportation, de transit et d'importation ainsi que points d'en

8) Description générale des déchets (état physique, appellation exacte et classe d'expédition ONU, numéro ONU, numéro Y et numéro H le cas échéant)

9) Renseignements sur les dispositions particulières relatives à la manipulation, y compris mesures d'intervention en cas d'accident

10) Type et nombre de colis

11) Quantité en poids/volume

12) Déclaration du producteur ou de l'exportateur certifiant l'exactitude des informations

13) Déclaration du producteur ou de l'exportateur certifiant l'absence d'objections de la part des autorités compétentes de tous les Etats concernés qui sont parties

14) Attestation de l'éliminateur de la réception à l'installation d'élimination désignée et indication de la méthode d'élimination et de la date approximative d'élimination.

Notes

Les informations à fournir sur le document de mouvement devraient, chaque fois que possible, être rassemblées dans un seul et même document avec celles exigées par la réglementation des transports. En cas d'impossibilité, ces informations devraient compléter et non répéter celles exigées par la réglementation des transports. Le document de mouvement contiendra des instructions quant à la personne habilitée à fournir les renseignements et à remplir les formulaires.

[1]   Nom et adresse complets, numéros de téléphone, de télex ou de télécopieur, ainsi que nom, adresse et numéro de téléphone, de télex ou de télécopieur de la personne à contacter en cas d'urgence.

ANNEXE VI

ARBITRAGE

Article premier

Sauf dispositions contraires de l'accord prévu à l'article 20 de la convention, la procédure d'arbitrage est conduite conformément aux dispositions des articles 2 à 10 ci-après.

Article 2

La partie requérante notifie au Secrétariat que les parties sont convenues de soumettre le différend à l'arbitrage conformément au paragraphe 2 ou au paragraphe 3 de l'article 20 de la convention, en indiquant notamment les articles de la convention dont l'interprétation ou l'application sont en cause. Le Secrétariat communique les informations ainsi reçues à toutes les parties à la convention.

Article 3

Le tribunal arbitral est composé de trois membres. Chacune des parties au différend nomme un arbitre et les deux arbitres ainsi nommés désignent d'un commun accord le troisième arbitre, qui assume la présidence du tribunal. Ce dernier ne doit pas être ressortissant de l'une des parties au différend, ni avoir sa résidence habituelle sur le territoire de l'une de ces parties, ni se trouver au service de l'une d'elles, ni s'être déjà occupé de l'affaire à aucun titre.

Article 4

1.   Si, dans un délai de deux mois après la nomination du deuxième arbitre, le président du tribunal arbitral n'est pas désigné, le secrétaire général de l'Organisation des Nation unies procède, à la requête de l'une des deux parties, à sa désignation dans un nouveau délai de deux mois.

2.   Si, dans un délai de deux mois après la réception de la requête, l'une des parties au différend ne procède pas à la nomination d'un arbitre, l'autre partie peut saisir le secrétaire général de l'Organisation des Nations unies, qui désigne le président du tribunal arbitral dans un nouveau délai de deux mois. Dès sa désignation, le président du tribunal arbitral demande à la partie qui n'a pas nommé d'arbitre de le faire dans un délai de deux mois. Passé ce délai, il

115

saisit le secrétaire général de l'Organisation des Nations unies, qui procède à cette nomination dans un nouveau délai de deux mois.

Article 5

1.   Le tribunal rend sa sentence conformément au droit international et aux dispositions de la présente convention.

2.   Tout tribunal arbitral constitué aux termes de la présente annexe établit ses propres règles de procédure.

Article 6

1.   Les décisions du tribunal arbitral, tant sur la procédure que sur le fond, sont prises à la majorité des voix de ses membres.

2.   Le tribunal peut prendre toutes mesures appropriées pour établir les faits. Il peut, à la demande de l'une des parties, recommander les mesures conservatoires indispensables.

3.   Les parties au différend fourniront toutes facilités nécessaires pour la bonne conduite de la procédure.

4.   L'absence ou le défaut d'une partie au différend ne fait pas obstacle à la procédure.

Article 7

Le tribunal peut connaître et décider des demandes reconventionnelles directement liées à l'objet du différend.

Article 8

À moins que le tribunal d'arbitrage n'en décide autrement en raison des circonstances particulières de l'affaire, les dépenses du tribunal, y compris la rémunération de ses membres, sont prises en charge à parts égales par les parties au différend. Le tribunal tient un relevé de toutes ses dépenses et en fournit un état final aux parties.

Article 9

Toute partie ayant, en ce qui concerne l'objet du différend, un intérêt d'ordre juridique susceptible d'être affecté par la décision peut intervenir dans la procédure avec le consentement du tribunal.

Article 10

1.   Le tribunal prononce la sentence dans un délai de cinq mois à partir de la date à laquelle il est créé, à moins qu'il n'estime nécessaire de prolonger ce délai pour une période qui ne devrait pas excéder cinq mois.

2.   La sentence du tribunal arbitral est motivée. Elle est définitive et obligatoire pour les parties au différend.

3.   Tout différend qui pourrait surgir entre les parties concernant l'interprétation ou l'exécution de la sentence peut être soumis par l'une des deux parties au tribunal arbitral qui l'a rendue, ou, si ce dernier ne peut en être saisi, à un autre tribunal arbitral constitué à cet effet de la même manière que le premier.

117

COUNCIL 94/C 211/01[1]
Information concerning the entry into force for the European Community of the Convention on the control of transboundary movements of hazardous wastes and their disposal (Basel Convention)

With the President of the Council having deposited the instrument of approval, on the Community's behalf, of the above Convention[2] on 7 February 1994, the Convention entered into force for the Community on 7 May 1994, in accordance with Article 25 (2) thereof.

---

[1] OJ No C 211, 2. 8. 1994, p. 1.
[2] OJ No L 39, 16. 2. 1993, p. 1.

COUNCIL REGULATION (EEC) No 259/93[1]
of 1 February 1993
on the supervision and control of shipments of waste within, into and out of the European Community

THE COUNCIL OF THE EUROPEAN COMMUNITIES,

Having regard to the Treaty establishing the European Economic Community, and in particular Article 130s thereof,

Having regard to the proposal from the Commission[2],

Having regard to the opinion of the European Parliament[3],

Having regard to the opinion of the Economic and Social Committee[4],

Whereas the Community has signed the Basle Convention of 22 March 1989 on the control of transboundary movements of hazardous wastes and their disposal;

Whereas provisions concerning waste are contained in Article 39 of the ACP-EEC Convention of 15 December 1989;

Whereas the Community has approved the Decision of the OECD Council of 30 March 1992 on the control of transfrontier movements of wastes destined for recovery operations;

Whereas, in the light of the foregoing, Directive 84/631/EEC[5], which organizes the supervision and control of transfrontier shipments of hazardous waste, needs to be replaced by a Regulation;

Whereas the supervision and control of shipments of waste within a Member State is a national responsibility; whereas, however, national systems for the supervision and control of shipments of waste within a Member State should comply with minimum criteria in order to ensure a high level of protection of the environment and human health;

---

[1] OJ No L 30, 6. 2. 1993, p.1.
[2] OJ No C 115, 6. 5. 1992, p. 4.
[3] OJ No C 94, 13. 4. 1992, p. 276 and opinion delivered on 20 January 1993 (not yet published in the *Official Journal*).
[4] OJ No C 269, 14. 10. 1991, p. 10.
[5] OJ No L 326, 13. 12. 1984, p. 31. Directive as last amended by Directive 91/692/EEC (OJ No L 377, 31. 12. 1991, p. 48).

Whereas it is important to organize the supervision and control of shipments of wastes in a way which takes account of the need to preserve, protect and improve the quality of the environment;

Whereas Council Directive 75/442/EEC of 15 July 1975 on waste[1] lays down in its Article 5 (1) that an integrated and adequate network of waste disposal installations, to be established by Member States through appropriate measures, where necessary or advisable in cooperation with other Member States, must enable the Community as a whole to become self-sufficient in waste disposal and the Member States to move towards that aim individually, taking into account geographical circumstances or the need for specialized installations for certain types of waste; whereas Article 7 of the said Directive requests the drawing up of waste management plans, if appropriate in cooperation with the Member States concerned, which shall be notified to the Commission, and stipulates that Member States may take measures necessary to prevent movements of waste which are not in accordance with their waste management plans and that they shall inform the Commission and the other Member States of any such measures;

Whereas it is necessary to apply different procedures depending on the type of waste and its destination, including whether it is destined for disposal or recovery;

Whereas shipments of waste must be subject to prior notification to the competent authorities enabling them to be duly informed in particular of the type, movement and disposal or recovery of the waste, so that these authorities may take all necessary measures for the protection of human health and the environment, including the possibility of raising reasoned objections to the shipment;

Whereas Member States should be able to implement the principles of proximity, priority for recovery and self-sufficiency at Community and national levels - in accordance with Directive 75/442/EEC - by taking measures in accordance with the Treaty to prohibit generally or partially or to object systematically to shipments of waste for disposal, except in the case of hazardous waste produced in the Member State of dispatch in such a small quantity that the provision of new specialized disposal installations within that State would be uneconomic; whereas the specific problem of disposal of such small quantities requires cooperation between the Member States concerned and possible recourse to a Community procedure;

---

[1] OJ No L 194, 25. 7. 1975, p. 39. Directive as amended by Directive 91/156/EEC (OJ No L 78, 26. 3. 1991, p. 32).

Whereas exports of waste for disposal to third countries must be prohibited in order to protect the environment of those countries; whereas exceptions shall apply to exports to EFTA countries which are also Parties to the Basle Convention;

Whereas exports of waste for recovery to countries to which the OECD Decision does not apply must be subject to conditions providing for environmentally sound management of waste;

Whereas agreements or arrangements on exports of waste for recovery with countries to which the OECD Decision does not apply must be subject to periodic review by the Commission leading, if appropriate, to a proposal by the Commission to reconsider the conditions under which such exports take place, including the possibility of a ban;

Whereas shipments of waste for recovery listed on the green list of the OECD Decision shall be generally excluded from the control procedures of this Regulation since such waste should not normally present a risk to the environment if properly recovered in the country of destination; whereas some exceptions to this exclusion are necessary in accordance with Community legislation and the OECD Decision; whereas some exceptions are also necessary in order to facilitate the tracking of such shipments within the Community and to take account of exceptional cases; whereas such waste shall be subject to Directive 75/442/EEC;

Whereas exports of waste for recovery listed on the OECD green list to countries to which the OECD Decision does not apply must be subject to consultation by the Commission with the country of destination; whereas it may be appropriate in the light of such consultation that the Commission make proposals to the Council;

Whereas exports of waste for recovery to countries which are not parties to the Basle Convention must be subject to specific agreements between these countries and the Community; whereas Member States must, in exceptional cases, be able to conclude after the date of application of this Regulation bilateral agreements for the import of specific waste before the Community has concluded such agreements, in the case of waste for recovery in order to avoid any interruption of waste treatment and in the case of waste for disposal where the country of dispatch does not have or cannot reasonably acquire the technical capacity and necessary facilities to dispose of the waste in an environmentally sound manner;

Whereas provision must be made for the waste to be taken back or to be disposed of or recovered in an alternative and environmentally sound manner if the shipment cannot be completed in accordance with the terms of the consignment note or the contract;

Whereas, in the event of illegal traffic, the person whose action is the cause of such traffic must take back and/or dispose of or recover the waste in an alternative and environmentally sound manner; whereas, should he fail to do so, the competent authorities of dispatch or destination, as appropriate, must themselves intervene;

Whereas it is important for a system of financial guarantees or equivalent insurance to be established;

Whereas Member States must provide the Commission with information relevant to the implementation of this Regulation;

Whereas the documents provided for by this Regulation must be established and the Annexes adapted within a Community procedure,

HAS ADOPTED THIS REGULATION:

TITLE I
SCOPE AND DEFINITIONS

Article 1

1.   This Regulation shall apply to shipments of waste within, into and out of the Community.

2.   The following shall be excluded from the scope of this Regulation:

a)   the offloading to shore of waste generated by the normal operation of ships and offshore platforms, including waste water and residues, provided that such waste is the subject of a specific binding international instrument;

b)   shipments of civil aviation waste;

c)   shipments of radioactive waste as defined in Article 2 of Directive 92/3/Euratom of 3 February 1992 on the supervision and control of shipments of radioactive waste between Member States and into and out of the Community[1];

d)   shipments of waste mentioned in Article 2 (1) (b) of Directive 75/442/EEC, where they are already covered by other relevant legislation;

e)   shipments of waste into the Community in accordance with the requirements of the Protocol on Environmental Protection to the Antarctic Treaty.

3.

a)   Shipments of waste destined for recovery only and listed in Annex II shall also be excluded from the provisions of this Regulation except as provided for in subparagraphs (b), (c), (d) and (e), in Article 11 and in Article 17 (1), (2) and (3).

b)   Such waste shall be subject to all provisions of Directive 75/442/EEC. It shall in particular be:

- destined for duly authorized facilities only, authorized according to Article 10 and 11 of Directive 75/442/EEC,

- subject to all provisions of Articles 8, 12, 13 and 14 of Directive 75/442/EEC.

c)   However, certain wastes listed in Annex II may be controlled, if, among other reasons, they exhibit any of the hazardous characteristics listed in

---

[1]   OJ No L 35, 12. 2. 1992, p. 24.

Annex III of Council Directive 91/689/EEC[1], as if they had been listed in Annex III or IV.

These wastes and the decision about which of the two procedures should be followed shall be determined in accordance with the procedure laid down in Article 18 of Directive 75/442/EEC. Such wastes shall be listed in Annex II (a).

d) In exceptional cases, shipments of wastes listed in Annex II may, for environmental or public health reasons, be controlled by Member States as if they had been listed in Annex III or IV.

Member States which make use of this possibility shall immediately notify the Commission of such cases and inform other Member States, as appropriate, and give reasons for their decision. The Commission, in accordance with the procedure laid down in Article 18 of Directive 75/442/EEC, may confirm such action including, where appropriate, by adding such wastes to Annex II.A.

e) Where waste listed in Annex II is shipped in contravention of this Regulation or of Directive 75/442/EEC, Member States may apply appropriate provisions of Articles 25 and 26 of this Regulation.

Article 2   *For the purposes of this Regulation:*

a) waste is as defined in Article 1 (a) of Directive 75/442/EEC;

b) competent authorities means the competent authorities designated by either the Member States in accordance with Article 36 or non-Member States;

c) competent authority of dispatch means the competent authority, designated by the Member States in accordance with Article 36, for the area from which the shipment is dispatched or designated by non-Member States;

d) competent authority of destination means the competent authority, designated by the Member States in accordance with Article 36, for the area in which the shipment is received, or in which waste is loaded on board before disposal at sea without prejudice to existing conventions on disposal at sea or designated by non-Member States;

e) competent authority of transit means the single authority designated by Member States in accordance with Article 36 for the State through which the shipment is in transit;

---

[1] OJ No L 377, 31. 12. 1991, p. 20.

f) correspondent means the central body designated by each Member State and the Commission, in accordance with Article 37;

g) notifier means any natural person or corporate body to whom or to which the duty to notify is assigned, that is to say the person referred to hereinafter who proposes to ship waste or have waste shipped:

    i) the person whose activities produced the waste (original producer); or

    ii) where this is not possible, a collector licensed to this effect by a Member State or a registered or licensed dealer or broker who arranges for the disposal or the recovery of waste; or

    iii) where these persons are unknown or are not licensed, the person having possession or legal control of the waste (holder); or

    iv) in the case of import into or transit through the Community of waste, the person designated by the laws of the State of dispatch or, when this designation has not taken place, the person having possession or legal control of the waste (holder);

h) consignee means the person or undertaking to whom or to which the waste is shipped for recovery or disposal;

i) disposal is as defined in Article 1 (e) of Directive 75/442/EEC;

j) authorized centre means any establishment or undertaking authorized or licensed pursuant to Article 6 of Directive 75/439/EEC[1], Articles 9, 10 and 11 of Directive 75/442/EEC and Article 6 of Directive 76/403/EEC[2];

k) recovery is as defined in Article 1 (f) of Directive 75/442/EEC;

l) State of dispatch means any State from which a shipment of waste is planned or made;

m) State of destination means any State to which a shipment of waste is planned or made for disposal or recovery, or for loading on board before disposal at sea without prejudice to existing conventions on disposal at sea;

n) State of transit means any State, other than the State of dispatch or destination, through which a shipment of waste is planned or made;

o) consignment note means the standard consignment note to be drawn up in accordance with Article 42;

---

[1] OJ No L 194, 25. 7. 1975, p. 23.
Directive as last amended by Directive 91/692/EEC
(OJ No L 377, 31. 12. 1991, p. 48).

[2] OJ No L 108, 26. 4. 1976, p. 41.

p) the Basle Convention means the Basle Convention of 22 March 1989 on the control of transboundary movements of hazardous wastes and their disposal;

q) the fourth Lomé Convention means the Lomé Convention of 15 December 1989;

r) the OECD Decision means the decision of the OECD Council of 30 March 1992 on the control of transfrontier movements of wastes destined for recovery operations.

TITLE II
SHIPMENTS OF WASTE BETWEEN MEMBER STATES

Chapter A   *Waste for disposal*

Article 3

1.   Where the notifier intends to ship waste for disposal from one Member State to another Member State and/or pass it in transit through one or several other Member States, and without prejudice to Articles 25 (2) and 26 (2), he shall notify the competent authority of destination and send a copy of the notification to the competent authorities of dispatch and of transit and to the consignee.

2.   Notification shall mandatorily cover any intermediate stage of the shipment from the place of dispatch to its final destination.

3.   Notification shall be effected by means of the consignment note which shall be issued by the competent authority of dispatch.

4.   In making notification, the notifier shall complete the consignment note and shall, if requested by competent authorities, supply additional information and documentation.

5.   The notifier shall supply on the consignment note information with particular regard to:

—   the source, composition and quantity of the waste for disposal including, in the case of Article 2 (g) (ii), the producer's identity and, in the case of waste from various sources a detailed inventory of the waste and, if known, the identity of the original producers,

—   the arrangements for routing and for insurance against damage to third parties,

—   the measures to be taken to ensure safe transport and, in particular, compliance by the carrier with the conditions laid down for transport by the Member States concerned,

—   the identity of the consignee of the waste, the location of the disposal centre and the type and duration of the authorization under which the centre operates. The centre must have adequate technical capacity for the disposal of the waste in question under conditions presenting no danger to human health or to the environment,

127

— the operations involving disposal as referred to in Annex II.A to Directive 75/442/EEC.

6.   The notifier must make a contract with the consignee for the disposal of the waste.

The contract may include some or all of the information referred to in paragraph 5.

The contract must include the obligation:

—   of the notifier, in accordance with Articles 25 and 26 (2), to take the waste back if the shipment has not been completed as planned or if it has been effected in violation of this Regulation,

—   of the consignee, to provide as soon as possible and no later than 180 days following the receipt of the waste a certificate to the notifier that the waste has been disposed of in an environmentally sound manner.

A copy of this contract must be supplied to the competent authority on request.

Should the waste be shipped between two establishments under the control of the same legal entity, this contract may be replaced by a declaration by the entity in question undertaking to dispose of the waste.

7.   The information given in accordance with paragraphs 4 to 6 shall be treated confidentially in accordance with existing national regulations.

8.   A competent authority of dispatch may, in accordance with national legislation, decide to transmit the notification itself instead of the notifier to the competent authority of destination, with copies to the consignee and to the competent authority of transit.

The competent authority of dispatch may decide not to proceed with notification if it has itself immediate objections to raise against the shipment in accordance with Article 4 (3). It shall immediately inform the notifier of these objections.

Article 4

1.   On receipt of the notification, the competent authority of destination shall, within three working days, send an acknowledgement to the notifier and copies thereof to the other competent authorities concerned and to the consignee.

2.

- a)   The competent authority of destination shall have 30 days following dispatch of the acknowledgement to take its decision authorizing the shipment, with or without conditions, or refusing it. It may also request additional information.

     It shall give its authorization only in the absence of objections on its part or on the part of the other competent authorities. The authorization shall be subject to any transport conditions referred to in (d).

     The competent authority of destination shall take its decision not earlier than 21 days following the dispatch of the acknowledgement. It may, however, take its decision earlier if it has the written consent of the other competent authorities concerned.

     The competent authority of destination shall send its decision to the notifier in writing, with copies to the other competent authorities concerned.

- b)   The competent authorities of dispatch and transit may raise objections within 20 days following the dispatch of the acknowledgement. They may also request additional information. These objections shall be conveyed in writing to the notifier, with copies to the other competent authorities concerned.

- c)   The objections and conditions referred to in (a) and (b) shall be based on paragraph 3.

- d)   The competent authorities of dispatch and transit may, within 20 days following the dispatch of the acknowledgement, lay down conditions in respect of the transport of waste within their jurisdiction.

     These conditions must be notified to the notifier in writing, with copies to the competent authorities concerned, and entered in the consignment note. They may not be more stringent than those laid down in respect of similar shipments occurring wholly within their jurisdiction and shall take due account of existing agreements, in particular relevant international conventions.

3.

a)

    i) In order to implement the principles of proximity, priority for recovery and self-sufficiency at Community and national levels in accordance with Directive 75/442/EEC, Member States may take measures in accordance with the Treaty to prohibit generally or partially or to object systematically to shipments of waste. Such measures shall immediately be notified to the Commission, which will inform the other Member States.

    ii) In the case of hazardous waste (as defined in Article 1 (4) of Directive 91/689/EEC) produced in a Member State of dispatch in such a small quantity overall per year that the provision of new specialized disposal installations within that State would be uneconomic, (i) shall not apply.

    iii) The Member State of destination shall cooperate with the Member State of dispatch which considers that (ii) applies, with a view to resolving the issue bilaterally. If there is no satisfactory solution, either Member State may refer the matter to the Commission, which will determine the issue in accordance with the procedure laid down in Article 18 of Directive 75/442/EEC.

b) The competent authorities of dispatch and destination, while taking into account geographical circumstances or the need for specialized installations for certain types of waste, may raise reasoned objections to planned shipments if they are not in accordance with Directive 75/442/EEC, especially Articles 5 and 7:

    i) in order to implement the principle of self-sufficiency at Community and national levels;

    ii) in cases where the installation has to dispose of waste from a nearer source and the competent authority has given priority to this waste;

    iii) in order to ensure that shipments are in accordance with waste management plans.

c) Furthermore, the competent authorities of dispatch, destination and transit may raise reasoned objections to the planned shipment if:

- it is not in accordance with national laws and regulations relating to environmental protection, public order, public safety or health protection,

- the notifier or the consignee was previously guilty of illegal trafficking.

- In this case, the competent authority of dispatch may refuse all shipments involving the person in question in accordance with national legislation,

or

- the shipment conflicts with obligations resulting from international conventions concluded by the Member State or Member States concerned.

4. If, within the time limits laid down in paragraph 2, the competent authorities are satisfied that the problems giving rise to their objections have been solved and that the conditions in respect of the transport will be met, they shall immediately inform the notifier in writing, with copies to the consignee and to the other competent authorities concerned.

If there is subsequently any essential change in the conditions of the shipment, a new notification must be made.

5. The competent authority of destination shall signify its authorization by appropriately stamping the consignment note.

Article 5

1. The shipment may be effected only after the notifier has received authorization from the competent authority of destination.

2. Once the notifier has received authorization, he shall insert the date of shipment and otherwise complete the consignment note and send copies to the competent authorities concerned three working days before the shipment is made.

3. A copy or, if requested by the competent authorities, a specimen of the consignment note, together with the stamp of authorization, shall accompany each shipment.

4. All undertakings involved in the operation shall complete the consignment note at the points indicated, sign it and retain a copy thereof.

5. Within three working days following receipt of the waste for disposal, the consignee shall send copies of the completed consignment note, except for the certificate referred to in paragraph 6, to the notifier and the competent authorities concerned.

6. As soon as possible and not later than 180 days following the receipt of the waste, the consignee shall, under his responsibility, send a certificate of

disposal to the notifier and the other competent authorities concerned. This certificate shall be part of or attached to the consignment note which accompanies the shipment.

Chapter B   *Waste for recovery*

Article 6

1.   Where the notifier intends to ship waste for recovery listed in Annex III from one Member State to another Member State and/or pass it in transit through one or several other Member States, and without prejudice to Articles 25 (2) and 26 (2), he shall notify the competent authority of destination and send copies of the notification to the competent authorities of dispatch and transit and to the consignee.

2.   Notification shall mandatorily cover any intermediary stage of the shipment from the place of dispatch to its final destination.

3.   Notification shall be effected by means of the consignment note which shall be issued by the competent authority of dispatch.

4.   In making notification, the notifier shall complete the consignment note and shall, if requested by competent authorities, supply additional information and documentation.

5.   The notifier shall supply on the consignment note information with particular regard to:

—   the source, composition and quantity of the waste for recovery, including the producer's identity and, in the case of waste from various sources, a detailed inventory of the waste and, if known, the indentity of the original producer,

—   the arrangements for routing and for insurance against damage to third parties,

—   the measures to be taken to ensure safe transport and, in particular, compliance by the carrier with the conditions laid down for transport by the Member States concerned,

—   the identity of the consignee of the waste, the location of the recovery centre and the type and duration of the autorization under which the centre operates. The centre must have adequate technical capacity for the recovery of the waste in question under conditions presenting no danger to human health or to the environment,

— the operations involving recovery as contained in Annex II.B to Directive 75/442/EEC,

— the planned method of disposal for the residual waste after recycling has taken place,

— the amount of the recycled material in relation to the residual waste,

— the estimated value of the recycled material.

6.   The notifier must conclude a contract with the consignee for the recovery of the waste.

The contract may include some or all of the information referred to in paragraph 5.

The contract must include the obligation:

— of the notifier, in accordance with Articles 25 and 26 (2), to take the waste back if the shipment has not been completed as planned or if it has been effected in violation of this Regulation,

— of the consignee to provide, in the case of retransfer of the waste for recovery to another Member State or to a third country, the notification of the initial country of dispatch,

— of the consignee to provide, as soon as possible and not later than 180 days following the receipt of the waste, a certificate to the notifier that the waste has been recovered in an environmentally sound manner.

A copy of this contract must be supplied to the competent authority on request.

Should the waste be shipped between two establishments under the control of the same legal entity, this contract may be replaced by a declaration by the entity in question undertaking to recover the waste.

7.   The information given in accordance with paragraphs 4 to 6 shall be treated confidentially in accordance with existing national regulations.

8.   A competent authority of dispatch may, in accordance with national legislation, decide to transmit the notification itself instead of the notifier to the competent authority of destination, with copies to the consignee and to the competent authority of transit.

Article 7

1.   On receipt of the notification the competent authority of destination shall send, within three working days, an acknowledgement to the notifier and copies thereof to the other competent authorities and to the consignee.

2.   The competent authorities of destination, dispatch and transit shall have 30 days following dispatch of the acknowledgement to object to the shipment. Such objection shall be based on paragraph 4. Any objection must be provided in writing to the notifier and to other competent authorities concerned within the 30-day period.

The competent authorities concerned may decide to provide written consent in a period less than the 30 days.

Written consent or objection may be provided by post, or by telefax followed by post. Such consent shall expire within one year unless otherwise specified.

3.   The competent authorities of dispatch, destination and transit shall have 20 days following the dispatch of the acknowledgement in which to lay down conditions in respect of the transport of waste within their jurisdiction.

These conditions must be notified to the notifier in writing, with copies to the competent authorities concerned, and entered in the consignment note. They may not be more stringent that those laid down in respect of similar shipments occuring wholly within their jurisdiction and shall take due account of existing agreements, in particular relevant international conventions.

4.

    a) The competent authorities of destination and dispatch may raise reasoned objections to the planned shipment:

—   in accordance with Directive 75/442/EEC, in particular Article 7 thereof,

      or

—   if it is not in accordance with national laws and regulations relating to environmental protection, public order, public safety or health protection,

      or

—   if the notifier or the consignee has previously been guilty of illegal trafficking. In this case, the competent authority of dispatch may refuse all shipments involving the person in question in accordance with national legislation,

      or

— if the shipment conflicts with obligations resulting from international conventions concluded by the Member State or Member States concerned,

or

— if the ratio of the recoverable and non-recoverable waste, the estimated value of the materials to be finally recovered or the cost of the recovery and the cost of the disposal of the non recoverable fraction do not justify the recovery under economic and environmental considerations.

b) The competent authorities of transit may raise reasoned objections to the planned shipment based on the second, third and fourth indents of (a).

5.   If within the time limit laid down in paragraph 2 the competent authorities are satisfied that the problems giving rise to their objections have been solved and that the conditions in respect of the transport will be met, they shall immediately inform the notifier in writing, with copies to the consignee and to the other competent authorities concerned.

If there is subsequently any essential change in the conditions of the shipment, a new notification must be made.

6.   In case of prior written consent, the competent authority shall signify its authorization by appropriately stamping the consignment note.

Article 8

1.   The shipment may be effected after the 30-day period has passed if no objection has been lodged. Tacit consent, however, expires within one year from that date.

Where the competent authorities decide to provide written consent, the shipment may be effected immediately after all necessary consents have been received.

2.   The notifier shall insert the date of shipment and otherwise complete the consignment note and send copies to the competent authorities concerned three working days before the shipment is made.

3.   A copy or, if requested by the competent authorities, a specimen of the consignment note shall accompany each shipment.

4.   All undertakings involved in the operation shall complete the consignment note at the points indicated, sign it and retain a copy thereof.

5.   Within three working days following receipt of the waste for recovery, the consignee shall send copies of the completed consignment note, except for the certificate referred to in paragraph 6, to the notifier and to the competent authorities concerned.

6.   As soon as possible and not later than 180 days following receipt of the waste the consignee, under his responsability, shall send a certificate of recovery of the waste to the notifier and the other competent authorities concerned. This certificate shall be part of or attached to the consignment note which accompanies the shipment.

Article 9

1.   The competent authorities having jurisdiction over specific recovery facilities may decide, notwithstanding Article 7, that they will not raise objections concerning shipments of certain types of waste to a specific recovery facility. Such decisions may be limited to a specific period of time; however, they may be revoked at any time.

2.   Competent authorities which select this option shall inform the Commission of the recovery facility name, address, technologies employed, waste types to which the decision applies and the period covered. Any revocations must also be notified to the Commission.

The Commission shall send this information without delay to the other competent authorities concerned in the Community and to the OECD Secretariat.

3.   All intended shipments to such facilities shall require notification to the competent authorities concerned, in accordance with Article 6. Such notification shall arrive prior to the time the shipment is dispatched.

The competent authorities of the Member States of dispatch and transit may raise objections to any such shipment, based on Article 7 (4), or impose conditions in respect of the transport.

4.   In instances where competent authorities acting under terms of their domestic laws are required to review the contract referred to in Article 6 (6), these authorities shall so inform the Commission. In such cases, the notification plus the contracts or portions thereof to be reviewed must arrive seven days prior to the time the shipment is dispatched in order that such review may be appropriately performed.

5.   For the actual shipment, Article 8 (2) to (6) shall apply.

Article 10

Shipments of waste for recovery listed in Annex IV and of waste for recovery which has not yet been assigned to Annex II, Annex III or Annex IV shall be subject to the same procedures as referred to in Articles 6 to 8 except that the consent of the competent authorities concerned must be provided in writing prior to commencement of shipment.

Article 11

1.   In order to assist the tracking of shipments of waste for recovery listed in Annex II, they shall be accompanied by the following information, signed by the holder:

a)   the name and address of the holder;

b)   the usual commercial description of the waste;

c)   the quantity of the waste;

d)   the name and address of the consignee;

e)   the operations involving recovery, as listed in Annex II.B to Directive 75/442/EEC;

f)   the anticipated date of shipment.

2.   The information specified in paragraph 1 shall be treated confidentially in accordance with existing national regulations.

Chapter C   *Shipment of waste for disposal and recovery between Member States with transit via third States*

Article 12

Without prejudice to Articles 3 to 10, where a shipment of waste takes place between Member States with transit via one or more third States,

a)   the notifier shall send a copy of the notification to the competent authority(ies) of the third State(s);

b)   the competent authority of destination shall ask the competent authority in the third State(s) whether it wishes to send its written consent to the planned shipment:

—   in the case of parties to the Basle Convention, within 60 days, unless it has waived this right in accordance with the terms of that Convention, or

—   in the case of countries not parties to the Basle Convention, within a period agreed between the competent authorities.

In both cases the competent authority of destination shall, where appropriate, wait for consent before giving its authorization.

TITLE III
SHIPMENTS OF WASTE WITHIN MEMBER STATES

Article 13

1.   Titles II, VII and VIII shall not apply to shipments within a Member State.

2.   Member States shall, however, establish an appropriate system for the supervision and control of shipments of waste within their jurisdiction. This system should take account of the need for coherence with the Community system established by this Regulation.

3.   Member States shall inform the Commission of their system for the supervision and control of shipments of waste. The Commission shall inform the other Member States thereof.

4.   Member States may apply the system provided for in Titles II, VII and VIII within their jurisdiction.

TITLE IV
EXPORTS OF WASTE

Chapter A   *Waste for disposal*

Article 14

1.   All exports of waste for disposal shall be prohibited, except those to EFTA countries which are also parties to the Basle Convention.

2.   However, without prejudice to Articles 25 (2), and 26 (2), exports of waste for disposal to an EFTA country shall also be banned:

    a) where the EFTA country of destination prohibits imports of such wastes or where it has not given its written consent to the specific import of this waste;

    b) if the competent authority of dispatch in the Community has reason to believe that the waste will not be managed in accordance with environmentally sound methods in the EFTA country of destination concerned.

3.   The competent authority of dispatch shall require that any waste for disposal authorized for export to EFTA countries be managed in an environmentally sound matter throughout the period of shipment and in the State of destination.

Article 15

1.   The notifier shall send the notificaion to the com-petent authority of dispatch by means of the consignment note in accordance with Article 3 (5), with copies to the other competent authorities concerned and to the consignee. The consignment note shall be issued by the competent authority of dispatch.

On receipt of the notification, the competent authority of dispatch shall within three working days send the notifier a written acknowledgement of the notification, with copies to the other competent authorities concerned.

2.   The competent authority of dispatch shall have 70 days following dispatch of the acknowledgement to take its decision authorizing the shipment, with or without conditions, or refusing it. It may also request additional information.

It shall give its authorization only in the absence of objections on its part or on the part of the other competent authorities and if it has received from the notifier the copies referred to in paragraph 4. The authorization shall, where applicable, be subject to any transport conditions referred to in paragraph 5.

The competent authority of dispatch shall take its de-cision no earlier than 61 days following the dispatch of the acknowledgement.

It may, however, take its decision earlier if it has the written consent of the other competent authorities.

It shall send a certified copy of the decision to the other competent authorities concerned, to the customs office of departure from the Community and to the consignee.

3.   The competent authorities of dispatch and transit in the Community may, within 60 days following the dispatch of the acknowledgement, raise objections based on Article 4 (3). They may also request additional informa-tion. Any objection must be provided in writing to the notifier, with copies to the other competent authorities concerned.

4.   The notifier shall provide to the competent authority of dispatch a copy of:

a) the written consent of the EFTA country of destination to the planned shipment;

b) the confirmation from the EFTA country of destination of the existence of a contract between the notifier and the consignee specifying environ-mentally sound management of the waste in question; a copy of the contract must be supplied, if requested.

The contract shall also specify that the consignee be required to provide:

- within three working days following the receipt of the waste for dis-posal, copies of the fully completed consignment note, except for the certification referred to in the second indent, to the notifier and to the competent authority concerned,

- as soon as possible and not later than 180 days following the receipt of the waste, a certificate of disposal under his responsability to the notifier and to the competent authority concerned. The form of this certificate shall be part of the consignment note which accompanies the shipment.

The contract shall, in addition, stipulate that if a consignee issues an incorrect certificate with the consequence that the financial guarantee is released he shall bear the costs arising from the duty to return the waste to the area of jurisdiction of the competent authority of dispatch and its disposal in an alternative and environmentally sound manner;

c) written consent to the planned shipment from the other State(s) of transit, unless this (these) State(s) is (are) a Party (Parties) to the Basle Convention and has (have) waived this in accordance with the terms of that Convention.

5.   The competent authorities of transit in the Community shall have 60 days following the dispatch of the acknowledgement in which to lay down conditions in respect of the shipments of waste in their area of jurisdi-ction.

These conditions, which shall be forwarded to the notifier, with copies to the other competent authorities concerned, may not be more stringent than those laid down in respect of similar shipments effected wholly within the area of jurisdiction of the competent authority in question.

6.   The competent authority of dispatch shall signify its authorization by appropriately stamping the consignment note.

7.   The shipment may be effected only after the notifier has received authorization from the competent authority of dispatch.

8.   Once the notifier has received authorization, he shall insert the date of shipment and otherwise complete the consignment note and send copies to the competent authorities concerned three working days before the shipment is made. A copy or, if requested by the competent authorities, a specimen of the consignment note, together with the stamp of authorization, shall accompany each shipment.

All undertakings involved in the operation shall complete the consignment note at the points indicated, sign it and retain a copy thereof.

A specimen of the consignment note shall be delivered by the carrier to the last customs office of departure when the waste leaves the Community.

9.   As soon as the waste has left the Community, the customs office of departure shall send a copy of the consignment note to the competent authority which issued the authorization.

10.   If, 42 days after the waste has left the Community, the competent authority which gave the authorization has received no information from the consignee about his receipt of the waste, it shall inform without delay the competent authority of destination.

It shall take action in a similar way if, 180 days after the waste has left the Community, the competent authority which gave the authorization has not received from the consignee the certificate of disposal referred to in paragraph 4.

11.   A competent authority of dispatch may, in accordance with national legislation, decide to transmit the notification itself instead of the notifier, with copies to the consignee and the competent authority of transit.

The competent authority of dispatch may decide to proceed with any notification if it has itself immediate objections to raise against the shipment in accordance with Article 4 (3). It shall immediately inform the notifier of these objections.

12.   The information given in paragraphs 1 to 4 shall be treated confidentially in accordance with existing national regulations.

Chapter B   Waste for recovery

Article 16

1.   All exports of waste for recovery shall be prohibited except those to:

a) countries to which the OECD decision applies;

b) other countries:

-   which are Parties to the Basle Convention and/or with which the Community, or the Community and its Member States, have concluded bilateral or multilateral or regional agreements or arrangements in accordance with Article 11 of the Basle Convention and paragraph 2, or

-   with which individual Member States have concluded bilateral agreements and arrangements prior to the date of application of this Regulation, in so far as these are compatible with Community legislation and in accordance with Article 11 of the Basle Convention and paragraph 2. These agreements and arrangements shall be notified to the Commission within three months of the date of application of this Regulation or of their date of application, whichever is the earlier, and shall expire when agreements or arrangements are concluded in accordance with the first indent.

2.   The agreements and arrangements referred to in paragraph 1 (b) shall guarantee an environmentally sound management of the waste in accordance with Article 11 of the Basle Convention and shall, in particular:

a)   guarantee that the recovery operation is carried out in an authorized centre which complies with the requirements for environmentally sound management;

b)   fix the conditions for the treatment of the non-recoverable components of the waste and, if appropriate, oblige the notifier to take them back;

c)   enable, if appropriate, the examination of the com-pliance of the agreements on the spot in agreement with the countries concerned;

d)   be subject to periodic review by the Commission and for the first time not later than 31 December 1996, taking into account the experience gained and the ability of the countries concerned to carry out recovery activities in a manner which provides full guarantees of environmentally sound management. The Commission shall inform the European Par-liament and the Council about the results of this review. If such a review leads to the conclusion that environmental guarantees are insufficient, the con-tinuation of waste exports under such terms shall, on a proposal from the Commission, be reconsidered, including the possibility of a ban.

3.   However, without prejudice to Article 25 (2) and 26 (2), exports of waste for recovery to the countries referred to in paragraph 1 shall be prohibited:

a)   where such a country prohibits all imports of such wastes or where it has not given its consent to their specific import;

b)   if the competent authority of dispatch has reason to believe that the waste will not be managed in accordance with environmentally sound methods in such a country.

4.   The competent authority of dispatch shall require that any waste for recovery authorized for export be managed in an environmentally sound manner throughout the period of shipment and in the State of destination.

Article 17

1.   In respect of waste listed in Annex II, the Commission shall notify prior to the date of application of this Regulation to every country to which the OECD Decision does not apply the list of waste included in that Annex and request written confirmation that such waste is not subject to control in the

country of destination and that the latter will accept categories of such waste to be shipped without recourse to the control procedures which apply to Annex III or IV or that it indicate where such waste should be subject to either those procedures or the procedure laid down in Article 15.

If such confirmation is not received six months before the date of application of this Regulation, the Commission shall make appropriate proposals to the Council.

2.   Where waste listed in Annex II is exported, it shall be destined for recovery operations within a facility which under applicable domestic law is operating or is authorized to operate in the importing country. Furthermore, a surveillance system based on prior automatic export licensing shall be established in cases to be determined in accordance with the procedure laid down in Article 18 of Directive 75/442/EEC.

Such a system shall in each case provide that a copy of the export licence be forwarded without delay to the authorities of the country in question.

3.   Where such waste is subject to control in the country of destination or upon request of such a country in accordance with paragraph 1 or where a country of destination has notified under Article 3 of the Basle Convention that it regards certain kinds of waste listed in Annex II is hazardous, exports of such waste to that country shall be subjected to control. The Member State of export or the Commission shall notify all such cases to the committee established pursuant to Article 18 of Directive 75/442/EEC; the Commission shall determine in consultation with the country of destination which of the control procedures shall apply, that is those applicable to Annex III or IV or the procedure laid down in Article 15.

4.   Where waste listed in Annex III is exported from the Community for recovery to countries and through countries to which the OECD Decision applies, Articles 6, 7, 8 and 9 (1), (3), (4) and (5) shall apply, the provisions concerning the competent authorities of dispatch and transit applying only to the competent authorities in the Community.

5.   In addition, the competent authorities of the ex-porting and Community-transit countries shall be informed of the decision referred to in Article 9.

6.   Where the waste for recovery listed in Annex IV and waste for recovery which has not yet been assigned to Annex II, III or IV is exported for recovery to countries and through countries to which the OECD Decision applies, Article 10 shall apply by analogy.

7.   In addition, where waste is exported in accordance with paragraphs 4 to 6:

—   a specimen of the consignment note shall be delivered by the carrier to the last customs office of departure when the waste leaves the Community,

—   as soon as the waste has left the Community, the customs office of departure shall send a copy of the consignment note to the competent authority of export,

—   if, 42 days after the waste has left the Community, the competent authority of export has received no information from the consignee about this receipt of the waste, it shall inform without delay the competent authority of destination,

—   the contract shall stipulate that, if a consignee issues an incorrect certificate with the consequence that the financial guarantee is released, he shall bear the costs arising from the duty to return the waste to the area of jurisdiction of the competent authority of dispatch and its disposal or recovery in an alternative and environmentally sound manner.

8.   Where waste for recovery listed in Annex III and IV and waste for recovery which has not yet been assigned to Annex II, III or IV is exported to and through countries to which the OECD Decision does not apply:

—   Article 15, except for paragraph 3, shall apply by analogy,

—   reasoned objections may be raised in accordance with Article 7 (4) only,

save as otherwise provided for in bilateral or multilateral agreements entered into in accordance with Article 16 (1) (b) and on the basis of the control procedure of either paragraph 4 or 6 of this Article or Article 15.

Chapter C   *Export of waste to ACP States*

Article 18

1.   All exports of waste to ACP States shall be prohibited.

2.   This prohibition does not prevent a Member State to which an ACP State has chosen to export waste for processing from returning the processed waste to the ACP State of origin.

3.   In case of re-export to ACP States, a specimen of the consignmet note, together with the stamp of authoriz-ation, shall accompany each shipment.

TITLE V
IMPORTS OF WASTE INTO THE COMMUNITY

Chapter A   *Imports of waste for disposal*

Article 19

1.   All imports into the Community of waste for disposal shall be prohibited except those from:

    a) EFTA countries which are Parties to the Basle Convention;

    b) other countries:

       - - which are Parties to the Basle Convention,

    or

       - with which the Community, or the Community and its Member States, have concluded bilateral or multilateral agreements or arrangements compatible with Community legislation and in accordance with Article 11 of the Basle Convention gauranteeing that the disposal operations carried out in an authorized centre and complies with the requirements for environmentally sound management, or

       - with which individual Member States have concluded bilateral agreements or arrangements prior to the date of application of this Regulation, compatible with Community legislation and in accordance with Article 11 of the Basle Convention, containing the same guarantees as referred to above and guaranteeing that the waste originated in the country of dispatch and that disposal will be carried out exclusively in the Member State which has concluded the agreement or arrangement. These agreements or arrangements shall be notified to the Commission with in three months of the date of application of the Regulation or of their date of application, whichever is the earlier, and shall expire when agreements or arrangements are concluded in accordance with the second indent, or

       - with which individual Member States conclude bilateral agreements or arrangements after the date of application of this Regulation in the circumstances of paragraph 2.

2.   The Council hereby authorizes individual Member States to conclude bilateral agreements and arrangements after the date of application of this Reg-

ulation in exceptional cases for the disposal of specific waste, where such waste will not be managed in an environmentally sound manner in the country of dispatch. These agreements and arrangements shall comply with the conditions set out in paragraph 1 (b), third indent and shall be notified ot the Commission prior to their conclusion.

3.   The countries referred to in paragraph 1 (b) shall be required to present a duly motivated request beforehand to the competent authority of the Member State of destination on the basis that they do no have and cannot reasonable acquire the technical capacity and the necessary facilities in order to dispose of the waste in an environmentally sound manner.

4.   The competent authority of destination shall prohibit the bringing of waste into its area of jurisdiction if it has reason to believe that the waste will not be managed in an environmentally sound manner in its area.

Article 20

1.   Notification shall be made to the competent authority of destinations by means of the consignment note in accordance with Article 3 (5) with copies to the consignee of the waste and to the competent authorities of transit. The consignment note shall be issued by the competent authority of destination.

On receipt of the notification, the competent authority of destination shall, within three working days, send a written acknowledgement ot the notifier, with copies to the competent authorities of transit in the Community.

2.   The competent authority of destination shall authorize the shipment only in the absence of objections on its part or from the other competent authorities concerned. The authorization shall be subject to any transport conditions referred to in paragraph 5.

3.   The competent authorities of destination and transit in the Community may, within 60 days of dispatch of the copy of the acknowledgement, raise objections based on Article 4 (3).

They may also request additional information. These objections shall be conveyed in writing to the notifier, with copies to the other competent authorities concerned in the Community;

4.   The competent authority of destination shall have 70 days following dispatch of the acknowledgement to take its decision authorizing the shipment, with or without conditions, or refusing it. It may also request additional information.

It shall send certified copies of the decision to the competent authorities of transit in the Community, the consignee and the customs office of entry into the Community.

The competent authority of destination shall take its decision no earlier than 61 days following the dispatch of the acknowledgement. It may, however, take its decision earlier if it has the written consent of the other competent auhtorities.

The competent authority of destination shall signify its authorization by appropriately stamping the consignment note.

5.   The competent authority of destination and transit in the Community shall have 60 days following dispatch of the acknowledgement to lay down conditions in respect of the shipment of the waste. These conditions, which must be conveyed to the notifier, with copies to the competent authorities concerned, may not be more stringent than those laid down in respect of similar shipments occuring wholly within the jurisdiction of the competent authority in question.

6.   The shipment may be effected only after the notifier has received authorization from the competent authority of destination.

7.   Once the notifier has received authorization, he shall insert the date of the shipment and otherwise complete the consignment note and send copies to the competent authorities concerned three working days before the shipment is made. A specimen of the consignment note shall be delivered by the carrier to the customs office of entry into the Community.

A copy or, if requested by the competent authorities, a specimen of the consignment note, together with the stamp of authorization, shall accompany each shipment.

All undertakings involved in the operation shall complete the consignment note at the points indicated, sign it and retain a copy.

8.   Within three working days following receipt of the waste for disposal, the consignee shall send copies of the completed consignment note, except for the certificate referred to in paragraph 9, to the notifier and the com-petent authorities concerned;

9.   As soon as possible and not later than 180 days following the receipt of the waste, the consignee shall, under his responsibility, send a certificate of disposal to the notifier and the other competent authorities concerned. This certificate shall be part of or attached to the consignment note which accompanies the shipment.

Chapter B   Imports of waste for recovery

Article 21

1.   All imports of waste for recovery into the Community shall be prohibited, except those from:

a)   countries to which the OECD decision applies;

b)   other countries:

- which are Parties to the Basle Convention and/or with which the Community, or the Community and its Member States, have concluded bilateral or multilateral or regional agreements or arrangements compatible with Community legislation and in accordance with Article 11 of the Basle Convention, guaranteeing that the recovery operation is carried out in an authorized centre and complies with the requirements for environmentally sound management,

    or

- with which individual Member States have concluded bilateral agreements or arrangements prior to the date of application of this Regulation, where these are compatible with Community legislation and in accordance with Article 11 of the Basle Convention, containing the same guarantees as referred to above. These agreements or arrangements shall be notified to the Commission within three months of the date of application of this Regulation or of their date of application, whichever is the earlier, and shall expire when agreements or arrangements are concluded in accordance with the first indent,

    or

- with which individual Member States conclude bilateral agreements or arrangements after the date of application of this Regulation in the circumstances of paragraph 2.

2.   The Council hereby authorizes individual Member States to conclude after the date of applications of this Regulation bilateral agreements and arrangements in exceptional cases for the recovery of specific waste, where a Member State deems such agreements or arrangements necessary to avoid any interruption of waste treatment before the Community has concluded those agreements and arrangements. Such agreements and arrangements shall also be compatible with Community legislation and in accordance with Article 11 of the Basle Convention; they shall be notified to the Commission prior to their

conclusion and shall expire when agreements or arrangements are concluded in accordance with paragraph 1 (b), first indent.

Article 22

1.   Where waste is imported for recovery from countries and through countries to which the OECD Decision applies, the following control procedures shall apply by analogy:

a)   for waste listed in Annex III: Articles 6, 7, 8, 9 (1), (3), (4) and (5), and 17 (5);

b)   for waste listed in Annex IV and waste which has not yet been assigned to Annex II, III or IV: Article 10.

2.   Where waste for recovery listed in Annexes III and IV and waste which has not yet been assigned to Annex II, III or IV is imported from and through countries to the OECD Decision does not apply:

—   Article 20 shall apply by analogy,

—   reasoned objections may be raised in accordance with Article 7 (4) only,

save as otherwise provided for the bilateral or multilateral agreements entered into in accordance with Article 21 (1) (b) and on the basis of the control procedures of either paragraph 1 of this Article or Article 20.

TITLE VI
TRANSIT OF WASTE FROM OUTSIDE AND THROUGH THE COMMUNITY FOR DISPOSAL OR RECOVERY OUTSIDE THE COMMUNITY

Chapter A *Waste for disposal and recovery (except transit covered by Article 24)*

Article 23

1.	Where waste for disposal and, except in cases covered by Article 24, recovery is shipped through (a) Member State(s), notification shall be effected by means of the consignment note to the last competent authority of transit within the Community, with copies to the consignee, the other competent authorities concerned and the customs offices of entry into and departure from the Community.

2.	The last competent authority of transit within the Community shall promptly inform the notifier of receipt of the notification. The other competent authorities in the Community shall, on the basis of paragraph 5, convey their reactions to the last competent authority of transit in the Community, which shall then respond in writing to the notifier within 60 days, consenting to the shipment with or without reservations; or imposing, if appropriate, conditions laid down by the other competent authorites of transit, or withholding information. Any refusal or reservations must be justified. The competent authority shall send a certified copy of the decision to both the other competent authorities concerned and the customs offices of entry into and departure form the Community.

3.	Without prejudice to Articles 25 (2) and 26 (2), the shipment shall be admitted into the Community only if the notifier has received the written consent of the last competent authority of transit. This authority shall signify its consent by appropriately stamping the consignment note.

4.	The competent authorities of transit within the Community shall have 20 days following notification to lay down, if appropriate, any conditions attached to the transport of the waste.

These conditions, which must be conveyed to the notifier, with copies to the competent authorities concerned, may not be more stringent than those laid down in respect of similar shipments occurring wholly within the jurisdiction of the competent authority in question.

5.   The consignment note shall be issued by the last competent authority of transit within the Community.

6.   Once the notifier has received authorization, he shall complete the consignment note and send copies to the competent authorities concerned three working days before the shipment is made.

A specimen of the consignment note, together with the stamp of authorization, shall accompany each shipment.

A specimen of the consignment note shall be supplied by the carrier to the customs office of departure when the waste leaves the Community.

All undertakings involved in the operation shall complete the consignment note at the points indicated, sign it and retain a copy thereof.

7.   As soon as the waste has left the Community, the customs office of departure shall send a copy of the consignment note to the last competent authority of transit within the Community.

Furthermore, at the latest 42 days after the waste has left the Community, the notifier shall declare or certify to that competent authority, with copies to the other competent authorities of transit, that it has arrived at its intended destination.

Chapter B

Transit of waste for recovery from and to a country to which the OECD Decision applies

Article 24

1.   Transit of waste for recovery listed in Annexes III and IV from a country and transferred for recovery to a country to which the OECD Decision applies through (a) Member State(s) requires notification to all competent authorities of transit of the Member State(s) concerned.

2.   Notification shall be effected by means of the consignment note.

3.   On receipt of the notification the competent authority(ies) of transit shall send an acknowledgement to the notifier and to the consignee within three working days.

4. This competent authority(ies) of transit may raise reasoned objections to the planned shipment based on Article 7 (4). Any objection must be provided in writing to the notifier and to the competent authorities of transit of the other Member States concerned within 30 days of dispatch of the acknowledgement.

5. The competent authority of transit may decide to provide written consent in less than 30 days.

In the case of transit of waste listed in Annex IV and waste which has not yet been assigned to Annex II, III or IV, consent must be given in writing prior to commencement of the shipment.

6. The shipment may be effected only in the absence of any objection.

TITLE VII
COMMON PROVISIONS

Article 25

1.   Where a shipment of waste to which the competent authorities concerned have consented cannot be completed in accordance with the terms of the consignment note or the contract referred to in Articles 3 and 6, the competent authority of dispatch shall, within 90 days after it has been informed thereof, ensure that the notifier returns the waste to its area of jurisdiction or elsewhere within the State of dispatch unless it is satisfied that the waste can be disposed of or recovered in an alternative and environmentally sound manner.

2.   In cases referred to in paragraph 1, a further notification shall be made. No Member State of dispatch or Member State of transit shall oppose the return of this waste at the duly motivated request of the competent authority of destination and with an explanation of the reason.

3.   The obligation of the notifier and the subsidiary obligation of the State of dispatch to take the waste back shall end when the consignee has issued the certificate referred to in Articles 5 and 8.

Article 26

1.   Any shipment of waste effected:

a) without notification to all competent authorities concerned pursuant to the provisions of this Regulation;

    or

b) without the consent of the competent authorities concerned pursuant to the provisions of this Regulation;

    or

c) with consent obtained from the competent authorities concerned through falsification, misrepresentation or fraud;

    or

d) which is not specified in a material way in the consignment note;

    or

e) which results in disposal or recovery in contravention of Community or international rules;

or

f) contrary to Articles 14, 16, 19 and 21 shall be deemed to be illegal traffic.

2.   If such illegal traffic is the responsability of the notifier of the waste, the competent authority of dispatch shall ensure that the waste in question is:

a) taken back by the notifier or, if necessary, by the competent authority itself, into the State of dispatch, or if impracticable;

b) otherwise disposed of or recovered in an environmentally sound manner,

within 30 days from the time when the competent authority was informed of the illegal traffic or within such other period of time as may be agreed by the competent authorities concerned.

In this case a further notification shall be made. No Member State of dispatch or Member State of transit shall oppose the return of this waste at the duly motivated request of the competent authority of destination and with an explanation of the reason.

3.   If such illegal traffic is the responsability of the consignee, the competent authority of destination shall ensure that the waste in question is disposed of in an environmentally sound manner by the consignee or, if impracticable, by the competent authority itself within 30 days from the time it was informed of the illegal traffic or within any such other period of time as may be agreed by the competent authorities concerned. To this end, they shall cooperate, as necessary, in the disposal or recovery of the waste in an environmentally sound manner.

4.   Where responsibility for the illegal traffic cannot be imputed to either the notifier or the consignee, the competent authorities shall cooperate to ensure that the waste in question is disposed of or recovered in an environmentally sound manner. Guidelines for this cooperation shall be established in accordance with the procedure laid down in Article 18 of Directive 75/442/EEC.

5.   Member States shall take appropriate legal action to prohibit and punish illegal traffic.

Article 27

1.   All shipments of waste covered within the scope of this Regulation shall be subject to the provision of a financial guarantee or equivalent insurance covering costs for shipment, including cases referred to in Articles 25 and 26, and for disposal or recovery.

2.   Such guarantees shall be returned when proof has been furnished, by means of:

— the certificate of disposal or recovery, that the waste has reached its destination and has been disposed of or recovered in an environmentally sound manner,

— Control copy T 5 drawn up pursuant to Commission Regulation (EEC) No 2823/87[1] that, in the case of transit through the Community, the waste has left the Community.

3.   Each Member State shall inform the Commission of the provision which it makes in national law pursuant to this Article. The Commission shall forward this information to all Member States.

Article 28

1.   While respecting the obligations imposed on him by the applicable Articles 3, 6, 9, 15, 17, 20, 22, 23 and 24, the notifier may use a general notification procedure where waste for disposal or recovery having the same physical and chemical characteristics is shipped periodically to the same consignee following the same route. If, in the case of unforeseen circumstances, this route cannot be followed, the notifier shall inform the competent authorities concerned as soon as possible or before the shipment starts if the need for route modification is already known at this time.

Where the route modification is known before the shipment starts and this involves other competent authorities than those concerned in the general notification, this procedure shall not be used.

2.   Under a general notification procedure, a single notification may cover several shipments of waste over a maximum period of one year. The indicated period may be shortened by agreement between the competent authorities concerned.

---

[1]   OJ No L 270, 23. 9. 1987, p. 1.

3.   The competent authorities concerned shall make their agreement to the use of this general notification procedure subject to the subsequent supply of additional information. If the composition of the waste is not as notified or if the conditions imposed on its shipment are not respected, the competent authorities concerned shall withdraw their consent to this procedure by means of official notice to the notifier. Copies of this notice shall be sent to the other competent authorities concerned.

4.   General notification shall be made by means of the consignment note.

Article 29

Wastes which are the subject of different notifications shall not be mixed during shipment.

Article 30

1.   Member States shall take the measures needed to ensure that waste is shipped in accordance with the provisions of this Regulation. Such measures may include inspections of establishments and undertakings, in accordance with Article 13 of Directive 75/442/EEC, and spot checks of shipments.

2.   Checks may take place in particular:

—   at the point of origin, carried out with the producer, holder or notifier,

—   at the destination, carried out with the final consignee,

—   at the external frontiers of the Community,

—   during the shipment within the Community.

3.   Checks may include the inspection of documents, the confirmation of identity and, if appropriate, the physical control of the waste.

Article 31

1.   The consignment note shall be printed and completed and any further documentation and information referred to in Article 4 and 6 shall be supplied in a language which is acceptable to the competent authority of:

— dispatch, as referred to in Articles 3, 7, 15 and 17, in the case of both a shipment of waste within the Community and the export of waste,

— destination, as referred to in Articles 20 and 22, in the case of the import of waste,

— transit, as referred to in Articles 23 and 24.

A translation shall be supplied by the notifier at the request of the other competent authorities concerned in a language acceptable to them.

2.   Further details may be determined in accordance with the procedure laid down in Article 18 of Directive 75/442/EEC.

TITLE VIII
OTHER PROVISIONS

Article 32

The provisions of the international transport conventions listed in Annex I to which the Member States are parties shall be complied with in so far as they cover the waste to which this Regulation refers.

Article 33

1.　Appropriate administrative costs of implementing the notification and supervision procedure and usual costs of appropriate analyses and inspections may be charged to the notifier.

2.　Costs arising from the return of waste, including shipment, disposal or recovery of the waste in an alternative and environmentally sound manner pursuant to Articles 25 (1) and 26 (2), shall be charged to the notifier or, if impracticable, to the Member States concerned.

3.　Costs arising from disposal or recovery in an alternative and environmentally sound manner pursuant to Article 26 (3) shall be charged to the consignee.

4.　Costs arising from disposal or recovery, including possible shipment pursuant to Article 26 (4), shall be charged to the notifier and/or the consignee depending upon the decision by the competent authorities involved.

Article 34

1.　Without prejudice to the provisions of Article 26 and to Community and national provisions concerning civil liability and irrespective of the point of disposal or recovery of the waste, the producer of that waste shall take all the necessary steps to dispose of or recover or to arrange for disposal or recovery of the waste so as to protect the quality of the environment in accordance with Directives 75/442/EEC and 91/689/EEC.

2.　Member States shall take all necessary steps to ensure that the obligations laid down in paragraph 1 are carried out.

Article 35

All documents sent to or by the competent authorities shall be kept in the Community for at least three years by the competent authorities, the notifier and the consignee.

Article 36

Member States shall designate the competent authority or authorities for the implementation of this Regulation. A single competent authority of transit shall be designated by each Member State.

Article 37

1.   Member States and the Commission shall each designate at least one correspondent responsible for informing or advising persons or undertakings who or which make enquiries. The Commission correspondent shall forward to the correspondents of the Member States any questions put to him which concern the latter, and vice versa.

2.   The Commission shall, if requested by Member States or if otherwise appropriate, periodically hold a meeting of the correspondents to examine with them the questions raised by the implementation of this Regulation.

Article 38

1.   Member States shall notify the Commission not later than three months before the date of application of this Regulation of the name(s), address(es) and telephone and telex/telefax number(s) of the competent authorities and of the correspondents, together with the stamp of the competent authorities.

Member States shall notify the Commission annually of any changes in this information.

2.   The Commission shall send the information without delay to the other Member States and to the Secretariat of the Basle Convention.

The Commission shall furthermore send to Member States the waste management plans referred to in Article 7 of Directive 75/442/EEC.

Article 39

1. Member States may designate customs offices of entry into and departure from the Community for shipments of waste entering and leaving the Community and inform the Commission thereof.

The Commission shall publish the list of these offices in the *Official Journal of the European Communities* and, if appropriate, update this list.

2. If Member States decide to designate the custom offices referred to in paragraph 1, no shipment of waste shall be allowed to use any other frontier crossing points within a Member State for entering or leaving the Community.

Article 40

Member States, as appropriate and necessary in liaison with the Commission, shall cooperate with other parties to the Basle Convention and inter-State organizations directy or through the Secretariat of the Basle Convention, inter alia, via the exchange of information, the promotion of environmentally sound technologies and the development of appropriate codes of good practice.

Article 41

1. Before the end of each calendar year, Member States shall draw up a report in accordance with Article 13 (3) of the Basle Convention and send it to the Secretariat of the Basle Convention and a copy thereof to the Commission.

2. The Commission shall, based on these reports, establish every three years report on the implementation of this Regulation by the Community and its Member States. It may request to this end additional information in accordance with Article 6 of Directive 91/692/EEC[1].

Article 42

1. The Commission shall draw up not later than three months before the date of application of this Regulation and adapt if appropriate afterwards, in accordance with the procedure laid down in Article 18 of Directive 75/442/EEC, the standard consignment note, including the form of the certificate of disposal and recovery (either integral to the consignment note or, meanwhile, attached to the existing consignment note under Directive 84/631/EEC) taking account in particular of:

---

[1]   OJ No L 377, 31. 12. 1991, p. 48.

— the relevant Articles of this Regulation,

- the relevant international Conventions and agreements.

2.   The existing form of the consignment note shall apply by analogy until the new consignment note has been drawn up. The form of the certificate of disposal and recovery to be attached to the existing consignment note shall be drawn up as soon as possible.

3.   Without prejudice to the procedure laid down in Article 1 (3) (c) and (d) regarding Annex II.A, Annexes II, III and IV shall be adapted by the Commission in accordance with the procedure laid down in Article 18 of Directive 75/442/EEC only to reflect changes already agreed under the review mechanism of the OECD.

4.   The procedure referred to in paragraph 1 shall apply also to define environmentally sound management, taking into account the relevant international conventions and agreements.

Article 43

Directive 84/631/EEC is hereby repealed with effect from the date of application of this Regulation. Any shipment pursuant to Articles 4 and 5 of that Directive shall be completed not later than six months from the date of application of this Regulation.

Article 44

This Regulation shall enter into force on the third day following its publication in the *Official Journal of the European Communities*.

It shall apply 15 months after publication.

This Regulation shall be binding in its entirety and directly applicable in all Member States.

Done at Brussels, 1 February 1993.

For the Council

The President

N. HELVEG PETERSEN

ANNEX I

LIST OF INTERNATIONAL TRANSPORT CONVENTIONS REFERRED TO IN ARTICLE 32[1]

1. ADR:

European Agreement concerning the international carriage of dangerous goods by road (1957).

2. Cotif:

Convention concerning the international carriage of dangerous goods by rail (1985).

RID:

Regulation on the international carriage by rail of dangerous goods (1985).

3. Solas Convention:

International Convention for the safety of life at sea (1974).

4. IMDG Code[2]:

International maritime dangerous goods code.

5. Chicago Convention:

Convention on international civil aviation (1944), Annex 18 to which deals with the carriage of dangerous goods by air (TI: Technical instructions for the safe transport of dangerous goods by air).

6. Marpol Convention:

International Convention for the prevention of pollution from ships (1973 to 1978).

7. ADNR:

Regulations of the carriage of dangerous substances on the Rhine (1970).

---

[1] This list contains those Conventions in force at the time of adoption of this Regulation.

[2] Since 1 January 1985, the IMDG code has been incorporated in the Solas Convention.

ANNEX II

GREEN LIST OF WASTESw[1]

A. METAL AND METAL-ALLOY WASTES IN METALLIC, NON DISPERSIBLE FORM[2]

The following waste and scrap of precious metals and their alloys:

7112 10	- Of gold
7112 20	- Of platinum (the expression 'platinum' includes platinum, iridium, osmium, palladium, rhodium and ruthenium)
7112 90	- Of other precious metal, e.g., silver

NB: 1. Mercury is specifically excluded as a component of these metals.

2. Electrical assemblies wastes and electronic scrap shall consist only of metals or alloys

3. Electrical scrap (meeting specifications laid down by the Review Mechanism).

The following ferrous waste and scrap; remelting scrap ingots of iron or steel:

7204 10	- Waste and scrap of cast iron
7204 21	- Waste and scrap of stainless steel
7204 29	- Waste and scrap of other alloy steels
7204 30	- Waste and scrap of tinned iron or steel
7204 41	- Turnings, shavings, chips, milling waste, filings, trimmings and stampings, whether or not in bundles
7204 49	- Other ferrous waste and scrap

---

[1] The indicative 'ex' identifies a specific item contained within the harmonized customs code heading.

[2] 'Non-dispersible' does not include any wastes in the form of powder, sludge, dust or solid items containing encased hazardous waste liquids.

| | 7204 50 | - Remelting scrap ingots |
| ex | 7302 10 | - Used iron and steel rails |

The following waste and scrap of non-ferrous metals and their alloys:

	7404 00	- Copper waste and scrap
	7503 00	- Nickel waste and scrap
	7602 00	- Aluminium waste and scrap
ex	7802 00	- Lead waste and scrap
	7902 00	- Zinc waste and scrap
	8002 00	- Tin waste and scrap
ex	8101 91	- Tungsten waste and scrap
ex	8102 91	- Molybdenum waste and scrap
ex	8103 10	- Tantalum waste and scrap
	8104 20	- Magnesium waste and scrap
ex	8105 10	- Cobalt waste and scrap
ex	8106 00	- Bismuth waste and scrap
ex	8107 10	- Cadmium waste and scrap
ex	8108 10	- Titanium waste and scrap
ex	8109 10	- Zirconium waste and scrap
ex	8110 00	- Antimony waste and scrap
ex	8111 00	- Manganese waste and scrap
ex	8112 11	- Beryllium waste and scrap
ex	8112 20	- Chromium waste and scrap
ex	8112 30	- Germanium waste and scrap
ex	8112 40	- Vanadium waste and scrap

ex   8112 91   Wastes and scrap of:

                        - Hafnium

                        - Indium

                        - Niobium

                        - Phenium

                        - Gallium

                        - Thallium

ex   2805 30   Thorium and rare earths waste and scrap

ex   2804 90   Selenium waste and scrap

ex   2804 50   Tellurium waste and scrap

B.   OTHER METAL BEARING WASTES ARISING FROM MELTING, SMELTING AND REFINING OF METALS

          2620 11   Hard zinc spelter

                    Zinc containing drosses:

                    - Galvanizing slab zinc top dross (> 90 % Zn)

                    - Galvanizing slab zinc bottom dross (> 92 % Zn)

                    - Zinc die cast dross (> 85 % Zn)

                    - Hot dip galvanizers slab zinc dross (batch) (> 92 % Zn)

                    - Zinc skimmings

                    Aluminium skimmings

ex   2620 90   Slags from precious metals and copper processing for further refining

C.   WASTES FROM MINING OPERATIONS: THESE WASTES TO BE IN NON-DISPERSIBLE FORM

ex	2504 90	Natural graphite waste
ex	2514 00	Slate waste, whether or not roughly trimmed or merely cut, by sawing or otherwise
	2525 30	Mica waste
ex	2529 21	Feldspar; leucite; nepheline and nepheline syenite; fluor spar - containing by weight 97 % or less of calcium fluoride
ex	2804 61	ex 2804 69 Silica wastes in solid form excluding those used in foundry operations

D.   SOLID PLASTIC WASTES

Including, but not limited to:

3915	Waste, parings and scrap of plastics:
3915 10	- Of polymers of ethylene
3915 20	- Of polymers of styrene
3915 30	- Of polymers of vinyl chloride
3915 90	Polymerized or co-polymerized:

- Polypropylene

- Polyethylene terephthalate

- Acrylonitrile copolymer

- Butadiene copolymer

- Styrene copolymer

- Polyamides

- Polybutylene terephthalates

- Polycarbonates

- Polyphenylene sulphides

169

- Acrylic polymers

- Paraffins (C10-C13)

- Polyurethane (not containing chlorofluorocarbons)

- Polysilozalanes (silicones)

- Polymethyl methacrylate

- Polyvinyl alcohol

- Polyvinyl butyral

- Polyvinyl acetate

- Fluorinated polytetrafluoroethylene (Teflon, PTFE)

3915 90	Resins or condensation products of:

- Urea formaldehyde resins

- Phenol formaldehyde resins

- Melamine formaldehyde resins

- Epoxy resins

- Alkyd resins

- Polyamides

E. PAPER, PAPERBOARD AND PAPER PRODUCT WASTES

4707 00	Waste and scrap of paper or paperboard:
4707 10	- Of unbleached kraft paper or paperboard or of corrugated paper or paperboard
4707 20	- Of other paper or paperboard, made mainly of bleached chemical pulp, not colored in the mass
4707 30	- Of paper or paperboard made mainly of mechanical pulp (for example, newspapers, journals and similar printed matter)
4707 90	- Other, including but not limited to:

1) Laminated paperboard

2) Unsorted waste and scrap

F.   GLASS WASTE IN NON-DISPERSIBLE FORM

ex   7001 00   Cullet and other waste and scrap of glass except for

glass from cathode-ray tubes and other activated glasses

Fibre glass wastes

G.   CERAMIC WASTES IN NON-DISPERSIBLE FORM

ex   6900 00   Wastes of ceramic which have been fired after shaping, including ceramic vessels

ex   8113 00   Cermets waste and scrap

Ceramic based fibres not otherwise listed

H.   TEXTILE WASTES

5003   Silk waste (including cocoons unsuitable for reeling, yarn waste and garnetted stock):

5003 10   - Not carded or combed

5003 90   - Other

5103   Waste of wool or of fine or coarse animal hair, including yarn waste but excluding garnetted stock:

5103 10   - Noils of wool or of fine animal hair

5103 20   - Other waste of wool or of fine animal hair

5103 30   - Waste of coarse animal hair

5202   Cotton waste (including yarn waste and garnetted stock):

5202 10   - Yarn waste (including thread waste)

5202 91   - Garnetted stock

5202 99   - Other

5301 30   Flax tow and waste

ex	5302 90 T	ow and waste (including yarn waste and garnetted stock) of true hemp (Cannabis sativa L.)
ex	5303 90	Tow and waste (including yarn waste and garnetted stock) of jute and other textile bast fibres (excluding flax, true hemp and ramie)
ex	5304 90	Tow and waste (including yarn waste and garnetted stock) of sisal and other textile fibres of the genus Agave
ex	5305 19	Tow, noils and waste (including yarn waste and garnetted stock) of coconut
ex	5305 29	Tow, noils and waste (including yarn waste and garnetted stock) of abaca (Manila hemp or Musa textilis Nee)
ex	5305 99	Tow, noils and waste (including yarn waste and garnetted stock) of ramie and other vegetable textile fibres, not else where specified or included
	5505	Waste (including noils, yarn waste and garnetted stock) of man-made fibres:
	5505 10	- Of synthetic fibres
	5505 20	- Of artificial fibres
	6309 00	Worn clothing and other worn textile articles
	6310	Used rags, scrap twine, cordage, rope and cables and worn out articles of twine, cordage, rope or cables of textile materials:
	6310 10	- Sorted
	6310 90	- Other

I.   RUBBER WASTES

	4004 00	Waste, parings and scrap of rubber (other than hard rubber) and granules obtained therefrom
	4012 20	Used pneumatic tyres
ex	4017 00	Waste and scrap of hard rubber (for example, ebonite)

J.   UNTREATED CORK AND WOOD WASTES

4401 30   Wood waste and scrap, whether or not agglomerated in logs, briquettes, pellets or similar forms

4501 90   Cork waste; crushed, granulated or ground cork

K.   WASTES ARISING FROM AGRO-FOOD INDUSTRIES

2301 00   Dried, sterilized and stabilized flours, meals and pellets, of meat or meat offal, of fish or of crustaceans, molluscs or other aquatic invertebrates, unfit for human consumption but fit for animal feed or other purposes; greaves

2302 00   Bran, sharps and other residues, whether or not in the form of pellets derived from the shifting, milling or other working of cereals or of leguminous plants

2303 00   Residues of starch manufacture and similar residues, beet-pulp, bagasse and other waste of sugar manufacture, brewing or distilling dregs and waste, whether or not in the form of pellets

2304 00   Oil-cake and other solid residues, whether or not ground or in the form of pellets, resulting from the extraction of soya-bean oil, used for animal feed

2305 00   Oil-cake and other solid residues, whether or not ground or in the form of pellets, resulting from the extraction of ground-nut (peanut) oil, used for animal feed

2306 00   Oil-cake and other solid residues, whether or not ground or in the form of pellets, resulting from the extraction of vegetable oil, used for animal feed

ex   2307 00   Wine lees

ex   2308 00   Dried and sterilized vegetable waste, residues and byproducts, whether or not in the form of pellets, of a kind used in animal feeding, not elsewhere specified or included

1522 00   Degras; residues resulting from the treatment of fatty substances or animal or vegetable waxes

1807 00   Cocoa shells, husks, skins and other cocoa waste

L. WASTES ARISING FROM TANNING AND FELLMONGERY OPERATIONS AND LEATHER USE

0502 00	Waste of pigs', hogs' or boars' bristles and hair or of badger hair and other brush-making hair
0503 00	Horsehair waste, whether or not put up as a layer with or without supporting material
0505 90	Waste of skins and other parts of birds, with their feathers or down, of feathers and parts of feathers (whether or not with trimmed edges) and down, not further worked than cleaned, disinfected or treated for preservation
0506 90	Waste of bones and horn-cores, unworked, defatted, simply prepared (but not cut to shape), treated with acid or degelatinized
4110 00	Parings and other waste of leather or of composition leather, not suitable for the manufacture of leather articles, excluding leather sludges

M. OTHER WASTES

	8908 00	Vessels and other floating structures for breaking up, properly emptied of any cargo which may have been classified as a dangerous substance or waste
		Motor vehicle wrecks, drained of liquids
	0501 00	Waste of human hair
ex	0511 91	Fish waste
		Anode butts of petroleum coke and/or bitumen
		Flue gas desulphurisation (FGD) gypsum
		Waste gypsum wallboard or plasterboard arising from the demolition of buildings
ex	2621	Coal fired power station fly ash, bottom ash and slag tap[1]

---

[1] Must be subject to certain specifications, these to be reviewed by the Review Mechanism.

Waste straw

Broken concrete

Spent catalysts:

- Fluid catalytic cracking (FCC) catalysts

- Precious metal bearing catalysts

- Transition metal catalysts

Deactivated fungus mycelium from penicillin production to be used as animal feed

	2618 00	Granulated slag arising from the manufacture of iron and steel
ex	2619 00	Slag arising from the manufacture of iron or steel[1]
	3103 20	Basic slag arising from the manufacture of iron or steel for phosphate fertilizer and other use
	ex 2621 00	Slag from copper production, chemically stabilized, having a high iron content (above 20 %) and processed according to industrial specifications (e.g. DIN 4301 and DIN 8201) mainly for construction and abrasive applications
ex	2621 00	Neutralized red mud from alumina production
ex	2621 00	Spent activated carbon

Sulphur in solid form

---

[1] This entry covers the use of such slags as a source of titanium dioxide and vanadium.

ex   2836 50   Limestone from the production of calcium cyanamide (having a pH less than 9)

Sodium, calcium, potassium chlorides

Waste photographic film base and waste photographic film not containing silver

Single use cameras without batteries

ex   2818 10   Carborundum

ANNEX III

AMBER LIST OF WASTES[1]

ex	2619 00	Dross, scalings and other wastes from the manufacture of iron and steel[2]
	2620 19	Zinc ash and residues
	2620 20	Lead ash and residues
	2620 30	Copper ash and residues
	2620 40	Aluminium ash and residues
	2620 50	Vanadium ash and residues
	2620 90	Ash and residue containing metals or metal compounds not specified elsewhere
		Residues from alumina production not specified elsewhere
	2621 00	Other ash and residues, not specified elsewhere
		Residues arising from the combustion of municipal wastes
	2713 90	Waste from the production/processing of petroleum coke and bitumen, excluding anode butts
		Lead-acid batteries, whole or crushed
		Waste oils unfit for their originally intended use
		Waste oils/water, hydrocarbons/water mixtures, emulsions
		Wastes from production, formulation and use of inks, dyes, pigments, paints, lacquers, varnish

---

[1] The indicative 'ex' identifies a specific item contained within the harmonized customs code heading.

[2] This listing includes ash, residue, slag, dross, skimming, scaling, dust, sludge and cake, unless a material is expressly listed elsewhere.

Wastes from production, formulation and use of resins, latex, plasticizers, glues and adhesives

Wastes from production, formulation and use of reprographic and photographic chemicals and processing materials not otherwise listed

Single use cameras with batteries

Wastes from non-cyanide-based systems which arise from surface treatment of metals and plastics

Asphalt cement wastes

Phenols, phenol compounds including chlorophenol in the form of liquids or sludges

Treated cork and wood wastes

Used batteries or accumulators, whole or crushed, other than lead-acid batteries, and waste and scrap arising from the production of batteries and accumulators, not otherwise listed

ex	3915 90	Nitrocellulose
ex	7001 00	Glass from cathode-ray tubes and other activated glasses
ex	4110 00	Leather dust, ash, sludges and flours
ex	2529 21	Calcium fluoride sludge

Other inorganic fluorine compounds in the form of liquids or sludges

Zinc slags containing up to 18 weight percent zinc

Galvanic sludges

Liquors from the pickling of metals

Sands used in foundry operations

Thallium compounds

Polychlorinated naphtalenes

Ethers

Precious metal bearing residues in solid form which contain traces of inorganic cyanides

Hydrogen peroxide solutions

Triethylamine catalyst for setting foundry sands

| ex | 2804 80 | Arsenic waste and residue |
| ex | 2805 40 | Mercury waste and residue |

Precious metal ash, sludge, dust and other residues such as:

- Ash from incineration of printed circuit boards

- Film ash

Waste catalysts not on the green list

Leaching residues from zinc processing, dusts and sludges such as jarosite, hematite, goethite, etc.

Waste hydrates of aluminium

Waste alumina

Wastes that contain, consist of or are contaminated with any of the following:

- Inorganic cyanides, excepting precious metal-bearing residues in solid form containing traces or inorganic cyanides

- Organic cyanides

Wastes of an explosible nature, when not subject to specific other legislation

Wastes from the manufacture, formulation and use of wood preserving chemicals

Leaded petrol (gasoline) sludges

Used blasting grit

Chlorofluorocarbons

Halons

Fluff - light fraction from metal shredding

Thermal (heat transfer) fluids

Hydraulic fluids

Brake fluids

Antifreeze fluids

Ion exchange resins

Wastes on the amber list which will be re-examined as a priority matter by the Review Mechanism of the OECD

Organic phosphorous compounds

Non-halogenated solvents

Halogenated solvents

Halogenated or unhalogenated non-aqueous distillation residues arising from organic solvent recovery operations

Liquid pig manure; feces

Sewage sludge

Household wastes

Wastes from the production, formulation and use of biocides and phytopharmaceuticals

Wastes from the production and preparation of pharmaceutical products

Acidic solutions

Basic solutions

Surface active agents (surfactants)

Inorganic balide compounds, not specified elsewhere

Wastes from industrial pollution control devices for cleaning of industrial off-gases, not specified elsewhere

Gypsum arising from chemical industry processes

ANNEX IV

RED LIST OF WASTES

Wastes, substances and articles containing, consisting of or contaminated with polychlorinated biphenyl (PCB) and/or polychlorinated terphenyl (PCT) and/or polybrominated biphenyl (PBB), including any other polybrominated analogues of these compounds, at a concentration level of 50 mg/kg or more

Wastes that contain, consist of or are contaminated with any of the following:

— Any congenor of polychlorinated dibenzo-furan

— Any congenor of polychlorinated dibenzo-dioxin

Asbestos (dusts and fibres)

Ceramic based fibres similar to those of asbestos

Leaded anti-knock compound sludges

Wastes on the red list which will be re-examined as a priority matter by the Review Mechanism of the OECD

Waste tarry residues (excluding asphalt cements) arising from refining, distillation and any pyrolitic treatment

Peroxides other than hydrogen peroxide

DECISION 94/1/ECSC, EC[1] OF THE COUNCIL AND THE COMMISSION
of 13 December 1993
on the conclusion of the Agreement on the European Economic Area between the European Communities, their Member States and the Republic of Austria, the Republic of Finland, the Republic of Iceland, the Principality of Liechtenstein, the Kingdom of Norway, the Kingdom of Sweden and the Swiss Confederation

THE COUNCIL OF THE EUROPEAN UNION,

THE COMMISSION OF THE EUROPEAN COMMUNITIES,

Having regard to the Treaty establishing the European Coal and Steel Community,

Having regard to the Treaty establishing the European Community, and in particular Article 238 in conjunction with Article 228 (3), second subparagraph thereof,

Having regard to the assent of the European Parliament[2],

Whereas the Agreement on the European Economic Area between the European Communities, their Member States and the Republic of Austria, the Republic of Finland, the Republic of Iceland, the Principality of Liechtenstein, the Kingdom of Norway, the Kingdom of Sweden and the Swiss Confederation, signed in Oporto on 2 May 1992 should be approved,

HAVE DECIDED AS FOLLOWS:

Article 1

The Agreement on the European Economic Area between the European Communities, their Member States and the Republic of Austria, the Republic of Finland, the Republic of Iceland, the Principality of Liechtenstein, the Kingdom of Norway, the Kingdom of Sweden and the Swiss Confederation, the Protocols, the Annexes annexed thereto and the Declarations, the Agreed Minutes and exchanges of letters attached to the Final Act are hereby approved

---

[1]   OJ No L 1, 3. 1. 1994.
[2]   OJ No C 305, 23. 11. 1992, p. 66.

on behalf of the European Community and the European Coal and Steel Community.

The texts of the acts referred to in the first paragraph are attached to this Decision.

Article 2

The act of approval provided for in Article 129 of the Agreement shall be deposited by the President of the Council on behalf of the European Community and by the President of the Commission on behalf of the European Coal and Steel Community[1].

Done at Brussels, 13 December 1993.

For the Council	*For the Commission*
The President	*The President*
Ph. MAYSTADT	J. DELORS

---

[1] See page 606 of this Official Journal. (OJ No L 1, 3. 1. 1994)

AGREEMENT ON THE EUROPEAN ECONOMIC AREA

CHAPTER 3   ENVIRONMENT

Article 73

1)   Action by the Contracting Parties relating to the environment shall have the following objectives:

a) to preserve, protect and improve the quality of the environment;

b) to contribute towards protecting human health;

c) to ensure a prudent and rational utilization of natural resources.

2.   Action by the Contracting Parties relating to the environment shall be based on the principles that preventive action should be taken, that environmental damage should as a priority be rectified at source, and that the polluter should pay. Environmental protection requirements shall be a component of the Contracting Parties' other policies.

Article 74

Annex XX contains the specific provisions on protective measures which shall apply pursuant to Article 73.

Article 75

The protective measures referred to in Article 74 shall not prevent any Contracting Party from maintaining or introducing more stringent protective measures compatible with this Agreement.

ANNEX XX

ENVIRONMENT

List provided for in Article 74

INTRODUCTION

When the acts referred to in this Annex contain notions or refer to procedures which are specific to the Community legal order, such as

- preambles;

- the addressees of the Community acts;

- references to territories or languages of the EC;

- references to rights and obligations of EC Member States, their public entities, undertakings or individuals in relation to each other; and

- references to information and notification procedures;

Protocol 1 on horizontal adaptations shall apply, unless otherwise provided for in this Annex.

SECTORAL ADAPTATION

For the purposes of this Annex and notwithstanding the provisions of Protocol 1, the term 'Member State(s)' contained in the acts referred to shall be understood to include, in addition to its meaning in the relevant EC acts, Austria, Finland, Iceland, Liechtenstein, Norway, Sweden and Switzerland.

ACTS REFERRED TO

I.   **General**

1)   **385 L 0337:** Council Directive 85/337/EEC of 27 June 1985 on the assessment of the effects of certain public and private projects on the environment (OJ No L 175, 5.7.1985, p. 40).

2)   **390 L 0313:** Council Directive 90/313/EEC of 7 June 1990 on freedom of access to information (OJ No L 158, 23.6.1990, p. 56).

II.   **Water**

3)   **375 L 0440:** Council Directive 75/440/EEC of 16 June 1975 concerning the quality required of surface water intended for the abstraction of drinking water in the Member States (OJ No L 194, 25.7.1975, p. 26), as amended by:

—   **379 L 0869:** Council Directive 79/869/EEC of 9 October 1979
(OJ No L 271, 29.10.1979, p. 44).

4)   **376 L 0464:** Council Directive 76/464/EEC of 4 May 1976 on pollution caused by certain dangerous substances discharged into the aquatic environment of the Community (OJ L 129, 18.5.1976, p. 23).

The provisions of the Directive shall, for the purposes of the Agreement, be read with the following adaptation:

Iceland shall put into effect the measures necessary for it to comply with the provisions of this Directive as from 1 January 1995.

5)   **379 L 0869:** Council Directive 79/869/EEC of 9 October 1979 concerning the methods of measurement and frequencies of sampling and analysis of surface water intended for the abstraction of drinking water in the Member States (OJ L 271, 29.10.1979, p. 44), as amended by:

—   **381 L 0855:** Council Directive 81/855/EEC of 19 October 1981
(OJ No L 319, 7.11.1981, p. 16),

—   **1 85 I:** Act concerning the Conditions of Accession and Adjustments to the Treaties — Accession to the European Communities of the Kingdom of Spain and the Portuguese Republic
(OJ No L 302, 15.11.1985, p. 219).

6)   **380 L 0068:** Council Directive 80/68/EEC of 17 December 1979 on the protection of groundwater against pollution caused by certain dangerous substances (OJ No L 20, 26.1.1980, p. 43).

The provisions of the Directive shall, for the purposes of the Agreement, be read with the following adaptation:

the provisions of Article 14 shall not apply.

7)   **380 L 0778:** Council Directive 80/778/EEC of 15 July 1980 relating to the quality of water intended for human consumption
(OJ No L 229, 30.8.1980, p. 11), as amended by:

—   **381 L 0858:** Council Directive 81/858/EEC of 19 October 1981
(OJ No L 319, 7.11.1981, p. 19).

—   **1 85 I:** Act concerning the Conditions of Accession and Adjustments to the Treaties — Accession to the European Communities of the

Kingdom of Spain and the Portuguese Republic
(OJ No L 302, 15.11.1985, pp. 219, 397).

The provisions of the Directive shall, for the purposes of the Agreement, be read with the following adaptation:

the provisions of Article 20 shall not apply.

8) **382 L 0176:** Council Directive 82/176/EEC of 22 March 1982 on limit values and quality objectives for mercury discharges by the chlor-alkali electrolysis industry (OJ No L 81, 27.3.1982, p. 29).

The provisions of the Directive shall, for the purposes of the present Agreement, be read with the following adaptation:

Iceland shall put into effect the measures necessary for it to comply with the provisions of this Directive as from 1 January 1995.

9) **383 L 0513:** Council Directive 83/513/EEC of 26 September 1983 on limit values and quality objectives for cadmium discharges
(OJ No L 291, 24.10.1983, p. 1).

The provisions of the Directive shall, for the purposes of the Agreement, be read with the following adaptation:

Iceland shall put into effect the measures necessary for it to comply with the provisions of this Directive as from 1 January 1995.

10) **384 L 0156:** Council Directive 84/156/EEC of 8 March 1984 on limit values and quality objectives for mercury discharges by sectors other than the chlor-alkali electrolysis industry
(OJ No L 74, 17.3.1984, p. 49).

The provisions of the Directive shall, for the purposes of the Agreement, be read with the following adaptation:

Iceland shall put into effect the measures necessary for it to comply with the provisions of this Directive as from 1 January 1995.

11) **384 L 0491**: Council Directive 84/491/EEC of 9 October 1984 on limit values and quality objectives for discharges of hexachlorocyclohexane (OJ No L 274, 17.10.1984, p. 11).

The provisions of the Directive shall, for the purposes of the Agreement, be read with the following adaptation:

Iceland shall put into effect the measures necessary for it to comply with the provisions of this Directive as from 1 January 1995.

12) **386 L 0280:** Council Directive 86/280/EEC of 12 June 1986 on limit values and quality objectives for discharges of certain dangerous substances included in List I of the Annex to Directive 76/464/EEC
(OJ No L 181, 4.7.1986, p. 16), as amended by:

— **388 L 0347:** Council Directive 88/347/EEC of 16 June 1988 amending Annex II to Directive 86/280/EEC (OJ No L 158, 25.6.1988, p. 35),

— **390 L 0415:** Council Directive 90/415/EEC of 27 July 1990 amending Annex II to Directive 86/280/EEC (OJ No L 219, 14.8.1990, p. 49).

The provisions of the Directive shall, for the purposes of the Agreement, be read with the following adaptation:

Iceland shall put into effect the measures necessary for it to comply with the provisions of this Directive as from 1 January 1995.

13) **391 L 0271:** Council Directive 91/271/EEC of 21 May 1991 concerning urban waste water treatment (OJ No L 135, 30.5.1991, p. 40).

The provisions of the Directive shall, for the purposes of the Agreement, be read with the following adaptation:

Iceland shall put into effect the measures necessary for it to comply with the provisions of this Directive as from 1 January 1995.

III.   Air

14) **380 L 0779:** Council Directive 80/779/EEC of 15 July 1980 on air quality limit values and guide values for sulphur dioxide and suspended particulates (OJ No L 229, 30.8.1980, p. 30), as amended by:

— **381 L 0857:** Council Directive 81/857/EEC of 19 October 1981 (OJ No L 319, 7.11.1981, p. 18),

— **1 85 I:** Act concerning the Conditions of Accession and Adjustments to the Treaties — Accession to the European Communities of the Kingdom of Spain and the Portuguese Republic (OJ No L 302, 15.11.1985, p. 219),

— **389 L 0427:** Council Directive 89/427/EEC of 21 June 1989 (OJ No L 201, 14.7.1989, p. 53).

The provisions of the Directive shall, for the purposes of the Agreement, be read with the following adaptation:

Iceland shall put into effect the measures necessary for it to comply with the provisions of this Directive as from 1 January 1995.

15) **382 L 0884:** Council Directive 82/884/EEC of 3 December 1982 on a limit value for lead in the air (OJ No L 378, 31.12.1982, p. 15).

The provisions of the Directive shall, for the purposes of the Agreement, be read with the following adaptation:

Iceland shall put into effect the measures necessary for it to comply with the provisions of this Directive as from 1 January 1995.

16) **384 L 0360:** Council Directive 84/360/EEC of 28 June 1984 on the combating of air pollution from industrial plants
(OJ No L 188, 16.7.1984, p. 20).

The provisions of the Directive shall, for the purposes of the Agreement, be read with the following adaptation:

Iceland shall put into effect the measures necessary for it to comply with the provisions of this Directive as from 1 January 1995.

17) **385 L 0203:** Council Directive 85/203/EEC of 7 March 1985 on air-quality standards for nitrogen dioxide (OJ No L 87, 27.3.1985, p. 1), as amended by:

— **385 L 0580:** Council Directive 85/580/EEC of 20 December 1985 (OJ No L 372, 31.12.1985, p. 36).

The provisions of the Directive shall, for the purposes of the Agreement, be read with the following adaptation:

Iceland shall put into effect the measures necessary for it to comply with the provisions of this Directive as from 1 January 1995.

18) **387 L 0217:** Council Directive 87/217/EEC of 19 March 1987 on the prevention and reduction of environmental pollution by asbestos
(OJ No L 85, 28.3.1987, p. 40).

The provisions of the Directive shall, for the purposes of the Agreement, be read with the following adaptations:

a) in Article 9 'the Treaty' shall read 'the EEA Agreement';

b) Iceland shall put into effect the measures necessary for it to comply with the provisions of this Directive as from 1 January 1995.

19) **388 L 0609:** Council Directive 88/609/EEC of 24 November 1988 on the limitation of emissions of certain pollutants into the air from large combustion plants (OJ No L 336, 7.12.1988, p. 1).

The provisions of the Directive shall, for the purposes of the Agreement, be read with the following adaptations:

a) Article 3(5) shall be replaced by the following:

' 5 (a) If a substantial and unexpected change in energy demand or in the availability of certain fuels or certain generating installations creates serious technical difficulties for the implementation by a Contracting Party of the emission ceilings, such a Contracting Party may request a modification of the emission ceilings and/or dates set out in Annexes I and II. The procedure set out in (b) shall apply.

(b) The Contracting Party shall immediately inform the other Contracting Parties through the EEA Joint Committee of such action and give reasons for its decision. If a Contracting Party so requires, consultations on the appropriateness of the measures taken shall take place in the EEA Joint Committee. Part VII of the Agreement shall apply.';

b) the following shall be added to the table for ceilings and reduction targets in Annex I:

	0	1	2	3	4	5	6	7	8	9
Austria	171	102	68	51	-40	-60	-70	-40	-60	-70
Finland	90	54	36	27	-40	-60	-70	-40	-60	-70
Sweden	112	67	45	34	-40	-60	-70	-40	60	-70
Switzerland	28	14	14	14	-50	-50	-50	-50	-50	-50

';

c) the following is added to the table for ceilings and reduction targets in Annex II:

	0	1	2	3	4	5	6
Austria	81	65	48	-20	-40	-20	-40
Finland	19	15	11	-20	-40	-20	-40
Sweden	31	25	19	-20	-40	-20	-40
Switzerland	9	8	5	-10	-40	-10	-40

';

d) at the time of entry into force of the Agreement, Iceland, Liechtenstein and Norway do not have any large combustion plants as defined in Article 1. These States will comply with the Directive if and when they acquire such plants.

20) **389 L 0369:** Council Directive 89/369/EEC of 8 June 1989 on the prevention of air pollution from new municipal waste-incineration plants (OJ No L 163, 14.6.1989, p. 32).

The provisions of the Directive shall, for the purposes of the Agreement, be read with the following adaptation:

Iceland shall put into effect the measures necessary for it to comply with the provisions of this Directive as from 1 January 1995.

21) **389 L 0429:** Council Directive 89/429/EEC of 21 June 1989 on the reduction of air pollution from existing municipal waste-incineration plants (OJ No L 203, 15.7.1989, p. 50).

IV.   Chemicals, industrial risk and biotechnology

22) **376 L 0403:** Council Directive 76/403/EEC of 6 April 1976 on the disposal of polychlorinated biphenyls and polychlorinated terphenyls (OJ No L 108, 26.4.1976, p. 41).

The provisions of the Directive shall, for the purposes of the Agreement, be read with the following adaptation:

The EFTA States shall put into effect the measures necessary for them to comply with the provisions of this Directive as from 1 January 1995, subject to a review before that date.

23) **382 L 0501:** Council Directive 82/501/EEC of 24 June 1982 on the major accident hazards of certain industrial activities
(OJ No L 230, 5.8.1982, p. 1), as amended by:

— **1 85 I:** Act concerning the Conditions of Accession and Adjustments to the Treaties — Accession to the European Communities of the Kingdom of Spain and the Portuguese Republic
(OJ No L 302, 15.11.1985, p. 219),

— **387 L 0216:** Council Directive 87/216/EEC of 19 March 1987
(OJ No L 85, 28.3.1987, p. 36),

— **388 L 0610**: Council Directive 88/610/EEC of 24 November 1988
(OJ No L 336, 7.12.1988, p. 14).

24) **390 L 0219:** Council Directive 90/219/EEC of 23 April 1990 on the contained use of genetically modified micro-organisms
(OJ No L 117, 8.5.1990, p. 1).

The provisions of the Directive shall, for the purposes of the Agreement, be read with the following adaptation:

Austria, Finland, Iceland, Liechtenstein, Norway and Sweden shall put into effect the measures necessary for them to comply with the provisions of this Directive as from 1 January 1995.

25) **390 L 0220:** Council Directive 90/220/EEC of 23 April 1990 on the deliberate release into the environment of genetically modified organisms (OJ No L 117, 8.5.1990, p. 15).

The provisions of the Directive shall, for the purposes of the present Agreement, be read with the following adaptations:

a) Austria, Finland, Iceland, Liechtenstein, Norway and Sweden shall put into effect the measures necessary for them to comply with the provisions of this Directive as from 1 January 1995;

b) Article 16 shall be replaced by the following:

' 1. Where a Contracting Party has justifiable reasons to consider that a product which has been properly notified and has received written consent under this Directive constitutes a risk to human health or the environment, it may restrict or prohibit the use and/or sale of that product on its territory. It shall immediately inform the other Contracting Parties through the EEA Joint Committee of such action and give reasons for its decision.

2. If a Contracting Party so requires, consultations on the appropriateness of the measures taken shall take place in the EEA Joint Committee. Part VII of the Agreement shall apply.';

c) The Contracting Parties agree that the Directive only covers aspects relating to the potential risks to humans, plants, animals and the environment.

The EFTA States therefore reserve the right to apply their national legislation in this area in relation to other concerns than health and environment, in so far as it is compatible with this Agreement.

V. Waste

26) **375 L 0439:** Council Directive 75/439/EEC of 16 June 1975 on the disposal of waste oils (OJ No L 194, 25.7.1975, p. 23), as amended by:

— **387 L 0101:** Council Directive 87/101/EEC of 22 December 1986 (OJ No L 42, 12.2.1987, p. 43).

27) **375 L 0442:** Council Directive 75/442/EEC of 15 July 1975 on waste (OJ No L 194, 25.7.1975, p. 39), as amended by:

— **391 L 0156:** Council Directive 91/156/EEC of 18 March 1991 (OJ No L 78, 26.3.1991, p. 32).

The provisions of the Directive shall, for the purposes of the Agreement, be read with the following adaptation:

Norway shall put into effect the measures necessary for it to comply with the provisions of this Directive as from 1 January 1995, subject to a review before that date.

28) **378 L 0176:** Council Directive 78/176/EEC of 20 February 1978 on waste from the titanium-dioxide industry (OJ No L 54, 25.2.1978, p. 19), as amended by:

— **382 L 0883:** Council Directive 82/883/EEC of 3 December 1982 on procedures for the surveillance and monitoring of environments concerned by waste from the titanium-dioxide industry
(OJ No L 378, 31.12.1982, p. 1),

— **383 L 0029:** Council Directive 83/29/EEC of 24 January 1983
(OJ No L 32, 3.2.1983, p. 28).

29) **378 L 0319:** Council Directive 78/319/EEC of 20 March 1978 on toxic and dangerous waste (OJ No L 84, 31.3.1978, p. 43), as amended by:

— **1 79 H:** Act concerning the Conditions of Accession and Adjustments to the Treaties — Accession to the European Communities of the Hellenic Republic (OJ No L 291, 19.11.1979, p. 111),

— **1 85 I:** Act concerning the Conditions of Accession and Adjustments to the Treaties — Accession to the European Communities of the Kingdom of Spain and the Portuguese Republic
(OJ No L 302, 15.11.1985, pp. 219, 397).

The provisions of the Directive shall, for the purposes of the Agreement, be read with the following adaptation:

the EFTA States shall put into effect the measures necessary for them to comply with the provisions of this Directive as from 1 January 1995, subject to a review before that date.

30) **382 L 0883:** Council Directive 82/883/EEC of 3 December 1982 on procedures for the surveillance and monitoring of environments concerned by waste from the titanium-dioxide industry
(OJ No L 378, 31.12.1982, p. 1), as amended by:

— **1 85 I:** Act concerning the Conditions of Accession and Adjustments to the Treaties — Accession to the European Communities of the Kingdom of Spain and the Portuguese Republic
(OJ No L 302, 15.11.1985, p. 219).

31) **384 L 0631:** Council Directive 84/631/EEC of 6 December 1984 on the supervision and control within the European Community of the transfrontier shipment of hazardous waste (OJ No L 326, 13.12.1984, p. 31), as amended by:

— **385 L 0469:** Commission Directive 85/469/EEC of 22 July 1985
(OJ No L 272, 12.10.1985, p. 1),

— **386 L 0121:** Council Directive 86/121/EEC of 8 April 1986
(OJ No L 100, 16.4.1986, p. 20),

— **386 L 0279:** Council Directive 86/279/EEC of 12 June 1986
(OJ No L 181, 4.7.1986, p. 13).

The provisions of the Directive shall, for the purposes of the Agreement, be read with the following adaptations:

the following shall be added to box 36 of Annex I:

'

ÍSLENSKA	duft	duftkennt	fast	lúmkennt	seigfl-jótandi	bunnfl-jótandi	vökvi	loftkennt
NORSK	pulver-formet	stov-formet	fast	pasta-formet	viskost (tyktfly-tende)	slam-formet	flytende	gass-formet
SUOMESKI	jauhe-mäinen	pöly-mäinen	kiinteä	tahna-mäinen	siirappi-mäinen	liete-mäinen	neste-mäinen	kaasu-mäinen
SVENSKA	pulver-formigt	stoft	fast	pastöst	visköst	slamfor-migt	flytande	gasfor-migt

•unnfljótandi

støvformetviskøstl

';

d) the following new entries shall be added to the last sentence of provision 6 of Annex III: 'AU for Austria, SF for Finland, IS for Iceland, LI for Liechtenstein, NO for Norway, SE for Sweden and CH for Switzerland.';

e) the EFTA States shall put into effect the measures necessary for them to comply with the provisions of this Directive as from 1 January 1995, subject to a review before that date.

32) **386 L 0278:** Council Directive 86/278/EEC of 12 June 1986 on the protection of the environment, and in particular of the soil, when sewage sludge is used in agriculture (OJ No L 181, 4.7.1986, p. 6).

ACTS OF WHICH THE CONTRACTING PARTIES SHALL TAKE NOTE

The Contracting Parties take note of the content of the following acts:

33) **375 X 0436:** Council Recommendation 75/436/Euratom, ECSC, EEC of 3 March 1975 regarding cost allocation by public authorities on environmental matters (OJ No L 194, 25.7.1975, p. 1).

34) **379 X 0003:** Council Recommendation 79/3/EEC of 19 December 1978 to the Member States regarding methods of evaluating the cost of pollution control to industry (OJ No L 5, 9.1.1979, p. 28).

35)   **380 Y 0830(01):** Council Resolution of 15 July 1980 on transboundary air pollution by sulphur dioxide and suspended particulates (OJ No C 222, 30.8.1980, p. 1).

36)   **389 Y 1026(01):** Council Resolution (89/C 273/01) of 16 October 1989 on guidelines to reduce technological and natural hazards (OJ No C 273, 26.10.1989, p. 1).

37)   **390 Y 0518(01):** Council Resolution (90/C 122/02) of 7 May 1990 on waste policy (OJ No C 122, 18.5.1990, p. 2).

38)   **SEC (89) 934 final:** Communication from the Commission to the Council and to Parliament of 18 September 1989. 'A Community strategy for waste management'.

COMMISSION DECISION 94/3/EC[1]
of 20 December 1993
establishing a list of wastes pursuant to
Article 1 (a) of Council Directive 75/442/EEC
on waste

THE COMMISSION OF THE EUROPEAN COMMUNITIES,

Having regard to the Treaty establishing the European Community,

Having regard to Council Directive 75/442/EEC of 15 July 1975 on waste[2], and in particular Article 1 (a) thereof,

Whereas the aforesaid provision requires the Commission to draw up a list of wastes belonging to the categories listed in Annex I to the same Directive; whereas the Commission is assisted in this task by the Committee composed of representatives of the Member States and chaired by the representative of the Commission, established by Article 18 of the Directive;

Whereas the measures envisaged by this Decision are in accordance with the opinion expressed by the aforementioned Committee,

HAS ADOPTED THIS DECISION:

Article 1

The list contained in the Annex to this Decision is hereby adopted.

---

[1] OJ No L 5, 7. 1. 1994, p. 115.
[2] OJ No L 194, 25. 7. 1975, p. 47, as last amended by
     Directive 91/692/EEC (OJ No L 377, 31. 12. 1991, p. 48).

Article 2

This Decision is addressed to the Member States.

Done at Brussels, 20 December 1993.

For the Commission

Yannis PALEOKRASSAS

Member of the Commission

ANNEX

List of wastes pursuant to Article 1 (a) of Council Directive 75/442/EEC on waste

(EUROPEAN WASTE CATALOGUE)

Introductory note

1) Article 1 (a) of Directive 75/442/EEC defines the term 'waste' as: 'any substance or object in the categories set out in Annex I which the holder discards or intends or is required to discard'.

2) The second indent of Article 1 (a) requires the Commission, acting in accordance with the procedure laid down in Article 18, to draw up a list of waste belonging to the categories listed in Annex I. This list is commonly referred to as the European Waste Catalogue (EWC), and applies to all wastes, irrespective of whether they are destined for disposal or for recovery operations.

3) The EWC is an harmonized, non-exhaustive list of wastes, that is to say, a list which will be periodically reviewed and if necessary revised in accordance with the committee procedure.

4) However, the inclusion of a material in the EWC does not mean that the material is a waste in all circumstances. The entry is only relevant when the definition of waste has been satisfied.

5) The waste featuring in the EWC is subject to the provisions of the Directive unless Article 2 (1) (b) of this Directive applies.

6) The EWC is to be a reference nomenclature providing a common terminology throughout the Community with the purpose to improve the efficiency of waste management activities. In this respect the European Waste Catalogue should constitute the basic reference for the Community Programme on waste statistics launched pursuant to the Council resolution of 7 May 1990 on waste management policy[1].

7) The EWC will be subject to adaptation to scientific and technical progress in accordance with the procedure laid down in Article 18 of the Directive.

8) The reading of an individual code of waste in the EWC should not be isolated from its heading.

---

[1] OJ No C 122, 18. 5. 1990, p. 2.

9) The EWC does not prejudge the list of 'hazardous wastes' as required by Article 1 (4) of Council Directive 91/689/EEC of 12 December 1991 on hazardous waste[1].

INDEX

---

[1] OJ No L 377, 31. 12. 1991, p. 20.

15 00 00	Packaging; absorbents, wiping cloths, filter materials and protective clothing not otherwise specified
16 00 00	Waste not otherwise specified in the catalogue
17 00 00	Construction and demolition waste (including road construction)
18 00 00	Wastes from human or animal health care and/or related research (excluding kitchen and restaurant wastes which do not arise from immediate health care)
19 00 00	Wastes from waste treatment facilities, off-site waste water treatment plants and the water industry
20 00 00	Municipal wastes and similar commercial, industrial and institutional wastes including separately collected fractions

01 00 00   **WASTE RESULTING FROM EXPLORATION, MINING, DRESSING AND FURTHER TREATMENT OF MINERALS AND QUARRY**

01 01 00   **waste from mineral excavation**

01 01 01   waste from mineral metaliferous excavation

01 01 02   waste from mineral non-metaliferous excavation

01 02 00   **waste from mineral dressing**

01 02 01   waste from the dressing of metalferous minerals

01 02 02   waste from the dressing of non-metalferous minerals

01 03 00   **waste from further physical and chemical processing of metaliferous minerals**

01 03 01   tailings

01 03 02   dusty and powdery waste

01 03 03   red mud from the alumina production

01 03 99   wastes not otherwise specified

01 04 00   **waste from further physical and chemical processing of non metaliferous minerals**

01 04 01   waste gravel and crushed rocks

01 04 02   waste sand and clays

01 04 03   dusty and powdery waste

01 04 04   waste from potash and rock salt processing

01 04 05   waste from washing and cleaning of minerals

01 04 06   waste from stone cutting and sawing

01 04 99   wastes not otherwise specified

01 05 00   **drilling muds and other drilling wastes**

01 05 01   oil-containing drilling muds and wastes

01 05 02	barite-containing drilling muds and wastes
01 05 03	chloride-containing drilling muds and wastes
01 05 04	fresh-water drilling muds and wastes
01 05 99	wastes not otherwise specified

02 00 00 **WASTE FROM AGRICULTURAL, HORTICUL-TURAL, HUNTING, FISHING AND AQUACUL-TURE PRIMARY PRODUCTION, FOOD PREPARATION AND PROCESSING**

02 01 00 **primary production waste**

02 01 01	sludges from washing and cleaning
02 01 02	animal tissue waste
02 01 03	plant tissue waste
02 01 04	waste plastics (excluding packaging)
02 01 05	agrochemical wastes
02 01 06	animal feces, urine and manure (including spoiled straw), effluent, collected separately and treated off-site
02 01 07	waste from forestry exploitation
02 01 99	wastes not otherwise specified

02 02 00 **wastes from the preparation and processing of meat, fish and other foods of animal origin**

02 02 01	sludges from washing and cleaning
02 02 02	animal tissue waste
02 02 03	materials unsuitable for consumption or processing
02 02 04	sludges from on-site effluent treatment
02 02 99	wastes not otherwise specified

02 03 00   **wastes from fruit, vegetables, cereals, edible oils, cocoa, coffee and tobacco preparation, processing; conserve production; tobacco processing**

02 03 01   sludges from washing, cleaning, peeling, centrifuging and separation

02 03 02   wastes from preserving agents

02 03 03   wastes from solvent extraction

02 03 04   materials unsuitable for consumption or processing

02 03 05   sludges from on-site effluent treatment

02 03 99   wastes not otherwise specified

02 04 00   **wastes from sugar processing**

02 04 01   soil from cleaning and washing beet

02 04 02   off specification calcium carbonate

02 04 03   sludges from on-site effluent treatment

02 04 99   wastes not otherwise specified

02 05 00   **wastes from the dairy products industry**

02 05 01   materials unsuitable for consumption or processing

02 05 02   sludges from on-site effluent treatment

02 05 99   wastes not otherwise specified

02 06 00   **wastes from the baking and confectionery industry**

02 06 01   materials unsuitable for consumption or processing

02 06 02   wastes from preserving agents02 06 03sludges from on-site effluent treatment

02 06 99   wastes not otherwise specified

02 07 00   **wastes from the production of alcoholic and non-alcoholic beverages (excluding coffee, tea and cocoa)**

02 07 01	wastes from washing, cleaning and mechanical reduction of the raw material
02 07 02	wastes from spirits distillation
02 07 03	waste from chemical treatment
02 07 04	materials unsuitable for consumption or processing
02 07 05	sludges from on-site effluent treatment
02 07 99	wastes not otherwise specified

03 00 00 **WASTES FROM WOOD PROCESSING AND THE PRODUCTION OF PAPER, CARDBOARD, PULP, PANELS AND FURNITURE**

03 01 00 **wastes from wood processing and the production of panels and furniture**

03 01 00	waste bark and cork
03 01 02	sawdust
03 01 03	shavings, cuttings, spoiled timber/particle board/veneer
03 01 99	wastes not otherwise specified

03 02 00 **wood preservation waste**

03 02 01	non-halogenated organic wood preservatives
03 02 02	organochlorinated wood preservatives
03 02 03	organometallic wood preservatives
03 02 04	inorganic wood preservatives

03 03 00 **wastes from pulp, paper and cardboard production and processing**

03 03 01	bark
03 03 02	dregs and green liquor sludge (from black liquor treatment)

03 03 03	bleaching sludges from hypochlorite and chlorine processes
03 03 04	bleaching sludges from other bleaching processes
03 03 05	de-inking sludges from paper recycling
03 03 06	fibre and paper sludge
03 03 07	rejects from paper and cardboard recycling
03 03 99	wastes not otherwise specified
04 00 00	**WASTES FROM THE LEATHER AND TEXTILE INDUSTRIES**
04 01 00	wastes from the leather industry
04 01 01	fleshings and lime split waste
04 01 02	liming waste
04 01 03	degreasing wastes containing solvents without a liquid phase
04 01 04	tanning liquor containing chromium
04 01 05	tanning liquor free of chromium
04 01 06	sludges containing chromium
04 01 07	sludges free of chromium
04 01 08	waste tanned leather (blue sheetings, shavings, cuttings, buffing dust) containing chromium
04 01 09	wastes from dressing and finishing
04 01 99	wastes not otherwise specified
04 02 00	**wastes from textile industry**
04 02 01	wastes from unprocessed textile fibres and other natural fibrous substances mainly of vegetable origin
04 02 02	wastes from unprocessed textile fibres mainly of animal origin

04 02 03	wastes from unprocessed textile fibres mainly artificial or synthetic
04 02 04	wastes from unprocessed mixed textile fibres before spinning and weaving
04 02 05	wastes from processed textile fibres mainly of vegetable origin
04 02 06	wastes from processed textile fibres mainly of animal origin
04 02 07	wastes from processed textile fibres mainly of artificial or synthetic origin
04 02 08	wastes from processed mixed textile fibres
04 02 09	wastes from composite materials (impregnated textile, elastomer, plastomer)
04 02 10	organic matter from natural products (e.g. grease, wax)
04 02 11	halogenated wastes from dressing and finishing
04 02 12	non-halogenated wastes from dressing and finishing
04 02 13	dye stuffs and pigments
04 02 99	wastes not otherwise specified
05 00 00	**WASTES FROM PETROLEUM REFINING, NATURAL GAS PURIFICATION AND PYROLYTIC TREATMENT OF COAL**
05 01 00	**Oily sludges and solid wastes**
05 01 01	sludges from on-site effluent treatment
05 01 02	desalter sludges
05 01 03	tank bottom sludges
05 01 04	acid alkyl sludges
05 01 05	oil spills

05 01 06	sludges from plant, equipment and maintenance operations
05 01 07	acid tars
05 01 08	other tars
05 01 99	wastes not otherwise specified
05 02 00	**Non oily sludges and solid wastes**
05 02 01	boiler feedwater sludges
05 02 02	waste from cooling columns
05 02 99	wastes not otherwise specified
05 03 00	**spent catalysts**
05 03 01	spent catalysts containing precious metals
05 03 02	other spent catalysts
05 04 00	**spent filter clays**
05 04 01	spent filter clays
05 05 00	**oil desulphurisation waste**
05 05 01	waste containing sulphur
05 05 99	wastes not otherwise specified
05 06 00	**waste from the pyrolytic treatment of coal**
05 06 01	acid tars
05 06 02	asphalt
05 06 03	other tars
05 06 04	waste from cooling columns
05 06 99	wastes not otherwise specified
05 07 00	**wastes from natural gas purification**
05 07 01	sludges containing mercury

05 07 02	wastes containing sulphur
05 07 99	wastes not otherwise specified
05 08 00	**wastes from oil regeneration**
05 08 01	spent filter clays
05 08 02	acid tars
05 08 03	other tars
05 08 04	aqueous liquid waste from oil regeneration
05 08 99	wastes not otherwise specified
06 00 00	**WASTES FROM INORGANIC CHEMICAL PROCESSES**
06 01 00	**waste acidic solutions**
06 01 01	sulphuric acid and sulphurous acid
06 01 02	hydrochloric acid
06 01 03	hydrofluoric acid
06 01 04	phosphoric and phosphorous acid
06 01 05	nitric acid and nitrous acid
06 01 99	waste not otherwise specified
06 02 00	**waste alkaline solutions**
06 02 01	calcium hydroxide
06 02 02	soda
06 02 03	ammonia
06 02 99	wastes not otherwise specified
06 03 00	**waste salts and their solutions**
06 03 01	carbonates (except 02 04 02 and 19 10 03)

06 03 02	saline solutions containing sulphates, sulphites or sulphides
06 03 03	solid salts containing sulphates, sulphites or sulphides
06 03 04	saline solutions containing chlorides, fluorides and halides
06 03 05	solid salts containing chlorides, fluorides and other halogenated solid salts
06 03 06	saline solutions containing phosphates and related solid salts
06 03 07	phosphates and related solid salts
06 03 08	saline solutions containing nitrates and related compounds
06 03 09	solid salts containing nitrides (nitrometallic)
06 03 10	solid salts containing ammonium
06 03 11	salts and solutions containing cyanides
06 03 12	salts and solutions containing organic compounds
06 03 99	wastes not otherwise specified
06 04 00	**metal-containing wastes**
06 04 01	metallic oxides
06 04 02	metallic salts (except 06 03 00)
06 04 03	wastes containing arsenic
06 04 04	wastes containing mercury
06 04 05	wastes containing other heavey metals
06 04 99	wastes not otherwise specified
06 05 00	**sludges from on-site effluent treatment**
06 05 01	sludges from on-site effluent treatment

06 06 00   **wastes from sulphur chemical processes (production and transformation) and desulphurisation processes**

06 06 01   waste containing sulphur

06 06 99   wastes not otherwise specified

06 07 00   **wastes from halogen chemical processes**

06 07 01   wastes containing asbestos from electrolysis

06 07 02   activated carbon from chlorine production

06 07 99   wastes not otherwise specified

06 08 00   **wastes from production of silicon and silicon derivatives**

06 08 01   wastes from production of silicon and silicon derivatives

06 09 00   **wastes from phosphorus chemical processes**

06 09 01   phosphogypsum

06 09 02   phosphorous slag

06 09 99   wastes not otherwise specified

06 10 00   **wastes from nitrogen chemical processes and fertilizer manufacture**

06 10 01   waste from nitrogen chemical processes and fertilizer manufacture

06 11 00   **wastes from the manufacturing of inorganic pigments and opacificiers**

06 11 01   gypsum from titanium dioxide production

06 11 99   wastes not otherwise specified

06 12 00   **wastes from production, use and regeneration of catalysts**

06 12 01   spent catalysts containing precious metals

06 12 02   other spent catalysts

06 13 00	**wastes from other inorganic chemical processes**
06 13 01	inorganic pesticides, biocides and wood preserving agents
06 13 02	spent activated carbon (except 06 07 02)
06 13 03	carbon black
06 13 99	wastes not otherwise specified
07 00 00	**WASTES FROM ORGANIC CHEMICAL PROCESSES**
07 01 00	**waste from the manufacture, formulation, supply and use (MFSU) of basic organic chemicals**
07 01 01	aqueous washing liquids and mother liquors
07 01 02	sludges from on-site effluent treatment
07 01 03	organic halogenated solvents, washing liquids and mother liquors
07 01 04	other organic solvents, washing liquids and mother liquors
07 01 05	spent catalysts containing precious metals
07 01 06	other spent catalysts
07 01 07	halogenated still bottoms and reaction residues
07 01 08	other still bottoms and reaction residues
07 01 09	halogenated filter cakes, spent absorbents
07 01 10	other filter cakes, spent absorbents
07 01 99	wastes not otherwise specified
07 02 00	**waste from the MFSU of plastics, synthetic rubber and man-made fibres**
07 02 01	aqueous washing liquids and mother liquors
07 02 02	sludges from on-site effluent treatment

07 02 03	organic halogenated solvents, washing liquids and mother liquors
07 02 04	other organic solvents, washing liquids and mother liquors
07 02 05	spent catalysts containing precious metals
07 02 06	other spent catalysts
07 02 07	halogenated still bottoms and reaction residues
07 02 08	other still bottoms and reaction residues
07 02 09	halogenated filter cakes, spent absorbents
07 02 10	other filter cakes, spent absorbents
07 02 99	wastes not otherwise specified
07 03 00	**waste from the MFSU of organic dyes and pigments (excluding 06 11 00)**
07 03 01	aqueous washing liquids and mother liquors
07 03 02	sludges from on-site effluent treatment
07 03 03	organic halogenated solvents, washing liquids and mother liquors
07 03 04	other organic solvents, washing liquids and mother liquors
07 03 05	spent catalysts containing precious metals
07 03 06	other spent catalysts
07 03 07	halogenated still bottoms and reaction residues
07 03 08	other still bottoms and reaction residues
07 03 09	halogenated filter cakes, spent absorbents
07 03 10	other filter cakes, spent absorbents
07 03 99	wastes not otherwise specified

07 04 00	**waste from the MFSU of organic pesticides (except 02 01 05)**
07 04 01	aqueous washing liquids and mother liquors
07 04 02	sludges from on-site effluent treatment
07 04 03	organic halogenated solvents, washing liquids and mother liquors
07 04 04	other organic solvents, washing liquids and mother liquors
07 04 05	spent catalysts containing precious metals
07 04 06	other spent catalysts
07 04 07	halogenated still bottoms and reaction residues
07 04 08	other still bottoms and reaction residues
07 04 09	halogenated filter cakes, spent absorbents
07 04 10	other filter cakes, spent absorbents
07 04 99	wastes not otherwise specified
07 05 00	**waste from the MFSU of pharmaceuticals**
07 05 01	aqueous washing liquids and mother liquors
07 05 02	sludges from on-site effluent treatment
07 05 03	organic halogenated solvents, washing liquids and mother liquors
07 05 04	other organic solvents, washing liquids and mother liquors
07 05 05	spent catalysts containing precious metals
07 05 06	other spent catalysts
07 05 07	halogenated still bottoms and reaction residues
07 05 08	other still bottoms and reaction residues
07 05 09	halogenated filter cakes, spent absorbents

07 05 10	other filter cakes, spent absorbents
07 05 99	wastes not otherwise specified
07 06 00	**waste from the MFSU of fats, grease, soaps, detergents disinfectants and cosmetics**
07 06 01	aqueous washing liquids and mother liquors
07 06 02	sludges from on-site effluent treatment
07 06 03	organic halogenated solvents, washing liquids and mother liquors
07 06 04	other organic solvents, washing liquids and mother liquors
07 06 05	spent catalysts containing precious metals
07 06 06	other spent catalysts
07 06 07	halogenated still bottoms and reaction residues
07 06 08	other still bottoms and reaction residues
07 06 09	halogenated filter cakes, spent absorbents
07 06 10	other filter cakes, spent absorbents
07 06 99	wastes not otherwise specified
07 07 00	**waste from the MFSU of fine chemicals and chemical products not otherwise specified**
07 07 01	aqueous washing liquids and mother liquors
07 07 02	sludges from on site effluent treatment
07 07 03	organic halogenaged solvents, washing liquids and mother liquors
07 07 04	other organic solvents, washing liquids and mother liquors
07 07 05	spent catalysts containing precious metals
07 07 06	other spent catalysts

07 07 07	halogenated still bottoms and reaction residues
07 07 08	other still bottoms and reaction residues
07 07 09	halogenated filter cakes, spent absorbents
07 07 10	other filter cakes, spent absorbents
07 07 99	wastes not otherwise specified

08 00 00 **WASTES FROM THE MANUFACTURE, FORMU-LATION, SUPPLY AND USE (MFSU) OF COATINGS (PAINTS, VARNISHES AND VITREOUS ENAMELS), ADHESIVE, SEALANTS AND PRINTING INKS**

08 01 00 **wastes from MFSU of paint and varnish**

08 01 01	waste paints and varnish containing halogenated solvents
08 01 02	waste paints and varnish free of halogenated solvents
08 01 03	waste from water-based paints and varnishes
08 01 04	powder paints
08 01 05	hardened paints and varnishes
08 01 06	sludges from paint or varnish removal containing halogenated solvents
08 01 07	sludges from paint or varnish removal free of halogenated solvents
08 01 08	aqueous sludges containing paint or varnish
08 01 09	waste from paint or varnish removal (except 08 01 05 and 08 01 06)
08 01 10	aqueous suspensions containing paint or varnish
08 01 99	wastes not otherwise specified

08 02 00 **wastes from MFSU of other coating (including ceramic materials)**

08 02 01	waste coating powders

08 02 02	aqueous sludges containing ceramic materials
08 02 03	**aqueous suspensions containing ceramic materials**
08 02 99	wastes not otherwise specified
08 03 00	waste from MFSU of printing inks
08 03 01	waste ink containing halogenated solvents
08 03 02	waste ink free of halogenated solvents
08 03 03	waste from water-based ink
08 03 04	dried ink
08 03 05	ink sludges containing halogenated solvents
08 03 06	ink sludges free of halogenated solvents
08 03 07	aqueous sludges containing ink
08 03 08	aqueous liquid waste containing ink
08 03 09	waste printing toner (including cartridges)
08 03 99	wastes not otherwise specified
08 04 00	**wastes from MFSU of adhesives and sealants (including waterproofing products)**
08 04 01	waste adhesives and sealants containing halogenated solvents
08 04 02	waste adhesives and sealants free of halogenated solvents
08 04 03	wastes from water-based adhesives and sealants
08 04 04	hardened adhesives and sealants
08 04 05	adhesives and sealants sludges containing halogenated solvents
08 04 06	adhesives and sealants sludges free of halogenated solvents
08 04 07	aqueous sludges containing adhesives and sealants

08 04 08	aqueous liquid wastes containing adhesives and sealants
08 04 99	wastes not otherwise specified

09 00 00 WASTES FROM THE PHOTOGRAPHIC INDUSTRY

09 01 00 wastes from photographic industry

09 01 01	water based developer and activator solutions
09 01 02	water based offset plate developer solutions
09 01 03	solvent based developer solutions
09 01 04	fixer solutions
09 01 05	bleach solutions and bleach fixer solutions
09 01 06	waste containing silver from on-site treatment of photographic waste
09 01 07	photographic film and paper containing silver or silver compounds
09 01 08	photographic film and paper free of silver or silver compounds
09 01 09	single-use cameras with batteries
09 01 10	single use cameras without batteries
09 01 99	wastes not otherwise specified

10 00 00 INORGANIC WASTES FROM THERMAL PROCESSES

10 01 00 wastes from power station and other combustion plants (except 19 00 00)

10 01 01	bottom ash
10 01 02	coal fly ash
10 01 03	peat fly ash
10 01 04	oil fly ash

10 01 05	calcium based reaction wastes from flue gas desulphurisation in solid form
10 01 06	other solid wastes from gas treatment
10 01 07	calcium based reaction wastes from flue gas desulphurisation in sludge form
10 01 08	other sludges from gas treatment
10 01 09	sulphuric acid
10 01 10	spent catalysts e.g. from removal of NO_x
10 01 11	aqueous sludges from boiler cleansing
10 01 12	spent linings and refractories
10 01 99	wastes not otherwise specified
10 02 00	**wastes from the iron and steel industry**
10 02 01	waste from the processing of slag
10 02 02	unprocessed slag
10 02 03	solid wastes from gas treatment
10 02 04	sludges from gas treatment
10 02 05	other sludges
10 02 06	spent linings and refractories
10 02 99	wastes not otherwise specified
10 03 00	**wastes from aluminium thermal metallurgy**
10 03 01	tars and other carbon-containing wastes from anode manufacture
10 03 02	anode scraps
10 03 03	skimmings
10 03 04	primary smelting slags/white drosses
10 03 05	alumina dust

10 03 06	used carbon strips and fireproof materials from electrolysis
10 03 07	spent pot linings
10 03 08	salt slags from secondary smelting
10 03 09	black drosses from secondary smelting
10 03 10	waste from treatment of salt slags and black drosses treatment
10 03 11	flue gas dust
10 03 12	other particulates and dust (including ball mill dust)
10 03 13	solid waste from gas treatment
10 03 14	sludges from gas treatment
10 03 99	wastes not otherwise specified
10 04 00	**wastes from lead thermal metallurgy**
10 04 01	slags (first and second smelting)
10 04 02	dross and skimmings (first and second smelting)
10 04 03	calcium arsenate
10 04 04	flue gas dust
10 04 05	other particulates and dust
10 04 06	solid waste from gas treatment
10 04 07	sludges from gas treatment
10 04 08	spent linings and refractories
10 04 99	wastes not otherwise specified
10 05 00	**wastes from zinc thermal metallurgy**
10 05 01	slags (first and second smelting)
10 05 02	dross and skimmings (first and second smelting)

10 05 03	flue gas dust
10 05 04	other particulates and dust
10 05 05	solid waste from gas treatment
10 05 06	sludges from gas treatment
10 05 07	spent linings and refractories
10 05 99	wastes not otherwise specified
10 06 00	**wastes from copper thermal metallurgy**
10 06 01	slags (first and second smelting)
10 06 02	dross and skimmings (first and second smelting)
10 06 03	flue gas dust
10 06 04	other particulates and dust
10 06 05	waste from electrolytic refining
10 06 06	solid waste from gas treatment
10 06 07	sludges from gas treatment
10 06 08	spent linings and refractories
10 06 99	wastes not otherwise specified
10 07 00	**wastes from silver, gold and platinum thermal metallurgy**
10 07 01	slags (first and second smelting)
10 07 02	dross and skimmings (first and second smelting)
10 07 03	solid waste from gas treatment
10 07 04	other particulates and dust
10 07 05	sludges from gas treatment
10 07 06	spent linings and refractories
10 07 99	wastes not otherwise specified

10 08 00	**wastes from other non-ferrous thermal metallurgy**
10 08 01	slags (first and second smelting)
10 08 02	dross and skimmings (first and second smelting)
10 08 03	flue gas dust
10 08 04	other particulates and dust
10 08 05	solid waste from gas treatment
10 08 06	sludges from gas treatment
10 08 07	spent linings and refractories
10 08 99	wastes not otherwise specified
10 09 00	**wastes from casting of ferrous pieces**
10 09 01	casting cores and moulds containing organic binders which have not undergone pouring
10 09 02	casting cores and moulds containing organic binders which have undergone pouring
10 09 03	furnace slag
10 09 04	furnace dust
10 09 99	wastes not otherwise specified
10 10 00	**wastes from casting of non-ferrous pieces**
10 10 01	casting cores and moulds containing organic binders which have not undergone pouring
10 10 02	casting cores and moulds containing organic binders which have undergone pouring
10 10 03	furnace slag
10 10 04	furnace dust
10 10 99	wastes not otherwise specified
10 11 00	**wastes from manufacture of glass and glass products**

10 11 01	waste preparation mixture before thermal processing
10 11 02	waste glass
10 11 03	waste glass-based fibrous materials
10 11 04	flue gas dust
10 11 05	other particulates and dust
10 11 06	solid waste from gas treatment
10 11 07	sludges from gas treatment
10 11 08	spent linings and refractories
10 11 99	wastes not otherwise specified
10 12 00	**wastes from manufacture of ceramic goods, bricks, tiles and constructions products**
10 12 01	waste preparation mixture before thermal processing
10 12 02	flue gas dust
10 12 03	other particulates and dust
10 12 04	solid waste from gas treatment
10 12 05	sludges from gas treatment
10 12 06	discarded moulds
10 12 07	spent linings and refractories
10 12 99	wastes not otherwise specified
10 13 00	**wastes from manufacture of cement, lime and plaster and articles and products made from them**
10 13 01	waste preparation mixture before thermal processing
10 13 02	wastes from asbestos-cement manufacture
10 13 03	wastes from other cement-based composite materials
10 13 04	waste from calcination and hydration of lime

10 13 05	solid waste from gas treatment
10 13 06	other particulates and dust1
0 13 07	sludges from gas treatment
10 13 08	spent linings and refractories
10 13 99	wastes not otherwise specified

11 00 00 **INORGANIC WASTE WITH METALS FROM METAL TREATMENT AND THE COATING OF METALS; NON-FERROUS HYDRO-METALLURGY**

11 01 00 **liquid wastes and sludges from metal treatment and coating of metals (eg. galvanic processes, zinc coating processes, pickling processes, etching, phosphatizing, alkaline degreasing)**

11 01 01	cyanidic (alkaline) wastes containing heavy metals other than chromium
11 01 02	cyanidic (alkaline) wastes which do not contain heavy metals
11 01 03	cyanide-free wastes containing chromium
11 01 04	cyanide-free wastes not containing chromium
11 01 05	acidic pickling solutions
11 01 06	acids not otherwise specified
11 01 07	alkalis not otherwise specified
11 01 08	phosphatizing sludges

11 02 00 **wastes and sludges from non-ferrous hydrometallurgical processes**

11 02 01	sludges from copper hydrometallurgy
11 02 02	sludges from zinc hydrometallurgy (including jarosite, goethite)

11 02 03	**wastes from the production of anodes for aqueous electrolytical processes**
11 02 04	sludges not otherwise specified
11 03 00	sludges and solids from tempering processes
11 03 01	wastes containing cyanide
11 03 02	other wastes
11 04 00	**other inorganic wastes with metals not otherwise specified**
11 04 01	other inorganic wastes with metals not otherwise specified
12 00 00	**WASTES FROM SHAPING AND SURFACE TREATMENT OF METALS AND PLASTICS**
12 01 00	**wastes from shaping (including forging, welding, pressing, drawing, turning, cutting and filing)**
12 01 01	ferrous metal filings and turnings
12 01 02	other ferrous metals particles
12 01 03	non-ferrous metal filings and turnings
12 01 04	other non-ferrous metal particules
12 01 05	plastics particles
12 01 06	waste machining oils containing halogens (not emulsioned)
12 01 07	waste machining oils free of halogens (not emulsioned)
12 01 08	waste machining emulsions containing halogens
12 01 09	waste machining emulsions free of halogens
12 01 10	synthetic machining oils
12 01 11	machining sludges
12 01 12	spent waxes and fats
12 01 13	welding wastes

12 01 99	wastes not otherwise specified
12 02 00	**wastes from mechanical surface treatment processes (blasting, grinding, honing, lapping, polishing)**
12 02 01	spent blasting grit
12 02 02	sludges from grinding, honing and lapping
12 02 03	polishing sludges
12 02 99	wastes not otherwise specified
12 03 00	**wastes from water and steam degreasing processes (except 11 00 00)**
12 03 01	aqueous washing liquids
12 03 02	steam degreasing wastes
13 00 00	**OIL WASTES (except edible oils, 05 00 00 and 12 00 00)**
13 01 00	**waste hydraulic oils and brake fluids**
13 01 01	hydraulic oils, containing PCBs or PCTs
13 01 02	other chlorinated hydraulic oils (not emulsions)
13 01 03	non chlorinated hydraulic oils (not emulsions)
13 01 04	chlorinated emulsions
13 01 05	non chlorinated emulsions
13 01 06	hydraulic oils containing only mineral oil
13 01 07	other hydraulic oils
13 01 08	brake fluids
13 02 00	**waste engine, gear & lubricating oils**
13 02 01	chlorinated engine, gear and lubricating oils
13 02 02	non-chlorinated engine, gear, lubricating oils
13 02 03	other engine, gear and lubricating oils

13 03 00   **waste insulating and heat transmission oils and other liquids**

13 03 01   insulating or heat transmission oils and other liquids containing PCBs or PCTs

13 03 02   other chlorinated insulating and heat transmission oils and other liquids

13 03 03   non-chlorinated insulating and heat transmission oils and other liquids

13 03 04   synthetic insulating and heat transmission oils and other liquids

13 03 05   mineral insulating and heat transmission oils

13 04 00   **bilge oils**

13 04 01   bilge oils from inland navigation

13 04 02   bilge oils from jetty sewers

13 04 03   bilge oils from other navigation

13 05 00   **oil/water separator contents**

13 05 01   oil/water separator solids

13 05 02   oil/water separator sludges

13 05 03   interceptor sludges

13 05 04   desalter sludges or emulsions

13 05 05   other emulsions

13 06 00   **oil waste not otherwise specified**

13 06 01   oil waste not otherwise specified

14 00 00   **WASTES FROM ORGANIC SUBSTANCES EMPLOYED AS SOLVENTS (except 07 00 00 and 08 00 00)**

14 01 00   **wastes from metal degreasing and machinery maintenance**

14 01 01	chlorofluorocarbons
14 01 02	other halogenated solvents and solvent mixes
14 01 03	other solvents and solvent mixes
14 01 04	aqueous solvent mixes containing halogens
14 01 05	aqueous solvent mixes free of halogens
14 01 06	sludges or solid wastes containing halogenated solvents
14 01 07	sludges or solid wastes free of halogenated solvents
14 02 00	**wastes from textile cleaning and degreasing of natural products**
14 02 01	halogenated solvents and solvent mixes
14 02 02	solvent mixes or organic liquids free of halogenated solvents
14 02 03	sludges or solid wastes containing halogenated solvents
14 02 04	sludges or solid wastes containing other solvents
14 03 00	**wastes from the electronic industry**
14 03 01	chlorofluorocarbons
14 03 02	other halogenated solvents
14 03 03	solvents and solvent mixes free of halogenated solvents
14 03 04	sludges or solid wastes containing halogenated solvents
14 03 05	sludges or solid wastes containing other solvents
14 04 00	**wastes from coolants, foam/aerosol propellents**
14 04 01	chlorofluorocarbons
14 04 02	other halogenated solvents and solvent mixes
14 04 03	other solvents and solvent mixes
14 04 04	sludges or solid wastes containing halogenated solvents

14 04 05	sludges or solid wastes containing other solvents
14 05 00	**wastes from solvent and coolant recovery (still bottoms)**
14 05 01	chlorofluorocarbons
14 05 02	halogenated solvents and solvent mixes
14 05 03	other solvents and solvent mixes
14 05 04	sludges containing halogenated solvents
14 05 05	sludges containing other solvents
15 00 00	**PACKAGING; ABSORBENTS, WIPING CLOTHS, FILTER MATERIALS AND PROTECTIVE CLOTHING NOT OTHERWISE SPECIFIED**
15 01 00	**packaging**
15 01 01	paper and cardboard
15 01 02	plastic
15 01 03	wooden
15 01 04	metallic
15 01 05	composite packaging
15 01 06	mixed
15 02 00	**absorbents, filter materials, wiping cloths and protective clothing**
15 02 01	absorbents, filter materials, wiping cloths, protective clothing
16 00 00	**WASTE NOT OTHERWISE SPECIFIED IN THE CATALOGUE**
16 01 00	**end of life vehicles**
16 01 01	catalysts removed from vehicles containing precious metals

16 01 02	other catalysts removed from vehicles
16 01 03	used tyres
16 01 04	discarded vehicles
16 01 05	light fraction from automobile shredding
16 01 99	wastes not otherwise specified
16 02 00	**discarded equipment and shredder residues**
16 02 01	transformers and capacitors containing PCB or PCTs
16 02 02	other discarded electronic equipment (e.g. printed circuit boards)
16 02 03	equipment containing chlorofluorocarbons
16 02 04	discarded equipment containing free asbestos
16 02 05	other discarded equipment
16 02 06	wastes from the asbestos processing industry
16 02 07	waste from the plastic convertor industry
16 02 08	shredder residues
16 03 00	**off-specification batches**
16 03 01	inorganic off-specification batches
16 03 02	organic off-specification batches
16 04 00	waste explosives
16 04 01	waste ammunition
16 04 02	fireworks waste
16 04 03	other waste explosives
16 05 00	**chemicals and gases in containers**
16 05 01	industrial gases in high pressure cylinders, LPG containers and industrial aerosol containers (including halons)

16 05 02	other waste containing inorganic chemicals, e.g. lab chemicals not otherwise specified, fire extinguishing powders
16 05 03	other waste containing organic chemicals, e.g. lab chemicals not otherwise specified
16 06 00	**batteries and accumulators**
16 06 01	lead batteries
16 06 02	Ni-Cd batteries
16 06 03	mercury dry cells
16 06 04	alkaline batteries
16 06 05	other batteries and accumulators
16 06 06	electrolyte from batteries and accumulators
16 07 00	**waste from transport and storage tank cleaning (except 05 00 00 and 12 00 00)**
16 07 01	waste from marine transport tank cleaning, containing chemicals
16 07 02	waste from marine transport tank cleaning, containing oil
16 07 03	waste from railway and road transport tank cleaning containing oil
16 07 04	waste from railway and road transort tank cleaning containing chemicals
16 07 05	waste from storage tank cleaning, containing chemicals
16 07 06	waste from storage tank cleaning, containing oil
16 07 07	solid wastes from ship cargoes
16 07 99	waste not otherwise specified
17 00 00	**CONSTRUCTION AND DEMOLITION WASTE (INCLUDING ROAD CONSTRUCTION)**

17 01 00	**concrete, bricks, tiles, ceramics, and gypsum based materials**
17 01 01	concret
17 01 02	bricks
17 01 03	tiles and ceramics
17 01 04	gypsum based construction materials
17 01 05	asbestos based construction materials
17 02 00	**wood, glass and plastic**
17 02 01	wood
17 02 02	glass
17 02 03	plastic
17 03 00	**asphalt, tar and tarred products**
17 03 01	asphalt containing tar
17 03 02	asphalt (not containing tar)
17 03 03	tar and tar products
17 04 00	**metals (including their alloys)**
17 04 01	copper, bronze, brass
17 04 02	aluminium
17 04 03	lead
17 04 04	zinc
17 04 05	iron and steel
17 04 06	tin
17 04 07	mixed metals
17 04 08	cables
17 05 00	**soil and dredging spoil**

17 05 01	soil and stones
17 05 02	dredging spoil
17 06 00	**insulation materials**
17 06 01	insulation materials containing asbestos
17 06 02	other insulation materials
17 07 00	**mixed construction and demolition waste**
17 07 01	mixed construction and demolition waste
18 00 00	**WASTES FROM HUMAN OR ANIMAL HEALTH CARE AND/OR RELATED RESEARCH (excluding kitchen and restaurant wastes which do not arise from immediate health care)**
18 01 00	**waste from natal care, diagnosis, treatment or prevention of disease in humans**
18 01 01	sharps
18 01 02	body parts and organs including blood bags and blood preserves
18 01 03	other wastes whose collection and disposal is subject to special requirements in view of the prevention of infection
18 01 04	wastes whose collection and disposal is not subject to special requirements in view of the prevention of infection (e.g. dressings, plaster casts, linen, disposable clothing, diapers)
18 01 05	discarded chemicals and medicines
18 02 00	**waste from research, diagnosis, treatment or prevention of disease involving animals**
18 02 01	sharps
18 02 02	other wastes whose collection and disposal is subject to special requirements in view of the prevention of infection
18 02 03	wastes whose collection and disposal is not subject to special requirements in view of the prevention of infection

| 18 02 04 | discarded chemicals |

19 00 00   **WASTES FROM WASTE TREATMENT FACILI-TIES, OFF-SITE WASTE WATER TREATMENT PLANTS AND THE WATER INDUSTRY**

19 01 00   **wastes from incineration or pyrolysis of municipal and similar commercial, industrial and institutional wastes**

19 01 01	bottom ash and slag
19 01 02	ferrous materials removed from bottom ash
19 01 03	fly ash
19 01 04	boiler dust
19 01 05	filter cake from gas treatment
19 01 06	aqueous liquid waste from gas treatment and other aqueous liquid wastes
19 01 07	solid waste from gas treatment
19 01 08	pyrolysis wastes
19 01 09	spent catalysts e.g. from NO_x removal
19 01 10	spent activated carbon from flue gas treatment
19 01 99	wastes not otherwise specified

19 02 00   **wastes from specific physico/chemical treatments of industrial wastes (e.g. dechromatation, decyanidation, neutralisation)**

| 19 02 01 | metal hydroxide sludges and other sludges from metal insolubilisation treatment |
| 19 02 02 | premixed wastes for final disposal |

19 03 00   **stabilized/solidified wastes**

| 19 03 01 | wastes stabilized/solidified with hydraulic binders |
| 19 03 02 | wastes stabilized/solidified with organic binders |

19 03 03	wastes stabilized by biological treatment
19 04 00	**vitrified wastes and wastes from vitrification**
19 04 01	vitrified wastes
19 04 02	fly ash and other flue gas treatment wastes
19 04 03	non-vitrified solid phase
19 04 04	aqueous liquid waste from vitrified waste tempering
19 05 00	**wastes from aerobic treatment of solid wastes**
19 05 01	non-composted fraction of municipal and similar wastes
19 05 02	non-composted fraction of animal and vegetable wastes
19 05 03	off specification compost
19 05 99	wastes not otherwise specified
19 06 00	**wastes from aneaerobic treatment of wastes**
19 06 01	anaerobic treatment sludges of municipal and similar wastes
19 06 02	anaerobic treatment sludges of animal and vegetal wastes
19 06 99	wastes not otherwise specified
19 07 00	**landfill leachate**
19 07 01	landfill leachate
19 08 00	**wastes from waste water treatment plants not otherwise specified**
19 08 01	screenings
19 08 02	wastes from desanding
19 08 03	grease and oil mixture from oil/waste water separation
19 08 04	sludges from the treatment of industrial waste water
19 08 05	sludges from treatment of urban waste water

19 08 06	saturated or spent ion exchange resins
19 08 07	solutions and sludges from regeneration of ion exchangers
19 08 99	wastes not otherwise specified
19 09 00	**wastes from the preparation of drinking water or water for industrial use**
19 09 01	solid wastes from primary filtration and screening
19 09 02	sludges from water clarification
19 09 03	sludges from decarbonation
19 09 04	spent activated carbon
19 09 05	saturated or spent ion exchange resins
19 09 06	solutions and sludges from regeneration of ion exchangers
19 09 99	wastes not otherwise specified
20 00 00	**MUNICIPAL WASTES AND SIMILAR COMMERCIAL, INDUSTRIAL AND INSTITUTIONAL WASTES INCLUDING SEPARATELY COLLECTED FRACTIONS**
20 01 00	**separately collected fractions**
20 01 01	paper and cardboard
20 01 02	glass
20 01 03	small plastics
20 01 04	other plastics
20 01 05	small metals (cans etc.)
20 01 06	other metals
20 01 07	wood

20 01 08	organic compostable kitchen waste (including frying oil and kitchen waste from canteens and restaurants)
20 01 09	oil and fat
20 01 10	clothes
20 01 11	textiles
20 01 12	paint, inks, adhesives and resins
20 01 13	solvents
20 01 14	acids
20 01 15	alkalines
20 01 16	detergents
20 01 17	photo chemicals
20 01 18	medicines
20 01 19	pesticides
20 01 20	batteries
20 01 21	fluorescent tubes and other mercury containing waste
20 01 22	aerosols
20 01 23	equipment containing chloroflurocarbons
20 01 24	electronic equipment (e.g. printed circuit boards)
20 02 00	**garden and park waste (including cemetery waste)**
20 02 01	compostable wastes
20 02 02	soil and stones
20 02 03	other non-compostable wastes

20 03 00	**other municipal waste**
20 03 01	mixed municipal waste
20 03 02	waste from markets
20 03 03	street cleaning residues
20 03 04	septic tank sludge
20 03 05	end of life vehicles

European Commission

**European Community environment legislation
Volume 6 — Waste**

Luxembourg: Office for Official Publications of the European Communities

1996 — xlviii, 239 pp. — 16.2 x 22.9 cm

ISBN 92-827-6882-1 (Volume 6)
ISBN 92-827-6828-7 (Volumes 1-7)

Price (excluding VAT) in Luxembourg: ECU 11 (Volume 6)
ECU 74 (Volumes 1-7)